Families and Food in Hard

Families and Food in Hard Times

European comparative research

Rebecca O'Connell and Julia Brannen

First published in 2021 by
UCL Press
University College London
Gower Street
London WC1E 6BT

Available to download free: www.uclpress.co.uk

A CIP catalogue record for this book is available from The British Library.

O'Connell, R. and Brannen, J. 2021. *Families and Food in Hard Times: European comparative research*. London: UCL Press. https://doi.org/10.14324/111.9781787356559

ISBN: 978-1-78735-657-3 (Hbk.)
ISBN: 978-1-78735-656-6 (Pbk.)
ISBN: 978-1-78735-655-9 (pdf)
ISBN: 978-1-78735-658-0 (epub)
ISBN: 978-1-78735-659-7 (mobi)
DOI: https://doi.org/10.14324/111.9781787356559

Se podes olhar, vê. Se podes ver, repara.
[If you can see, look. If you can look, observe.]

Livro dos Conselhos

Contents

List of figures

List of tables

Acknowledgements

First and foremost, we wish to thank the families who participated in the study. We would also like to thank and acknowledge the co-researchers with whom we carried out the research on which the book is based. The team included: in the UK, Laura Hamilton, Abigail Knight, Charlie Owen, Antonia Simon (Thomas Coram Research Unit, Institute of Education, UCL); in Portugal, Manuel Abrantes, Fábio Augusto, Sónia Cardoso, Vasco Ramos, Mónica Truninger and Karin Wall (Instituto de Ciências Sociais da Universidade de Lisboa); in Norway, Silje Skuland and Anine Frisland (Consumption Research Norway, Oslo Metropolitan University). Penny Mellor and Cécile Brémont provided administrative support. We are grateful for your commitment, flexibility and collegiality. We have learned a great deal from all of you.

The Advisory Group was supportive, challenging and vital to the study's success. Its members included Elizabeth Dowler, University of Warwick (Chair); Niall Cooper, Church Action on Poverty; Linda Hantrais, Loughborough University; Anne Harrop, Aga Khan Foundation; Lotte Holm, University of Copenhagen; Imran Hussain and Louisa McGeehan, Child Poverty Action Group; Virginia Morrow, University of Oxford; Matt Padley, University of Loughborough; Imogen Richmond-Bishop, Sustain; Robert Walker, University of Oxford; and Wendy Wills, University of Hertfordshire. Thank you all for your expert advice, keeping us on track and helping us make the findings useful. We are also grateful to Ruth Wright for valued comments on the draft, Daisy O'Connell for vignette drawings and our colleagues at the Thomas Coram Research Unit, for all their support.

Finally, thanks are of course due to the European Research Council (ERC), who funded the study under the European Union's Seventh Framework Programme (FP7/2007–2013), ERC grant agreement number 337977. The Starting Grant scheme provided the resources needed to support and foster the development of a community of practice that recognises the value of research mentorship. In the years since we

(Rebecca and Julia) travelled together to an ERC boardroom in Brussels with Rebecca's three-week-old baby in tow, much has changed. But our enjoyment in working together has not. We are very grateful for the opportunity to collaborate on the research and the book and hope it does justice to the stories of the children and families who took part.

In every country in every period of history there have been two flames burning: the flame of anger against injustice and the flame of hope that we can build a better world. Both of these flames have to be kept alive. (Tony Benn interviewed by Steve McGiffen 1999)

Introduction

In *Hard Times*, published in 1854, Charles Dickens set out some fundamental principles of what he called the 'Gradgrind philosophy', which, in some respects, bears a striking resemblance to the neoliberal capitalism that has dominated the world since the late 1970s:

> A fundamental principle of the Gradgrind philosophy [was] that everything was to be paid for. Nobody was ever on any account to give anybody anything, or render anybody help without purchase. Gratitude was to be abolished, and the virtues springing from it were not to be. Every inch of the existence of mankind, from birth to death, was to be a bargain across a counter. And if we didn't get to Heaven that way, it was not a politico-economical place, and we had no business there. (Dickens 1854, 340)

This book, *Families and Food in Hard Times*, is about our world in the second decade of the twenty-first century and how parents living on low incomes in wealthy societies manage to feed their families. Although very different from the world of Dickens, in some respects today's world mirrors elements of his time because of the harsh realities of poverty among large sections of the population in the Global North. Just as the poor in many of Dickens's novels struggle to keep their heads above water, to put food on the table and to hold on to their dignity, so too do the low-income families who have been living through the period since the 2008 global financial crisis. Now, as in the nineteenth century, food poverty in rich societies powerfully reveals 'the fundamental shortcomings of unbridled reliance on markets' (Poppendieck 2012, 565).

In Dickens's *Hard Times*, workers' aspirations for better standards of living were denigrated as unrealistic; entitlements to 'turtle soup and venison, with a gold spoon' were not for the likes of them. One hundred and sixty years later, in the same country in 2014, Conservative peer Baroness Jenkin (a panel member of the All-Party Parliamentary Inquiry into Hunger and Food Poverty) declared that the poor should 'eat porridge' instead of more expensive processed cereals (Wright 2014; Knight et al. 2018). Elsewhere in Europe, in 2012, President of the European Federation of Food Banks and President of the Portuguese Food Bank Isabel Jonet argued that the Portuguese would 'have to learn to live poorer' because 'they had been living above their possibilities'. She added, 'If you can't afford to eat beef steak every day, then you should refrain from eating it' (Barbosa 2012, n.p.). Through living – and eating – within their means, these actors suggest, the poor should know their place. For, as Dickens recognised, food is fundamentally a symbolic as well as material resource, an expression of a person's worth and a powerful lens through which to view the social order.

The context in which we are writing this Introduction is not only very different from Dickens's time; it is also very different from that in which we designed the study, carried out the research and wrote much of the book. The study on which the book is based was funded by the European Research Council, a public body that funds scientific and technological research conducted within the European Union (EU). It was conceived at a time (2012) when the UK was a member of the EU, an international commitment that we did not seriously think the UK government would terminate. Since the UK has left the European Union, the UK's future research is further compromised as the government proposes to fund UK researchers' participation in Horizon Europe from its existing (UKRI) research budget.

The idea for the research was generated in the aftermath of the global financial crisis that occurred in 2008. At that time, the consequences of this event were becoming increasingly evident across Europe, notably the detrimental effects on those who were already among the most disadvantaged in society. In particular, we were concerned about the evidence, often based on international media reports, of increasing numbers of children arriving at school hungry and of a dramatic rise in the number of food banks handing out food parcels to families forced to choose between 'heating and eating'. Little evidence existed, however, about the types of families to which belong the growing numbers of children who lack enough decent food to eat, or the particular ways in which food poverty manifests and is managed and experienced in different places. Hardly any research included the experiences of children and young people, an omission that, as members of the Thomas Coram Research Unit, which since 1973 has specialised in research on children and families, we were keen to address. This book charts the effects of the 2008 crisis on the lives of children and their parents in different communities in three European countries.

This book is being completed in a very different, even worse, time of crisis that is engulfing the globe. The Covid-19 pandemic and the public health measures implemented to mitigate its impact are having devastating effects not only on people's health but also on their freedom to interact with others and on their economic circumstances. How deep the effects of the pandemic on people's lives will be, or how long lasting, we currently have no idea. However, early evidence suggests that the crisis is exacerbating existing health and social inequalities. It is our hope that this book will alert the reader to some of the ways in which the pandemic is likely to disproportionately affect the lives of the most disadvantaged, such as the families we describe here.

In our research we chose to focus on three European countries: the UK, Portugal and Norway. We selected the UK and Portugal because both were greatly affected in adverse ways by the 2008 financial crisis. In the UK, the financial crisis was met by the government's imposition of stringent austerity measures that caused sharp falls in wages and productivity and growing labour market polarisation and social inequality. Meanwhile Portugal, because of financial speculation in 2011, faced bankruptcy following the 2008 crisis, with the result that a bailout programme was agreed between the Portuguese government and the 'Troika': the European Commission on behalf of the Eurogroup, the European Central Bank (ECB) and the International Monetary Fund (IMF). As a consequence of the ways in which the 2008 crisis was managed in both the UK and Portugal, we expected to find families in those countries to be at greater risk of poverty and food poverty than before the crisis.

To provide a contrasting context of a country less affected by the 2008 financial crisis we chose Norway, a society in which we expected to find families less at risk of poverty and food poverty than in the UK and Portugal. Norway is a country with a generous welfare state that partly results from the Norwegian government's foresight and determination to garner the economic benefits of exploiting the nation's oil reserves for the long-term benefit of current and future generations. In contrast to the UK's strategy towards its North Sea oil, Norway established the Norwegian Sovereign Wealth Fund in 1967 as a public savings account during the development of its considerable oil reserves. This fund and its linked global investment fund are able to protect Norway and its people from the effects of global shocks such as the 2008 crisis and the volatility of oil prices (Hippe et al. 2013).

Low-income families are at the centre of this book. However, as we will argue, it is important to place individuals and families in the wider contexts in which their everyday lives unfold. Indeed, this contextualisation is central to the relative deprivation approach we have taken to understanding children's and parents' experiences. We have therefore sought to flesh out the societal and historical contexts of the three countries in order to describe the local institutions and services that families have access to, including school and school meals policies, and the families' social networks of family and friends. In order to do this, we conducted both primary and secondary research. Existing national and international datasets were analysed in order to understand how prevalent low income and food poverty were in the three countries and which types of families were most at risk of food poverty. We also collected new data and conducted comparative case studies of families in the capital cities of each of the three countries and in rural or semi-rural areas near these cities. This involved intensive qualitative fieldwork with 133 households, carried out by an international team. Drawing on in-depth interviews with young people aged 11–15 years and their parents, and data obtained by a variety of other methods, the book examines the following questions:

- Which types of family are at risk of food poverty?
- Under what conditions do families go without enough money and food?
- How do mothers manage food provisioning in the context of a lack of income?
- What support and extra-household resources do mothers and children rely upon to get by?
- What part do school meals play in mitigating the effects of low income and poverty?
- How does low income affect parents' and children's social relations with others and their everyday lives outside the household?
- How does a lack of resources make children and mothers feel when they cannot live or eat according to a socially acceptable standard of living?

In Section 1 of the book we set the scene. Chapter 1 contextualises the research discussed in the book by introducing and comparing the three countries in which it was carried out. We examine their welfare regimes, the ways in which the 2008 financial crisis played out in the three countries, the countries' public policy responses to food insecurity and the evidence for food insecurity. In Chapter 2 we discuss the main research concepts that informed our interpretation of the data. Chapter 3 describes the research design through which we sought to capture the multiple levels on which people live their lives and that constrain their opportunities and resources. It outlines the comparative case approach we adopted, the multiple methods we used and how we approached the analysis. Chapter 4 draws on secondary analysis of an existing international dataset in order to compare low income and food poverty across the three countries and considers which types of families are most at risk of food poverty. The chapter also introduces the qualitative research that we carried out in the three countries and that provides the basis for the rest of the book.

By understanding households as resource units, Section 2 examines household income and its impact on domestic food provisioning. Each of the three chapters (5, 6 and 7) focuses on three families, one from each of the three countries. In each chapter we identify the resources available to the families, the ways in which mothers transform these resources into food for their families, the implications in terms of the quantity and quality of food eaten and how food is distributed. Chapter 5 focuses on unemployed lone mothers who are reliant on social benefits; Chapter 6 on dual-parent working families, a growing social group at risk of food poverty; and Chapter 7 is about undocumented migrants whose access to work and benefits is severely restricted. By comparing similar types of families across three countries we identify the social conditions that contribute to their different experiences of poverty and food poverty. As this section of the book demonstrates, income from employment and benefits is not enough to feed all the members of a household properly, and some families receive neither source of income and are barely able to feed themselves at all.

Section 3 focuses on the social dimensions of food poverty and the experience of social exclusion. In Chapter 8 we compare parents' and children's experiences of offering and accepting hospitality, their capacity to participate in eating out, the constraints upon these activities, and the consequences of social exclusion. We draw a distinction between families who experience poverty and deprivation as a long-term state and those in which a fall in fortunes has arisen from the financial crisis and the ensuing policy consequences or because of sudden personal or family change.

Section 4 examines the extra-household resources that families draw upon to feed their families. Chapter 9 focuses on the 'formal' support that families seek from local and civil society organisations and the more 'informal' (but no less substantial) support provided by extended families, friends and neighbours. The analysis examines the types of help drawn on by the study households in each country. We analyse six cases, two in each country, that exemplify these patterns. Among the resources that some families have access to in some countries, but not in others, are school meals. Given that school meals can protect children in low-income families from a poor diet, this is an important formal resource for families and the focus of Chapter 10.

The concluding chapter brings the threads of the book together, considering the ways in which different tiers of context shape the resources available to the low-income families as they struggle to feed their children, while also reflecting on the future.

Section 1
Setting the scene

Central to the book is an emphasis on context and contextualisation. One meaning of 'contextualisation' is to situate historically, economically, politically and culturally the social phenomenon under study. In empirical research, this involves making sense of what research informants say in relation to different aspects of wider contexts which they do not reference or may not be cognisant of. 'Contextualisation' also refers to reflexivity about the context of the analytic (thought) processes by which social scientists make sense of social phenomena. In putting our analysis of original data into context we necessarily select and reify aspects of social context at the same time as we must be attentive to the ways in which meaning develops and shifts; as ethnomethodologists have well understood, meaning attached to conversation and social interaction is continually emergent. Therefore, revisiting our own research at a later date, or studies previously conducted by others, may generate new meanings in a later historical context. Similarly, in cross-national research, interpretations of national contexts may come into focus differently when considered comparatively.

Just as social science knowledge is context dependent, so social scientists are part of the knowledge context – for example, in the kinds of values we bring to research; the research designs, methods and skills we apply to our studies; the claims we make on the basis of research; and how we respond to the question 'what is knowledge "for"?' (Mills 1983).

In a book about poverty it is perhaps appropriate to note the relation of knowledge to the moral positionings of social scientists in the societies to which they belong, and to questions about the role of social scientists. As C. Wright Mills sets out in *The Sociological Imagination*, social science cannot be neutral or value free. The goal of the social scientist, as Mills sees it, is to understand the interplay of people's personal troubles with social structure; that what are very often experienced as personal troubles are also problems shared by others and only solved by bringing about social change, as in the case discussed here concerning the need to eradicate food poverty. The job of a social scientist, therefore, in studying families living on low incomes and experiencing food poverty, is to examine the phenomenon from the perspective of it being a public as well as a private issue (Mills 1983, 207). The values that are 'intrinsic to research as a distinctive occupation' (or vocation) are characterised by 'a commitment to pursue knowledge and to respect truth' (Hammersley 2015, 443; Weber 2012).

The approach we adopt in this book is to describe, understand and contextualise the multiple realities of families' everyday lives – not only how people see the world but the social conditions and causes that shape their experiences. To this end we applied a comparative case study method to the design and analysis of the research. By studying cases, as against populations or statistical samples, context-dependent knowledge is generated. As Flyvbjerg argues, researchers learn experientially in case study research. Whereas rule-based research is context independent, case study research is context dependent, with the benefit of producing knowledge that is nuanced and specific (Flyvbjerg 2004, 422). Although not generalisable, such knowledge that is gained in one context can be compared with other similar contexts, especially if cases are carefully selected and matched across contexts and analysis is both deep and rigorous (Brannen and Nilsen 2011). Selecting which aspects of context are relevant to understanding social phenomena and personal experiences is a key step in developing causal explanations. The research described in this book is informed by our own values and the explicit and implicit theories that are operationalised in our research questions and that emerge from our engagement with the data.

We examine contexts in terms of 'levels' – macro, meso and micro – and use the comparative method at each level. We compare the macro-level context of the three countries in terms of their political, economic and social institutions, together with national discourses and policies related to poverty, food and nutrition. At the meso level, we take account of characteristics of the localities in which we selected the families: their housing, the children's schools and types of school food provided, shopping amenities and other local services. However, it was not practically possible to select similar neighbourhoods across countries. At the individual/household level of everyday family life, we applied strict criteria to our selection of families and, in the book, we try as far as possible to match cases for comparison – to compare like with like. This means that we can compare similar types of families in different local and national contexts in terms of their access to income and their expenditure on food, their everyday intra-household negotiations and practices in food provisioning, and the support they access from local social networks.

In Chapter 2 we describe the main conceptual units that frame our analysis and underpin our research questions. We set out our stall concerning our theorisation of poverty. We subscribe to Townsend's (1979, 31) definition of relative poverty: that is, when people 'lack the resources to obtain the types of diet, participate in the activities, and have the living conditions and amenities which are customary, or at least widely encouraged or approved, in the societies to which they belong'. We discuss our understanding of how food poverty, like poverty, is multi-dimensional. First, food is material in the sense of providing the nutrients for health and is a resource to be managed and savoured. Second, food is also central to social life; through symbolic and customary practices, it mediates social relations and can bestow social status. Third, food is a fundamental means by which people, especially mothers, are judged, and judge themselves; food poverty is thereby exclusionary and leads to social isolation and feelings of shame. Because of the implications for the ways in which people manage food poverty, we also suggest that account needs to be taken of the dynamics of poverty: What precipitates households into poverty or keeps them afloat, and for how long? How do families and children manage social expectations when their means are substantially reduced? Finally, as key actors in their families, children are at the heart of the book; they are considered not only as consumers of food but as contributors to households, engaging actively with what it means to be food poor. We also conceptualise children as actors outside their homes, both in relation to school meals systems and in their negotiations with friends.

As noted in the Introduction, Chapter 3 sets out the research design of the study through which we sought to capture the multiple levels on which people live their lives and that constrain their opportunities and resources. We outline the comparative case approach we adopted, the multiple methods we used and how we approached the analysis. Finally, in Chapter 4 we move to the data analysis. In order to compare low income and food poverty across the three countries, we examine which types of families are most at risk of food poverty though secondary analysis of an existing international dataset, the EU Statistics on Income and Living Conditions (EU-SILC). In this chapter we also introduce the qualitative research we carried out in the three countries that forms the basis for the rest of the book.

1
The national contexts: the UK, Portugal and Norway

In this chapter we address the national contexts in which the families in the book are situated. We first offer a broad overview of the history, characteristics and welfare regimes of the three countries. We then sketch the effects of the 2008 financial crisis that have contributed to the rise of poverty and how the crisis led to the growth of food insecurity. International and national evidence is scrutinised with respect to food insecurity and the different ways in which food insecurity is measured in different datasets. We also briefly discuss the public discourses that prevail in each country in relation to poverty and food poverty, and we outline the significance of food and food policy as it relates (or not) to food insecurity in each country. Finally, we consider the role that food aid plays in each of the three countries.

The UK, Portugal and Norway: their history, characteristics and welfare regimes

The three countries in which the families in the study live are all modern Western capitalist states. In their gross domestic product (GDP) per capita rankings in Europe, Norway is in third place, the UK is in fourteenth place and Portugal is in twenty-second place. The countries have different histories and governance structures. Their welfare regimes were established at different times and under different social conditions. The UK and Norwegian welfare states were established in the 'golden age' of high economic growth, low (male) unemployment and rapidly improving health in the post-1945 era. By contrast, the creation of the welfare state in Portugal followed in the wake of the 1974 revolution.

It was also shaped by the oil crises in the 1980s and 1990s, a period when neoliberal ideas and policies were in the ascendant worldwide (Silva 2013, 25 in Alves 2014, 19). The countries also differ in their food and agricultural policies. At the time the research was carried out the UK and Portugal were members of the EU, whereas Norway was a member of the European Economic Area (EEA), which means that it partially participates in the EU's single market and contributes to the EU budget. Despite the EU and the UK having negotiated a post-Brexit trade deal, the UK's ties to the EU are now severed.

The countries also differ in terms of their history of in-migration (Chapter 7). In the UK and Portugal, migration arose in the context of the countries' legacies as former colonial powers, although their ties to their former empires differ (Horta and White 2008).

In contrast to the UK and Portugal, which have high levels of in-migration from former colonies, Norway has experienced more emigration than immigration, although the trend has reversed in recent decades through its refugee programme (Cappelen et al. 2011).

Drawing its wealth and power built on colonisation, the slave trade and early industrialisation, the UK dominated the European and world economy during the nineteenth century. Its colonialist legacy means that today Britain has one of the world's most globalised economies. Its welfare state was established after the Second World War by the Labour government of 1945–51, which introduced several key acts recommended in the Beveridge Report (Beveridge 1942) to address five 'Giant Evils' in society: squalor, ignorance, want, idleness and disease. These acts included the National Insurance Act 1946 that brought in a scheme for social security, the National Service Act 1946, the Children Act 1948 and the National Assistance Act 1948, which repealed the Poor Laws. The legislation was underpinned by universalist principles to serve the whole population from the 'cradle to the grave', in contrast to the Poor Law model that provided only residual and minimal protection for those in desperate need and at risk of destitution. The dismantling of Britain's post-war welfare state began in 1979 with the first Thatcher government and the emergence of neoliberal ideas that introduced market forces into all areas of the economy and society. The subsequent 'New Labour' governments of 1997–2010 continued to endorse the principles of neoliberalism while also aiming to support families and children at the lower end of the income spectrum (Taylor-Gooby et al. 2004).

The effects of the recession of 2008 in the UK were distinctive from those in continental Europe and the US. In the UK, the 2008 recession also played out differently from the two previous recessions despite being deeper and more prolonged. Rapid job creation resulted in more than a million more workers being in employment than in the pre-crisis period, with a huge shift from public sector to private sector employment (Coulter 2016). However, this was at the cost of sharp falls in wages and productivity and growing labour market polarisation and social inequality. Most of the growth in jobs was in part-time positions and in self-employment, much of which was involuntary. These trends suggest that a fall in wages reflects the growth in underemployment (Coulter 2016). Many workers are on zero-hours contracts, 1.8 million of them in 2016 (ONS 2017). For lone parents especially, these contracts create job insecurity and reduce household income (Harkness 2013), and unpredictable and fluctuating wages are incompatible with meeting fixed costs such as childcare.

In the UK, as more generally in Europe, children are among those groups most at risk of poverty (living in households with an income that is less than 60 per cent of median income), especially in lone-parent families (Chapter 5). Reductions in relative income poverty among lone-parent households in the UK in the 2000s resulted from a mix of policies, including employment-related benefits and universal child benefit for lone parents (Bennett and Daly 2014). However, as discussed below, so-called 'austerity' measures have reversed these effects.

Poverty is also gendered and racialised; women are slightly more likely to be in poverty than men (Bennett and Daly 2014), and people in minority ethnic groups are more likely to be in poverty than people in the majority white British group. The rate of poverty among ethnic minority women in the UK is much higher than among white women, especially among Pakistanis and Bangladeshis (Kenway and Palmer 2007; ONS 2020a). The patterns for rates of child poverty reflect these trends; data from the Households Below Average Income (HBAI) survey show that the percentage of children living in low-income households (three-year average, 2016–18) is highest among Pakistani households (47 per cent) and Bangladeshi households (41 per cent), compared with 17 per cent of children in both white British households and Indian households. The ethnic groups designated as 'other' (36 per cent), 'mixed' (33 per cent) and 'black' (30 per cent) all have a higher percentage of children living in low-income households than the national average (ONS 2020a). Around half of the 'excess poverty' of minority ethnic groups can be explained by differences in age structure, family type and family work status (Kenway and Palmer 2007), with higher than average levels of unemployment and economic inactivity among the Pakistani and Bangladeshi population (ONS 2020a). But other factors that may be important include much higher rates of in-work poverty among Bangladeshi, Pakistani and black African groups, undoubtedly linked to their concentration in low-paid work (Kenway and Palmer 2007). Underlying these patterns are racialised and racist institutionalised processes including in access to employment, housing and education. Access to citizenship is also racialised and denied to some, predominantly black, migrant groups who, as we discuss in Chapter 7, are among the poorest groups in the UK, many of whom are living in destitution.

Like Britain, Portugal is a former imperial power, but with a quite different history and a more recently established welfare state. The Carnation Revolution of 1974 that overthrew the Salazar dictatorship resulted in rapid economic development and urbanisation, high employment and an improvement in the purchasing power of households (Alves 2014). The post-Salazar constitution promised 'to create and update a national minimum income' (Art. 59, quoted by Pereirinha 1992 in Gough 1996, 6) and the first benefits (for the elderly and disabled) were introduced in 1974. Since then, however, Portugal has gone further in setting up a range of specific non-contributory assistance schemes (Gough 1996, 6). Life expectancy, educational attainment and poverty rates markedly improved as social policies addressed healthcare, poverty alleviation and unemployment protection (Alves 2014, 20). However, these did little to address socioeconomic inequalities, which remain among the highest in Europe (Eurostat 2018). High social spending relative to GDP made a significant impact on poverty rates, but not among all groups (Alves 2014). Reasons for Portugal's high level of inequality include the pervasiveness of the 'shadow economy', significant differences between the pension system and other benefits, and a clientelist model (Alves 2014, 12) in which a person (or patron) provides resources of their own or resources they control to people with inferior positions (or clients) in return for their loyalty and service (Rana and Kamal 2018). Portugal has also undergone labour market deregulation. In the first decade of the twenty-first century, it saw the largest decline in employment protection among the Organisation for Economic Co-operation and Development (OECD) countries (Venn 2009 in Pedroso 2014).

Like other Southern European countries, Portugal has been classified as having a 'familialist' welfare state (for example, Esping Anderson 1990), in which extended family is assumed to compensate or substitute for a weak welfare safety net (Parsons 1943). However, Portugal differs from other countries in Southern Europe, not least in its high rate of women's full-time employment. Historically, this is a consequence of heavy male emigration, together with the participation of young men in the African colonial wars from 1960 to the mid-1970s, which led to more developed family policies and childcare services than in other Southern European countries (Guerreiro 2014). Wall and colleagues (2013) argue that, before the 2008 crisis, Portugal saw a shift from a 'breadwinner' to a 'mixed' welfare state model in which different actors – families and public, private profit and non-profit institutions – take joint responsibility for the care of young children and to a lesser extent the elderly. In contradiction to the substitution thesis (Parsons 1943), it has been argued that familial support does not compensate for a weak welfare state but, rather, amplifies social inequality (Wall et al. 2001). However, other evidence suggests that familial networks in Portugal are protective in times of austerity (Gregório et al. 2014a; 2014b; and see Chapter 9).

As in the UK, children in Portugal are at greater risk of poverty than the adult population. In 2012, almost a third of children under 17 years of age were at risk of income poverty (below 60 per cent of median income) (INE 2014 in Arnold and Rodrigues 2015). Moreover, Alves (2014) showed that the group most at risk of poverty after social transfers is, by a large margin, lone parents with dependent children, followed by single people, and families with dependent children, while the households most immune to the risk of poverty are those with two adults and no dependent children.

In contrast to UK research, with its wealth of large-scale datasets, Portuguese research is relatively silent on race and ethnicity. The official line is that migration is not a topic that causes conflict in Portugal and that racist attitudes towards people of African descent are not 'prominent', as noted by Farkas (2017) in a report on equality data collection practices in the EU. However, a Working Group on People of African Descent in Portugal reported that migrants of African descent, particularly irregular migrants, have difficulty finding employment and are being replaced in low-paid precarious jobs by the new waves of white, 'less visible' migrants (UN 2012)[1]. The EU-SILC provides information about the country of origin of a child's parents and about household income. In 2018 the proportion of children living in a household in income poverty in Portugal was 15 per cent for those whose parents' birthplace was a foreign country, compared with 19.2 per cent for those whose parents were born in Portugal.

Although country of origin is sometimes used as a proxy for race or ethnicity, indigenous Roma communities have been identified as an ethnic group exposed to high levels of vulnerability to poverty in Portuguese society (Costa et al. 2008; Baptista 2011; SOS Racismo 1992). A national study on the Roma communities in Portugal (see Farkas 2014, 29, note 103) collected data with the support of mediators from Roma communities and concluded that these communities suffer from discrimination and 'subtle racism' that affect participation in all areas of social life, including access to housing, education and employment (Almeida et al. 2002; ECRI 2007).

In contrast to the UK and Portugal, Norway adheres to the Nordic welfare model with a comprehensive welfare state that was established after the Second World War. 'Ideals of equality, social justice, social security, solidarity and social integration have largely been realised based on the prerequisite of a strong work ethic and commitment to full employment' (Walker 2014, 177). However, although universalism underpins welfare provision, citizenship is premised on a highly educated workforce as well as highly regulated employment. Those with no or limited employment record have access to only a basic level of social assistance.

On job quality, earnings and labour market security, Norway is among the top performers in the OECD (2019). Norway operates a multilevel system of collective bargaining, with a high percentage of the workforce unionised, which results in low income inequality, mostly through compressing the wage distribution (OECD 2019). However, there is also a comparatively high rate of sick leave and the share of the working-age population on disability support is large. Some have argued that, as in other Nordic countries, the tradition of full employment and universal welfare provision has 'relegated social assistance to the margins of social programmes' (Gough 1996, 12; see also Lødemel 1992; Lødemel and Schulte 1992).

Norway is a prosperous, egalitarian society where poverty and child poverty rates are much lower than in the UK and Portugal (Bradshaw et al. 2012). Much of its wealth comes from oil, and careful management of oil profits protects Norway from global financial shocks. Unlike the UK government, which also benefited from oil reserves discovered in the North Sea in the 1960s, the Norwegian government decided to retain substantial public/national ownership of oil and gas reserves, rather than sell off the licences to commercial and private interests, and, recognising that oil and gas were finite resources, invested and is continuing to invest the profits from the production of oil and gas into a public savings fund for current and future generations (Norges Bank 2019). Following the global financial crisis, in 2009 the government stimulated the economy by spending an unprecedented amount of Norway's oil wealth (Hippe et al. 2013). Norway is one of only three OECD countries in which the global financial crisis did not entail increasing public debt (Schäfer and Streeck 2013). Given the limited impact of the crisis on the economy or rates of employment, there has been little internal pressure for welfare retrenchment. However, immigration and work 'activation' policies are high on the political agenda (Sørvoll 2015).

Despite Norway's relatively generous welfare state, those who live in households whose main income is from welfare benefits are over-represented in the low-income group, especially lone-parent households. In 2016, 28.5 per cent of lone-parent households belonged to the low-income group compared with 8.6 per cent of dual-parent households (Statistics Norway 2018a). However, poverty is increasingly an ethnic minority phenomenon. Unemployment rates are significantly higher for immigrants; those who are foreign born are much more likely to be long-term unemployed than those born in Norway, the education levels and skills of immigrants being considerably lower than those of the rest of the population (OECD 2019). More than half of all children living in households with persistent low income have an immigrant background (Statistics Norway 2014). Children in families that have migrated from Somalia, Iraq and Afghanistan stand out as over-represented in the low-income group. Migrant families not only often tend to have a weak occupational status; they also often have many family members to support (Statistics Norway 2014). Not only do migrants in Norway experience discrimination in areas such as recruitment, housing and healthcare (Søholt and Wessel 2010); they also experience racist attitudes, as a survey by the research organisation Fafo (2019) revealed: 35 per cent of participants agreed completely or partially with a statement that a woman who wears a hijab can't expect to be treated in the same way as other women in Norway. The Norwegian government's Action Plan against Racism and Discrimination on the Grounds of Ethnicity and Religion (Norwegian Ministry of Culture 2020) acknowledges that 'discrimination on the basis of skin colour can affect both people who have immigrated to Norway and their descendants, as well as people who were born or have grown up in Norway with Norwegian parents' and that 'more research is needed on discrimination based on skin colour and other external characteristics' (Norwegian Ministry of Culture 2020, 23).

Poverty and inequality among families after the 2008 financial crisis

The global financial crisis of 2008, primarily caused by deregulation in the financial industry, led to 'one of the deepest and most extensive economic downturns in recent history' (Margerison-Zilko et al. 2016). For example, unemployment rose to 10 per cent in the US and the EU (UN 2011), and in the housing market over 15 per cent of mortgages in the US were either 'delinquent or foreclosed' by 2010 (Fligstein and Goldstein 2011). In response, many governments in Europe, either of their own volition or at the behest of the international financial institutions, adopted stringent 'austerity' measures (McKee et al. 2012). Although ostensibly designed to cut financial deficits, they were also arguably driven by the ideological goal of reducing the public sector (Windebank and Whitworth 2014; Alston 2019).

In the UK, employment grew in the post-crisis period, but at the cost of a sharp fall in wages and productivity, as noted above (Coulter 2016). In this period, successive UK governments introduced austerity measures, cutting benefits and funding to local authorities for expenditure on public services. Although this was accompanied by the rhetoric that 'we are all in it together', these cuts have particularly hit those already on low incomes, including large and lone-parent families. Deep welfare retrenchment, following the Welfare Reform Act 2012, introduced progressively harsher cuts to welfare spending, such as the freezing of child benefit for four years and the introduction of a 'benefit cap' on the overall value of benefits a family can receive, including a limit to the amount of housing benefit that can be claimed, despite rising rents. Under this act, the introduction of the under-occupancy penalty (known as the 'bedroom tax'), the implementation of Universal Credit and increasingly restricted access to Employment and Support Allowance (ESA) for disabled people were opposed unsuccessfully. More recently, in April 2017, the 'two-child limit' on the child elements of child tax credit and Universal Credit came into effect, discriminating against larger families.

It is also important to note that devolution in the UK has created policy differences around social security and some other areas. For example, the Scottish government took a decision to try to mitigate some of the negative outcomes of austerity measures introduced by the UK parliament, such as mitigating the 'bedroom tax'. Philip Alston, the then UN Special Rapporteur on extreme poverty and equal rights, commended the Scottish government in his report on their actions to try to alleviate child poverty in Scotland with the limited powers they have at their disposal (Alston 2019, 19). According to data from the HBAI survey, for a time, child poverty rates were lower in Scotland than the rest of the UK, although some of those gains have been eroding over recent years (JRF 2020). In addition, the Scottish government started routinely generating food insecurity estimates in the Scottish Health Survey in 2017, the first of the four UK nations to do so. One of the main driving forces behind this move were the recommendations emanating from a government-appointed short life working group on food insecurity (Independent Working Group on Food Poverty 2016).

There have been many analyses of the cumulative distributional consequences of national austerity measures in the UK, for example, by the Institute for Fiscal Studies (Hood and Waters 2017), the Institute for Public Policy Research (Tucker and Stirling 2017; Tucker 2017) and the Equality and Human Rights Commission (Portes et al. 2018). The conclusions are clear: that cuts to welfare spending have disproportionately affected families with children, particularly lone-parent families, which make up around 25 per cent of all families with children in the UK. Poverty and child poverty have risen and, with the UK's exit from the EU, the future, especially for those with the lowest incomes, looks bleak.

Cuts to welfare spending have not only reduced collective and household resources, but also changed the normative expectations of the post-war welfare state. As Philip Alston (2019, 5) said, following his visit to the UK in November 2018, a 'harsh and uncaring ethos' and a 'punitive, mean-spirited and often callous approach' have characterised welfare policy since 2010, leading to 'great misery'. He argues that the basis of this change is ideological rather than economic, designed to achieve social re-engineering and restructure the relationship between the people and the state.

The global financial crisis hit Portugal hard. The country entered a deep recession. In 2011, the Socialist Party government, pressured by high interest rates and social unrest, asked for a bailout loan from the IMF, the ECB and the European Commission (collectively the 'Troika'). The Memorandum of Agreement between the government and the Troika was ultimately followed by a right-wing coalition government that imposed a set of draconian policies including severe retrenchment of social welfare, reductions in benefit levels and reduced eligibility. In this context, Portugal has seen a slowdown in social and economic progress (Nunes 2018), with unemployment rising to unprecedented rates (Pires et al. 2014). Austerity policies had a negative impact on family incomes via unemployment and cuts to wages and social security. Although most families were affected, poorer families were hit the hardest, despite the official rhetoric, similar to that in the UK, that claimed 'sacrifices were being shared by all' (Rodrigues et al. 2016). Although lone parents in Portugal are not entitled to specific benefits, the cuts included restrictions and reductions to some family benefits that have special conditions or amounts for lone parents.[2] A widespread increase in the number of households in relative poverty (with household income less than 60 per cent of median equivalised household income) was a direct effect of cuts in social transfers, namely in family benefits and Social Insertion Income (Rodrigues et al. 2016). Since the election of a centre-left prime minister, António Costa, in 2015, as leader of a leftist alliance, some aspects of austerity have been removed or reversed.

Norway witnessed only a minor rise in unemployment following the 2008 recession, and a slight fall in economic growth (Midthjell 2011). It did not introduce austerity measures. However, neoliberal notions that paid work should be the central route to welfare had already gained political momentum in the 1990s (Richards et al. 2016). In October 2013, the majority centre-left coalition government lost office and was replaced by a minority right-wing coalition. One of the policies brought in by the former government – to give lone parents a 'transitional allowance' until the youngest child was three years old – was changed in a negative direction.[3] A further policy change was to impose a cap on the total value of benefits a family receiving a disability pension could claim. Although none of the policy legislation mentions the words 'immigrants' or 'integration', it has been argued that the issue of lone parenthood among migrants, particularly from Somalia, and the take-up of disability pensions by migrant fathers with three or more children were among the impetuses for these changes (Grødem 2017, 83).

Rising household food insecurity in Europe after the 2008 financial crisis

There is evidence that household food insecurity has risen in some European countries since the global recession, though definitions and methodologies for measuring it vary. Many researchers and policy actors draw on the Food and Agriculture Organisation's (FAO) definition of 'food insecurity' as 'being unable to consume an adequate quality or sufficient quantity of food for health, in socially acceptable ways, or the uncertainty that one will be able to do so' (Dowler et al. 2001).

The FAO's Voices of the Hungry survey includes the countries in this book: the UK, Portugal and Norway. Administered by Gallup World

Poll (GWP), the survey uses the Food Insecurity Experience Scale (FIES) survey module, which is derived from the US Department of Agriculture (USDA) Household Food Security Survey Module (HFSSM) and the Latin American and Caribbean Food Security Scale (Ballard et al. 2013). The FIES is composed of eight questions that have been validated for measuring the severity of food insecurity in different cultural, linguistic and development contexts. According to FAO estimates based on the FIES, in 2017 about 10 per cent of the world's population was exposed to 'severe food insecurity' (reducing quantities, skipping meals and experiencing hunger in the past year), corresponding to around 770 million people.[4] At the regional level, this ranges from almost 30 per cent of people in Africa to 1.4 per cent in North America and Europe (FAO et al. 2018). The average for Europe, based on data in 2015–17 is 1.5 per cent, with the highest rates found in Albania (10.5 per cent) and Romania (4.1 per cent) (FAO et al. 2018, 7–9).

Table 1.1 shows that, according to the FIES measure adopted by FAO, the prevalence of severe food insecurity in the total population in

Table 1.1 Severe food insecurity in the UK, Portugal and Norway according to the Food Insecurity Experience Scale: all households and households with children aged 15 and under.

	UK (%)	Portugal (%)	Norway (%)	European average (%)
All households (2015–17)	3.4	3.7	1.2	1.5
Households with children aged 15 and under (2014–15)	10.4	4.9	1.7	3.6

Source: Adapted from FAO et al. 2018; Pereira et al. 2017.
Notes: FAO have estimated the percentage of people in the total population living in households where at least one adult is food insecure. To reduce the impact of year-to-year sampling variability, estimates are presented as three-year averages. Country-level results are presented only for those countries for which estimates are based on official national data (Ecuador, Ghana, Malawi, Republic of Korea, Saint Lucia, Seychelles and the US) or as provisional estimates, based on FAO Voices of the Hungry data collected through the Gallup World Poll, for countries whose national statistical authorities (NSAs) provided permission to publish them. Note that consent to publication does not necessarily imply validation of the estimate by the NSAs and that the estimate is subject to revision as soon as suitable data from official national sources are available. Global, regional and subregional aggregates reflect data collected in approximately 150 countries.

2017 was slightly higher in Portugal (3.7 per cent) than the UK (3.4 per cent). Both countries have rates of severe food insecurity more than double the European average of 1.5 per cent. Norway, by contrast, is below the average, 1.2 per cent of the population having experienced severe food insecurity within the past year. However, an analysis of the 2014–15 data which focused on families that included children[5] (FAO et al. 2018) living with a severely food-insecure adult found that, in all three countries, families with children aged 15 years and under are at greater risk of severe food insecurity compared with all households in severe food insecurity (see Table 1.1). In the UK, rates of food insecurity among families with children are much higher than the European average and in the other two countries studied here (Pereira et al. 2017).

However, the findings do not tell us about the types of family at risk, for example whether they are headed by one or two parents; and, because the first surveys were conducted in 2014, they cannot tell us about change over time through the global recession of 2008. In the absence of comparative time series data, researchers have used a proxy for household food insecurity – 'being unable to afford a meal with a protein source every other day' – which is included in two European surveys: the EU-SILC and the European Quality of Life survey. Analysing the EU-SILC, Loopstra and colleagues (2015) found that, before 2009, the number of people across Europe reporting this experience was declining: between 2005 and 2009 the number fell from 12 per cent of the EU-27 population to 8.7 per cent. In 2010, this trend reversed: 'food insecurity' rose to 10.9 per cent in 2012. There were marked variations, however, between countries. In further analysis, Loopstra and colleagues (2016) examined the 'drivers' of these increases in food insecurity – in particular, unemployment and decline in wage levels – and evaluated whether differing types and degrees of social security spending helped mitigate or exacerbate the effects on household food security. Analysing the same indicator in three waves (2003, 2007 and 2011) of a different survey, the European Quality of Life survey, Davis and Geiger also explored whether food insecurity had risen since the 2008 crisis. Adopting a different analytic approach, they investigated the role of policy by examining variations across different welfare state regimes: 'Anglo-Saxon', 'Bismarckian', 'Scandinavian', 'Southern' and 'Eastern' (Davis and Geiger 2017, 347).

The results of both analyses are broadly similar. Loopstra and colleagues (2016, 47) found rising food insecurity overall, particularly in the UK, and concluded that 'rising food insecurity within European countries was closely linked to rising unemployment and falling wages'. However, they also found that, in countries where social protection spending had been high, rising unemployment did not lead to greater food insecurity. Conversely, where social protection spending was low, declining annual average wages were closely connected to increasing food insecurity. Davis and Geiger (2017) also found that food insecurity has risen across all welfare regimes but with variation between them. The overall prevalence of food insecurity was considerably higher in the Eastern European regime throughout 2003–11 than in other regimes, but, contrary to their expectations, the rise in food insecurity was sharpest in the Anglo-Saxon regime. The authors suggest that this is surprising given that the impact of the economic crisis has been less severe in the UK (except Northern Ireland initially) than in Southern Europe. They offer some possible explanations for this, including increased welfare conditionality in the UK and familialism in Southern Europe, issues that are taken up in this book. Furthermore, there are some inconsistencies in the results of analyses of the different datasets for some countries. In particular, Portugal seems to be an exception to the general trends identified by Loopstra and colleagues (2016), while Davis and Geiger note that their tests for conceptual validity suggest that their Portuguese findings should be treated with caution.

Food poverty and public discourse

The ways in which societies respond to food poverty reflect and shape broader discourses concerning 'the poor', for policies are primarily ways of framing social problems (Bacchi and Goodwin 2016; Sayer 2017). In the UK, those living in poverty are typically portrayed as blameworthy and as 'scroungers', 'sponging' off the state, 'frauds', unwilling to work and making the 'wrong choices' (Baillie 2011; Chase and Walker 2015; Patrick 2016). Such discourses perpetuate a narrative linking family dysfunction, worklessness and welfare dependency (Garrett 2015) and the 'othering' of people living in poverty (Lister 2004; Krumer-Nevo and Benjamin 2010). In the UK, the term 'food poverty' is synonymous with 'food banks'. In an analysis of relevant newspaper articles from different political perspectives, we found that most articles related to the growth in the numbers of food bank users, the need and reasons for their existence (benefit reform or supply fuelling demand), and the rise in malnutrition owing to the poor food provided (Knight et al. 2018). The experiences of families with children living in food poverty (whether or not they used a food bank), the multi-dimensional nature of food poverty, which includes food as a human right, and the social participatory aspects of food and eating were largely absent (Knight et al. 2018).

Poverty discourses in Portugal seem to place less emphasis on blaming those in poverty. As poverty rates rose in Portugal after the 2008 financial crisis, poverty was increasingly described in the media as 'worrying', 'disturbing' and 'a social emergency'. Food security as a phenomenon is largely absent from public discourse; it is both cognitively and geographically seen as relating to the Global South. In 2009 among charity organisations and opposition political parties a consensus emerged that intervention was necessary as poverty became widespread, while state actors downplayed the issue (Cardoso et al. 2017). With middle-class families also hit by the crisis, the term 'new poor' entered common parlance, a concept that also pointed to and resonated with the existing high level of social inequality that characterises Portuguese society. Between 2010 and 2012 charity organisations stressed the moral imperative of helping those 'in need', which ran alongside an emphasis on 'solidarity' as an intrinsic feature of Portuguese culture.

Official discourse relating to poverty is muted in Norway (Walker and Chase 2014), and state actors maintain that poverty and social deprivation have been eradicated by the establishment of a strong protective welfare state (Hagen and Lødemel 2003, 210). Instead, terms such as 'lack of opportunities and possibilities', 'participation on equal terms' and 'social exclusion' are current. Food poverty as a phenomenon is seen as belonging to the distant past (Skuland 2018; Borch and Kjaerness 2016). In the present day it is seldom understood to involve having insufficient food on the table, despite the high price of food in Norway, a subject that does arouse debate. Rather, charities are left to draw attention to families with children who cannot afford to eat properly. However, food poverty enters public debate indirectly in reportage of class and educational inequalities and their effects on health and diet, for example, obesity, lifestyle diseases and longevity, and the topic of universalising school meals was hotly debated in the 2013 election.

Food, food policy and responsibility for household food insecurity

The UK, Portugal and Norway have all ratified the International Covenant on Economic, Social and Cultural Rights (ICESCR), which includes the 'right to food': 'when every man, woman or child, alone or in community with others have physical and economic access at all times to adequate food or the means for its procurement'. However, there is little evidence that their national laws respect, reflect and enforce the ICESCR's obligations, and their food systems and policies differ.

Since food price increases disproportionately affect households with smaller incomes, part of the explanation for growing food insecurity in parts of Europe may be the rise and volatility of food prices relative to wages, especially following the food price shock of 2007–8 (Reeves et al. 2017). In Europe, food prices rose by approximately 13 per cent between 2005 and 2008, while other goods and services remained relatively flat (European Commission 2016 in Reeves et al. 2017, 1414). However, there are differences in the relative change of prices of different types of food, as well as their impacts on households in different countries, given the differences in their welfare systems (Reeves et al. 2017). Food prices are generally far higher in Norway than in the UK and Portugal (Eurostat 2019): Norwegian prices are more than 20 per cent above the EU average, whereas Portugal's and the UK's are 20 per cent below it. However, wages are much lower in Portugal. In the UK, there are large disparities between the food spending of those at the lower and higher ends of the income spectrum: an average 10.6 per cent of household income was spent on food between 2017 and 2018, compared with 15.2 per cent for the lowest 20 per cent of households (Defra 2020).

Britain's food supply is heavily dependent on imports: the agricultural sector produces only around half of the food eaten (Lang 2020). Since the 1970s, food and cuisine in the UK have become more varied largely as a consequence of the growth of imports, the commercialisation of food, the internationalisation of food preferences and the huge rise in eating out. These changes have led to dietary diversity ranging from varied cuisine based on fresh produce to reliance on highly or 'ultra' processed food (Monteiro et al. 2018). Given that research shows that in the UK healthier foods are more expensive than less healthy ones (Jones et al. 2014), it is unsurprising that there is a long-standing social gradient in diet (Dowler 2008; Maguire and Monsivais 2015).

Access to sufficient healthy or 'good' food has never been considered a matter for the UK government; no government department has explicit responsibility for food poverty or food insecurity (Dowler and O'Connor 2012; Lambie-Mumford and Dowler 2014). As is typical of a neoliberal welfare state, successive UK governments 'have long favoured what are often termed "cheap food" policies' that externalise environmental and other costs and contribute to keeping UK labour costs low (Lang et al. 2017, 10). In the context of this 'leave it to Tesco' approach to food policy (Lang 2020), 'it has been left to civil society, trades unions and academic researchers to make the case that neither welfare benefits nor statutory minimum wages are sufficient to enable people to purchase enough food for health, particularly in families with dependent children' (Dowler and O'Connor 2012, 48). Although some universal and targeted benefits do address food needs, these are the responsibility of the Department of Health (DH) and the Department for Education (DfE) rather than the Department of Work and Pensions (DWP) that is responsible for social security. These benefits include Healthy Start vouchers, a food benefit aimed at low-income mothers of young children (the responsibility of DH). Free school meals provision, funded by DfE, is provided for all children until age seven and means tested for older children in England (Chapter 10).

Food is at the heart of Portuguese culture, which has a broadly Mediterranean diet with a great range of domestically produced fruit and vegetables. Portugal's national cuisine has been recognised as part of its 'intangible heritage' (Sobral 2014, 109). Although it has been suggested that in its pure form a Mediterranean diet is today only to be found on 'the rich man's table' (Amilien 2012), there is little evidence that income plays an important role in dietary inequalities in Portugal (for example, Moreira and Padrão 2004). Data covering 2008–12 shows a falling away from the Mediterranean diet (already detected before the crisis), with a decrease in meat and fish and an increase in carbohydrates (National Institute of Statistics 2014). Smallholdings that are too small to make a living allow some people to produce fruit, vegetables and poultry for their own consumption (see Moreira and Padrao 2004). According to data from the Household Budget Survey (HBS 2017), expenditure on 'restaurants and hotels' in Portugal in 2017 was relatively high (around 12 per cent of household expenditure) compared with the UK (around 10 per cent) and Norway (7 per cent); much of this difference is likely explained by the common practice in Portugal of workers eating lunch in local canteens.

Adequate food is not included as a social or economic right in Portuguese constitutional law. Rather, food and nutrition have been linked to the right to health protection and health polices in general. Hence policy strategies in the field of food and nutrition do not directly address the barriers to healthy eating in low-income families (Gregório et al. 2014b). Means-tested school meals are available to children in Portuguese state schools and are funded by the government in combination with local municipalities, in line with national food-based standards and pricing. School meals provision is framed as a health intervention; in particular it aims to address rising levels of obesity and also promote the adoption of the Mediterranean diet (Truninger 2013; Truninger and Sousa 2019; see Chapter 10).

The origins of Norwegian cuisine lie in Norway's rural, non-colonial past, although growing urbanisation has resulted in fewer people being directly connected to agriculture and to food cultures based on the farm's or village's own products (Amilien 2012), and international trade and travel have influenced the preparation of 'traditional' foods such as salt cod (Notaker 2018). There is no distinctive Nordic cuisine, unlike the 'Mediterranean diet', and food preferences vary between the Nordic countries. Compared with Finland and Sweden, food in Norway (and Denmark) is 'modest' and 'simple', with sandwiches for lunch a norm and boiled vegetables, often potatoes, eaten with the evening meal (Holm et al. 2012). Potatoes, fruits and vegetables such as cabbage, carrots and onions are important ingredients. With the internationalisation of the food market the produce available has been greatly extended (Wandel 1995), but many types of imported fruits and vegetables are more expensive in Norway than in other Western countries (OECD 1993). Norway has experienced a rise in eating out, though this remains lower than in the other two countries studied here: less money is spent eating out than in the UK or Portugal, and research also suggests that less time is given to eating out and that it happens less frequently (Warde et al. 2007; Lund et al. 2017).

In Norway's social democratic welfare state, access to food as an entitlement was used as an argument for raising poor families' incomes to a socially acceptable level through a universal social security system (Richards et al. 2016). However, no official standards relating to food needs exist, and claims of a minimum standard have met strong political reservations concerning the definition of poverty (Richards et al. 2016, 66–7). In contrast to the UK, in Norway there is a consensus around 'sufficient income', rather than low food prices, reflecting a long-standing red–green alliance that supports agricultural and labour interests, that is, both high food prices and high wages. Typical of the Nordic welfare state, there is an emphasis in Norway on national wage negotiations and universal social rights (Richards et al. 2016, 66–7). However, in contrast to other Scandinavian countries (such as Sweden), no school meals are provided in Norway, where health discourses have historically promoted a cold lunch (see Chapter 10).

Food aid in austerity Europe

In the period since the global financial crisis, food 'aid', 'assistance' and 'charity' have become commonplace in many European countries as means of providing food for people who struggle to obtain enough by the usual means (Lambie-Mumford and Dowler 2015, 501–11; Richards et al. 2016; Riches 2018). These initiatives, developed originally to address 'emergencies' in times of recession and changing/shrinking welfare provision, are no longer relegated to the margins of welfare provision. As in North America, they have become institutionalised in parts of Europe.

It is difficult to estimate and compare the extent of food aid within and across countries, not least because of inconsistencies in terminology and lack of systematic data (Lambie-Mumford and Silvasti 2020). In practice, 'food assistance' may include a 'blend' of state and non-statutory providers: for example, government financial support to non-governmental organisations (NGOs) operating in this sector; or NGOs implementing government-led programmes, as in the cases of Poland (Gentilini 2013) and Portugal (see below).

In the UK, there is no formal state arrangement supporting the provision of food aid through charities, though the positioning of welfare rights advisors in food banks has made the distinction between charity and the public sector opaque. However, 'civil society intervention which redistributes so-called "surplus" foods to people in need, sourced either from the retail sector or from generous citizens, is growing and implicitly encouraged (for example, Fareshare and Trussell Trust)' (Dowler and O'Connor 2012, 48). Partnerships between food retailers and food poverty charities, such as Tesco and FareShare, normalise the redistribution of surplus food as a solution to food poverty (Caplan 2017). Although such interventions come in a variety of forms, community and cooked meals as well as food parcels, for example, food banks have become synonymous with poverty in the UK, where a growing body of evidence has documented rising numbers of food banks and of food bank usage since the 2010 set of welfare reforms. Trussell Trust, a network that includes around 60 per cent of food banks in the UK, reported that they had 65 food banks in early 2011 and this had risen to over 1,200 in early 2019 (Sosenko et al. 2019, 16).

In Portugal, the church and civil society have historically played an important part in local welfare systems (Gough 1996). The economic crisis led to a retrenchment in benefits for families, and public policy moved implicitly towards a residual model. As Wall and Correira (2014, 2) note, 'the new focus of family policies has underlined support for very poor families, the strengthening of selectivity mechanisms and a move away from state responsibility for families in general, by encouraging the non-governmental sector and families themselves to act as the "frontline" of support for persons "in need".' State responsibility for disadvantaged families has in effect been delegated to third-sector institutions (mostly private publicly subsidised NGOs) and to regional and municipal authorities (Wall and Correira 2014).

In 2012 the Social Emergency Programme (PES) was created in Portugal to minimise the negative impacts of the financial crisis on the most vulnerable, a strategy focused on emergency assistance. This included an emergency food programme based on a network of social canteens that provide meals to the most disadvantaged. The number of canteens has risen sharply between 2011 and 2015 (Perista and Baptista 2017). Social canteens provide at least one meal every day to recipients. The use of social canteens increased by 33 per cent from 2012 to 2017. However, in January 2017 the government announced the end of the programme (except for the elderly and the homeless) and replaced it with a programme involving the distribution of uncooked food (Perista and Baptista 2017). As in other countries, there has been a growth in the redistribution of surplus food as a means to alleviate food poverty. The charity Re-food was established in Lisbon in 2011 with the aim of redistributing surplus cooked food from restaurants and cafes to those in need. In five years (2011–16) the initiative grew from one to 4,000 volunteers, 34 to 2,500 beneficiaries, 1,000 to 46,000 meals served per month, and from one centre that covered 30 food sources to 25 centres covering 900 sources of food. Volunteers can collect food on foot, by bicycle or by car. The beneficiaries can be either occasional (those who access the initiative sporadically) or regular (those who are enrolled in the initiative and use it with some regularity). For people with reduced mobility, the initiative makes deliveries at home. There are also defined distribution points, usually places that do not have a Re-food centre nearby (Augusto forthcoming).

Food banks, too, have proliferated. One study estimated that 4.5 per cent of the Portuguese population were food bank beneficiaries in 2010 (Gentilini 2013). Data from Portugal's national federation of food banks draw attention to the growing number of people helped by these organisations. Before the economic crisis in 2008, food banks provided help for 249,593 individuals; this had grown to 384,930 people in 2014 (FEBA 2015). Journalists such as Mario Queiroz (2013) also report the resurgence of soup kitchens in Lisbon, bringing back the *sopa dos pobres* provided by Catholic organisations. These were widespread in the 1950s as a means of 'feeding the poor', when long lines of people would queue for their one hot meal of the day.

In Norway, by contrast, the welfare system is assumed to avoid absolute poverty of a kind that threatens food security (Richards et al. 2016, 67). Local authorities have the responsibility to provide social assistance within a national regulatory framework (Gough 1996, 12; see Chapter 7). The Norwegian Labour and Welfare Administration (NAV) was established in 2006 to bring employment and social security into one agency. As well as receiving their welfare benefits via NAV, people may apply for additional payments that are discretionary to meet extraordinary expenditure of various sorts (Frazer and Marlier 2016, 20).[6] The outcomes of such requests depend on the judgements of bureaucrats who can set conditions in accordance with recipients' circumstances. Interrogation about private matters can lead to feelings of shame and stigma (Walker 2014, 177; Goffman 1974).

Compared with Portugal and the UK, charity and the private sector play a marginal role in addressing poverty and food poverty in Norway (Richards et al. 2016). This does not mean that poverty does not exist, but that the Norwegian welfare system is assumed to prevent the kind of poverty that threatens food security (Richards et al. 2016, 67). However, food charity is to be found in Norway, often run by the Salvation Army and other voluntary organisations that provide soup kitchens and food banks. Many of the recipients are the homeless and others facing particularly acute hardship. In Oslo the Poor House (*Fattighuset*) is a volunteer organisation established in 1994 that provides clothing, food, dentistry and counselling to those in need. Although the Poor House relies on donations from supermarkets,[7] food businesses in Norway do not play a major role in addressing food insecurity as they do in Portugal and the UK. However, in recent years, conservative-led (centre-right) governments have given more weight to 'consumer interests' and cheap food, in contrast to previous policies that protected the food sector from competition from imports in the context of an organised labour market (Richards et al. 2016).

The EU's Common Agricultural Policy (CAP) distributes 'commodity intervention stocks' to participating member states through the Fund for European Aid to the Most Deprived (FEAD) (until 2013 the MDP [Most Deprived People] food programme) (Lambie-Mumford and Silvasti 2020, 20). Although the stated goals of the programme include market stabilisation, waste reduction and feeding deprived people, NGOs, academics and others have heavily criticised the increasing dominance of charity as a response to poverty in the Global North, including the normalisation and institutionalisation of food waste as a solution to food poverty (Caplan 2017). In response to these concerns, some have examined the potential value of, and organised around, the idea of a 'right to food' (Riches 2018; 2020). In the UK, the right to food is at the heart of campaigns such as those run by Church Action on Poverty, Sustain, and the Children's Future Food Inquiry. Recognising the importance of meeting households' immediate needs, 'right to food' activists argue that 'food responses' to food poverty are inconsistent with official definitions of food insecurity, such as those of the FAO, and contrary to the United Nations Committee on Economic, Social and Cultural Rights (UNESCR), which gives people the 'right to food', not the right to be fed (Lambie-Mumford 2013; Riches and Silvasti 2014). Many argue that food charity depoliticises food poverty, absolves governments from meeting their obligations to promote, protect and respect people's right to food and further marginalises those who are already materially and socially excluded.

In this chapter we have endeavoured to give the reader some broad understanding of the three countries that are the focus of the book. Their wealth, welfare regimes and the history of those regimes differ in significant ways. In effect they constitute a 'contrast of contexts' (Kohn 1987) in their welfare models: the UK's residual welfare state, Portugal's mixed economy of welfare (state, families and private and not-for-profit actors) and Norway's highly regulated solidaristic model that is typical of Nordic states. We have indicated that the exacerbation of poverty by the global financial crisis of 2008 played out differently in the three countries: Norway was affected very little by the crisis, and families with children were most affected in the UK and Portugal. The rise in food poverty which has occurred in many European countries since 2008 has not only brought different public policy responses to the crisis but has exposed the lack at the national level of policies concerning the social and economic right to food. As a consequence, the evidence relating to food insecurity is poor. This book will, we hope, contribute to understanding which families were most at risk of food poverty and how low-income families with children were affected in their experiences of accessing, sharing and eating food in their daily lives.

Notes

1. In Portugal, as in some other European countries, 'the issue of feasibility [of collecting data about race or ethnicity] conceals political choices not necessarily favouring the effective enforcement of EU nondiscrimination law'. A note in UN (2012, 6) suggests that, 'According to the Portuguese Report, the current Minister for Justice notes that the issue is not on the political agenda due to the existence of "a kind of counter-prejudice … there is an official and institutional discourse that problems of discrimination are not applicable to the Portuguese. This paralyses any possibility of debate on this matter."'

2. There are no specific benefits for lone-parent families. However, under certain conditions they are entitled to a higher allowance – for example, family allowance for disabled children. They have no right to alimony legally set by the courts (Browne et al. 2020; Duffy 2013, appendix 5).

3. It was changed to the youngest child turning three. Changes were also made to eligibility criteria. Norway is one of the few countries in the OECD that has a separate, subsistence-level benefit payable to lone parents, known as 'transitional allowance' (Skevik 2006).

4. The FIES Survey Module (FIES-SM) is available in individual-referenced and household-referenced versions. The FIES-SM applied in the GWP as part of the Voices of the Hungry project measures food insecurity at the individual level. Although the results can be disaggregated to identify which sub-groups within a country are most affected by food insecurity, this depends on sample size in each country, and the FAO report does not give the breakdown.

5. Although food insecurity among children cannot be directly measured using the FIES-SM, it is possible to estimate the percentage of children living in food-insecure households. To do so, data are needed on the number of children in each household surveyed. See Voices of the Hungry (2016, 48) and Fram and colleagues (2015) for more detailed discussion of the challenges of measuring child food insecurity.

6. In Norway, 'the national framework legislation on social assistance offers only very vague directions as to the level of benefits and eligibility criteria, leaving a large room of manoeuvre for municipal policy guidelines and discretion at the hands of individual case workers' (Frazer and Marlier 2016, 15). Social assistance consists of three main components: a standardised allowance for ordinary living expenses, support for housing and housing-related expenditure and support for extraordinary expenditure of various sorts (Frazer and Marlier 2016, 20).

7. In 2016, changes to rules about selling products at or past their expiry dates meant a reduction in donations to the Poor House (Husebø-Evensen 2016).

2
Research questions and concepts

The study, 'Families and Food in Hard Times', on which this book is based was located at the Thomas Coram Research Unit, Institute of Education, UCL, UK, and funded by the European Research Council from 2014 to 2019.[1] It was carried out by an international team whose members were located in the three countries and had a mix of disciplinary backgrounds and methodological expertise.[2]

In this chapter we set out the study's main research questions and the concepts we drew upon: the ways in which we understand food poverty and its different dimensions; how we conceptualise households as resource units; the temporal dimensions of food poverty; and our theoretical approach to children both as affected by food poverty and as active contributors to family life.

The study's research questions

The study was conceived in the period following the 2008 financial crisis when increasing evidence emerged in the UK and elsewhere in 'austerity Europe' of children going hungry and of families going to food banks. Its aim was to investigate the social conditions in which low-income families with children were unable to feed themselves adequately and the consequences for parents' and children's food practices and other aspects of their lives. Through a cross-national mixed-methods research design and a comparative approach, the study examined the extent of food insecurity for low-income families with children in three European countries impacted upon by, respectively, high-, medium- and low-level austerity measures: the UK, Portugal and Norway. Through analysis of large-scale datasets the project set out to identify which children and which types of households were at greatest risk of food insecurity and, in order to place these data in context, to compare public policy, charitable and other types of initiatives and provisions that aimed to address household food insecurity, including how food insecurity as a 'public issue' was framed discursively.

In framing the study's research questions, we recognised that living on a low income and experiencing food insecurity are not only variable but specific to the social conditions in which families find themselves in terms of the resources available to them and the ways in which they manage poverty. We therefore carried out intensive qualitative research with low-income families with children aged 11–15, including those families with one or more parent in employment and those who were reliant on benefits in each country. We also took account as far as possible of the local geographical contexts, and we selected low-income families in the same types of areas in each country (regions of capital cities and less urbanised areas).

The questions we sought to address in the qualitative study of families included: how food figured in children's and families' everyday routines and social relations; how families managed food in the context of poverty; the types of help they accessed; whether families relied on public and charitable sources of support; who took responsibility for food work, including children's contributions; and how far families drew on informal sources of help, for example, extended families and social networks. We investigated the ways in which households procured food, including the effects of local (un)availability of food. We looked at the effects of parents' paid employment and how far school meals mitigated food poverty for children. We examined the effects of food poverty on the social participation of both parents and children and the emotional consequences for children of social exclusion from their peer groups – for example, feelings of stigma and shame.

Food poverty: a relative and political approach

Definitions of poverty and food poverty have a long history (Maxwell 1996; Dowler et al. 2011; Kneafsey et al. 2012). A central component of any conceptualisation of poverty or food poverty is 'the notion of food scarcity or deprivation in the basic need for food' (Tarasuk 2001, 7). For example, Seebohm Rowntree's (1901) definition of poverty – based on the minimum income that people might expect to receive and below which no one could be expected to fall – included at its heart adequate food for 'physical efficiency'. Although there has been much debate about whether Rowntree's concept of 'primary poverty' represented a 'subsistence' level equivalent to 'absolute' poverty, he later explained that the line was drawn at this level for political reasons, to avoid being accused of 'crying for the moon' (Briggs 2000, 10). Rowntree's message was directed to the society of his time, when between a quarter and a third of the population of York were living in conditions that made it impossible for them to make a full contribution to the economic and military life of their country (Bradshaw and Sainsbury 2000). However, as Rowntree acknowledged, no one could really be expected to live on this 'primary poverty income' in real life. Rather, as Peter Townsend later pointed out, 'social pressures, to drink in the local pub, to buy presents for the children, to be a normal social being especially in adversity, required a higher budget' (Glennerster et al. 2004, 25).

Research in 1950s and 1960s Britain by Townsend and his colleague Abel-Smith (Abel-Smith and Townsend 1965; Townsend 1954, 2010, 1979) provided the basis for the now widely used concept of 'relative poverty'. According to Townsend (1979, 31), people can be said to be in poverty 'when they lack the resources to obtain the types of diet, participate in the activities, and have the living conditions and amenities which are customary, or at least widely encouraged or approved, in the societies to which they belong'. This approach to defining poverty in terms of relative deprivation established that people have social as well as physical needs and that these cannot be usefully divided since the ways in which seemingly 'basic' needs (for example, for nutrition) are met are mediated by social norms and fulfil social functions (Hick 2014, 301). Although a cup of tea, for instance, is nutritionally insignificant, in the UK drinking tea is widely regarded as a necessity of life and offering tea to visitors makes 'a small contribution … towards maintaining the threads of social relationships' (Townsend 1979, 50). The implication is that what constitutes a need, basic or otherwise, cannot be separated from the context in which it is defined as such.

The concept of 'food poverty' retains this concern with customary food practices. It is sometimes used interchangeably with the 'food insecurity', although the methods of measurement vary (Chapter 1). Reflecting Townsend's relative deprivation approach to poverty, and seminal work in the study of household experiences of food insecurity (Radimer et al. 1990), in this book we conceptualise food poverty as a multi-dimensional phenomenon including:

- the material dimension: reduced quantity and quality of food
- the social dimension: compromises in the social acceptability of food and exclusion from customary food practices

- the psychosocial or emotional dimension: worry, shame and stigma relating to lack of resources and lack of access to food and food-related practices.

The material dimension of food poverty

The material dimension of food poverty needs to be conceptually understood in two senses. First, food provides the *nutrients* needed for growth and development; hence lack of good food plays a critical role in poor health and health inequalities (Najman and Davey Smith 2000). Second, food is material in the sense that it is a *resource* that has to be managed at the household level, usually by mothers, through domestic food-provisioning (accessing, preparing and serving food) and through processes of intra-household distribution (the priorities of its allocation to different household members). This second sense of the material nature of food is discussed below and in Section 2, but a few comments are included here about its nutritional importance.

Malnutrition today, not only in Britain and the Global North, but in all parts of the world, looks very different from in Rowntree's time. In the context of the 'nutrition transition'[3] and food systems in which commercial interests are dominant, lack of money leads not only to an 'absolute' lack of food but also to reliance on 'cheap' food that is often high in saturated fat and added sugars and low in nutrients. Consequently, in most regions of the world, poverty is not only closely connected to being underweight but also to being overweight.

The harmful effects of poor diet and malnutrition, particularly for children, are well established and have long-term individual and societal implications. For individuals, research suggests that consequences include the increasing incidence of coronary heart disease, type II diabetes and cancer (Kirkpatrick et al. 2010). Sub-optimal diets and food habits such as skipping meals are also associated with poor cognition and lower academic achievement, since children's ability to concentrate is damaged by insufficient food or food of low nutritious value. In the longer term, poverty and food poverty have an impact on the body which persists and is passed on to the next generation. Indeed, there is evidence that it is harder to break intergenerational links in health than in wealth (Brown and Bambra 2019).

The impacts of low household income – as well as wider contextual influences such as the collective resources embodied in local services and facilities – on health and diet are recognised in systems approaches such as the Social Determinants of Health (Bambra 2019). Although this framework has gained popularity, particularly through its adoption by the World Health Organisation (WHO), countries vary in the degree to which social policies recognise or address the impacts of income on health and diet. Among our three countries, only the UK National Diet and Nutrition Survey reports nutritional intake by income; the Norwegian Norkost study reports it by education only; and the Portuguese National Food and Physical Activity Survey (*Inquerito Alimentar Nacional e de Actividade Fisica* – IAN-AF) reports neither (Rippin et al. 2017). Furthermore, the UK survey consistently shows a strong social gradient in nutritional intake, households in the lowest income groups purchasing foods that are furthest from dietary recommendations, but – in accordance with a neoliberal approach to responsibility for health – food and eating have largely been framed as problems of 'lifestyle' and mainly addressed through education and 'nudge' approaches (Dowler and O'Connor 2012). Only recently have more upstream approaches, such as a soft drinks levy, been introduced, albeit with vocal opposition from the food and drinks lobby using the charge of 'nanny statism' (MacKay and Quigley 2018).

The social dimension: exclusion from customary food practices

It is a matter of debate whether social exclusion is a part, or a consequence, of poverty. Certainly, people may be socially excluded without being poor. Reflecting Townsend's conception of poverty, we include exclusion from customary food practices owing to a lack of resources as part of a multi-dimensional understanding of food poverty, because eating the same food as others is 'a basic mark of belonging' (Stone 1988, 71).

It is difficult to establish what constitute customary food practices in a society. Cross-national comparisons of food norms and eating practices are even more difficult and surprisingly rare. One reason for this is the complexity of creating units of comparison, not to mention methods of measurement (Darmon and Warde 2014; Harvey 2014). Customary food and eating practices are also multi-dimensional and cover particular foods and cuisines, the structure of eating occasions, including patterns of meals and their components, as well as norms about who eats with whom, when and where (Holm et al. 2012).[4]

The social dimension of food poverty acknowledges, as anthropologist Audrey Richards recognised in her 1930s study of the Bemba, that, 'for men [sic], food acquires a series of values other than those which hunger provides' (Richards 2004, 9). From this perspective, to be excluded from eating culturally appropriate food and from participating in customary practices of sociability means being unable to meet social expectations and being poor in relation to others (Townsend 1979; Leather 1996; Lang 1997; Dowler and Leather 2000; Healy 2019; O'Connell et al. 2019a).

In consumer societies, exercising choice in the marketplace, including what food to buy and eat, is one means of enacting agency; exclusion from 'choice' means having to rely on food or ways of procuring food that are not widely seen as socially acceptable. The 'social' aspects of food and eating, including norms of sociality, eating out and celebrating special occasions, are recognised as important in, and are part of, the consensually determined minimum for a socially acceptable standard of living in both the UK and Portugal (Davis et al. 2012; Padley et al. 2015; Pereirinha et al. 2017); the different method used to calculate budget standards in Norway does not include the costs of these practices of sociality (see Section 2). However, there is evidence that those on low incomes reduce their expectations about consumption in the context of austerity (Davis et al. 2012; 2014).

The psychosocial dimension: worry and shame

Finally, overlapping with the social aspects of food poverty is the psychosocial dimension. This includes worry about where money and food will come from and the sense of shame about being unable to provide appropriate food for one's family or to meet food-related social norms of demonstrating care or reciprocity, such as showing hospitality or accepting invitations to eat out (Walker 2014).

Volatility of income and unexpected spending demands create considerable insecurity among low-income households (Hills et al. 2006). Kjell Underlid (2007, 73), a Norwegian researcher (cited in Lister 2015, 147), concludes that 'the sense of insecurity [generally accompanied by fear and anxiety] is an existential verity for the poor in affluent welfare states'. This extends to worrying about food running out before there is money to buy more and the psychological stress that may manifest in loss of interest in food or cooking, for example, or fear of losing custody of one's child (Hamelin et al. 2002).

Food and eating are a medium for expressing care for self and others and are deeply steeped in morality. Food practices are therefore a fundamental means by which people, especially mothers, are judged, and judge themselves. The psychosocial dimension of food poverty includes shame about being unable to provide for one's family's basic needs and having to rely on non-normative sources of food such as charity. To avoid shame, people may engage in strategies such as making excuses to 'save face' (Goffman 1967) or withdrawing from social life.

Understanding the household as a resource unit

In focusing on families with children, we have taken account of different family forms. Given that our interest is in food, our unit of analysis is the household in which people live and eat together. Households are conceptualised as resource units in which family members engage in the provisioning processes that are central to social reproduction (Narotzky and Besnier 2014). These include drawing on and making use of different material and non-material resources (sometimes referred to in livelihoods approaches as 'assets' or different types of 'capital'). These provisioning processes include obtaining food, transforming it into meals and distributing it to, and eating it with, other family members.

In the sociology of food and eating, Marjorie DeVault's (1991) research was seminal in examining 'domestic food provisioning' in families. The concept of food provisioning neatly bridges so-called public and private domains (Warde 2016, 26), indicating 'the conjunction of commercial provision and domestic use, with unpaid labour as a crucial intermediating process', and focusing attention on the visible and invisible food work that transforms income and other resources into meals. Between 1975 and 2000, time use data from the UK, US, Norway, Netherlands and France suggest that there was a reduction in time spent on domestic food work (cooking and washing up) in all five countries (Warde et al. 2007). Although there has been a small increase in men's contributions, the evidence is that the distribution of this work remains highly gendered and is overwhelmingly the responsibility of women, particularly when they are mothers (Warde et al. 2007; O'Connell and Brannen 2016).

Different responsibilities for food work and different entitlements to food are embedded in, and reproduce, relations of power, including those that are gendered (Sen 1981). As qualitative studies indicate, budgeting and the management of money in low-income families suggests a gendered pattern in which women bear most of the burden of responsibility for managing a restricted income (Goode at al. 1998; Scott et al.

1999; Snape et al. 1999; Sung and Bennett 2007). Women are the primary 'managers of poverty' within households (for example, Hanmer and Hearn 1999, 19). In these conditions, being in control of money is likely to be 'more of a burden than a source of power' (Bennett and Daly 2014, 57).

Control of resources can also be directed toward prioritising the needs of other household members and to deprioritising one's own. Much research on the topic finds that it is mothers who often go without food and other things to prioritise the needs of children and male partners – a strategy referred to as 'maternal sacrifice' (Attree 2005) or 'maternal altruism' (Whitehead 1984). As the social anthropologist Pat Caplan (1996, 218) notes, the expectation that mothers sacrifice their food intake for others is one that many 'women have internalised to the point where it becomes second nature, and they may even articulate a preference for less valued food'. Studies find that although parents try to protect children from the effects of poverty, women are more likely to go without or restrict their own and their partners' spending to try and ensure that there is enough money for their children's needs (Goode et al. 1998; Ridge 2009; Dowler and O'Connor 2012). Studies also suggest that lone mothers suffer most (Dowler and Calvert 1995; Millar and Ridge 2013), not only in being materially disadvantaged relative to partnered mothers (or solo women), but also in exclusion from social relations. For example, the UK's Poverty and Social Exclusion Millennium Survey found that lone mothers suffer exclusion from common social activities such as socialising with friends and family, owing to a lack of money. Just over a quarter were able to participate in all the activities listed in the survey, compared with over half of the partnered and solo women (Levitas et al. 2006, 415).

As many studies of low-income families have found, mothers engage in different ways of managing food and eating when there is not enough money or food to go round, for example 'shopping around', shopping often, shopping alone, avoiding waste by cutting back on perishable foods like fresh fruit and vegetables, relying on tinned and frozen foods and not experimenting with new foods or dishes.

The management of income and food resources can be understood in different ways. In her review of mothers living in poverty, Attree (2005, 230) identifies three overarching concepts relating to low-income mothers' management of poverty which exert an influence on diet and nutrition: (a) 'strategic adjustment' (McKendrick et al. 2003) – material strategies mothers adopt to cope with poverty; (b) 'resigned adjustment' – the ways in which, over time, 'managing' poverty and the lifestyle changes this entails can become routine; (c) 'maternal sacrifice' – those aspects of women's accounts which relate to social ideals of the 'good mother', the discourses they draw upon to make sense of their situations (Duncan and Edwards 1999) and how these shape diet and nutrition in low-income families.

Such 'coping strategies' are ways of 'getting by' that reflect one form of everyday agency within the constraints of poverty identified by Lister (2013). More strategic and less individualised forms of agency include 'getting organised' and are reflected in community 'livelihoods approaches' addressed by some NGOs (for example, May et al. 2009). In relation to families' food and eating practices, examples include community food cooperatives and neighbourhood food-growing and bulk-buying schemes (for example, Gordon et al. 2018). One critique of such approaches is that when agency and the mobilisation of a range of non-material resources by those living in poverty are privileged, linkages with the wider contexts and policies that explain their insufficient resources can become lost. Another criticism is the narrow economic approach that is implied by a focus on 'assets' or 'capital'. Hence, as we discuss in Chapter 5, we prefer to conceptualise as *resources* the various material, organisational and other goods that are drawn on in processes of domestic provisioning.

Food, poverty and change

A consistent finding that emerges from research on the experience of food poverty, and underpins the measurement of food insecurity, is that it is a 'managed process' (Radimer 1990; Radimer et al. 1990; 1992). This entails the observation that reductions in money and food follow a fairly predictable sequence, in which worry about running out of food is the first phase, and cutting back on food quality, reducing the frequency of meals, and going without enough or anything to eat are the progressively more severe stages.

This temporal dimension of food insecurity reflects wider research on the dynamics of poverty in general. It is established that poverty is a temporal phenomenon, that people move in and out of low income and that there is a lag between drop or increase in income and the experience or relief of material deprivation (for example, Saunders 2013). Although there is evidence that some families have always survived 'on the brink' (for example, Pember Reeves 1913, 210), a striking feature of poverty in contemporary neoliberal societies is the precarity of income in deregulated labour markets and the sense of insecurity this engenders. Whereas a good deal of the literature on the dynamics of poverty is quantitative, using longitudinal datasets to follow individuals as they move in and out of low income, more micro-level qualitative longitudinal studies generate important insights into the agency of those struggling to escape poverty and the toll it can take on them and their families (for example, Corden and Millar 2007; Millar 2007; Ridge 2007; Lister 2015). The latter kind of research brings together a focus on agency within structural constraints, for example, demonstrating how difficult it is in today's insecure labour market for people to get out of poverty, even when they are strongly motivated to do so (Shildrick et al. 2010).

For those who migrate to new countries to escape poverty, war or natural disaster, or for other reasons, changing fortunes are complicated by the expectations and norms of the new society as well as the situation and needs of family back home. Alongside the growth of globalisation and international migration there has been a rise in nationalism and in immigration policies that restrict citizenship entitlements to the most privileged. Although most Western countries depend heavily on immigration, often to fill demand for low-paid labour, popular concerns about the impact of immigration on employment, welfare systems, national security and identity mean that migrants and their descendants are subject to institutional and everyday practices of racism and discrimination. Racism that structures workplaces and hierarchies of employment limits migrants' opportunities for paid work and advancement, though some groups of workers have – with or without the help of trades unions – organised to eradicate inequalities (Anitha and Pearson 2018).

As much research on food and diaspora has found (for example, Ray 2004), food, especially 'homemade food', is widely regarded as a source of emotional connection with one's mother, family and culture (Moisio et al. 2004). For this reason, food practices are often one of the last traits to change in the aftermath of migration, albeit that the availability of ingredients – as well as aspirations, for example, regarding children's acculturation – influences the way that meals are made and shared (Tuomainen 2009). In contrast, some migrants may actively shun the foods of their childhood and homeland – for example, those who have fled civil war (Bajić-Hajduković 2013). Maintaining – or rejecting – food and eating practices may be a major way of coping with – or signifying – historical or life-course change (O'Connell and Brannen 2016). The promotion and popularity of particular, often unhealthy, foods among teenagers are among the ways in which young people express their distinctiveness as a social group (Lems et al. 2020).

Children and poverty

Children are greatly affected by low family income because of their relative immaturity and lack of social power (Boyden and Mann 2005). It is therefore important to understand how they experience disadvantage, how they make sense of it and which aspects of their lives mediate it. Similarly, it is important to take account of the contributions they make to their families. A crucial element of sociological thinking is that childhood is a generational concept and can only really be understood in the context of adult–child relations (Alanen 2003; Brannen 2020). It is important, some suggest, to consider children's practices in combination with adults', particularly in the field of consumption (Cook 2009). Since children usually lack independent means, their consumption of foods (and other goods) cannot usefully be understood without considering the resources their families have at their disposal.

Given a gendered pattern of disadvantage in which women tend to bear the burden of responsibility for managing restricted incomes, and the ethical and methodological challenges of interviewing children about lack of food, it is not surprising that a good deal of work on food insecurity does not address intra-household variation (Coates et al. 2006). The 'responsibilisation' of mothers for children's food and eating in public discourse and in practice means that other family members, including children, are often excluded from the research or are included by proxy. Although studies suggest that children are usually protected from food deprivation in low-income households, some research from the US suggests that the numbers experiencing malnutrition and related outcomes are higher than data about experiences of household food insecurity would suggest (Fram et al. 2011). The implication is that parental reports of children's experiences may intentionally or unwittingly minimise the impacts of low income on children's experiences of food insecurity and that it is important to seek the views of children themselves.

From the early 1990s, sociological approaches to childhood have foregrounded children's experiences, conceptualising them as social agents and experts in their own lives (Langsted 1994). At the same time, there is increasing recognition of the interdependence of children and parents within families (Thorne 2012), directing attention towards the value of understanding multiple perspectives (Ribbens McCarthy et al. 2003) within households, including those of children. The concept of 'family practices' also emphasises children's role as active family participants and suggests that the family may be seen as a process or achievement that is accomplished in everyday routines (Morgan 1996, 2011), including ones associated with food and eating, such as sharing meals (Jackson et al. 2009; O'Connell and Brannen 2016).

Although childhoods and children are diverse, children's lives and development share some common features, notably a marginalised structural position in relation to adults. Some qualitative research into children's perspectives of poverty shows the damaging effects on children of material disadvantage and social exclusion, and the ways that young people seek to manage and moderate the effects of poverty. The research also notes the economic and care contributions they make in families (for example, Brannen et al. 2000), especially where parents are in long-term receipt of benefits due to sickness and disability. Children's care contributions in families include caring for themselves and caring for others (Brannen and O'Brien 1996). As Ridge (2011, 82) notes, these strategies of survival 'involve mediation and moderation, concealment of needs, employment and attempts to gain some autonomous control of income and resources. However, these strategies ... are not without tensions and costs for children themselves.'

The impact of low household income can be particularly devastating at a time when 'a child or young person is developing a sense of her own identity' (Lister 2004, 69). Food as a marker of identity and symbol of belonging may be particularly important for children because they use food to forge and reject social relations with family and peers (James 1979; James et al. 2009; Brembeck 2009). As children grow older and gain more autonomy they may eat in an expanding range of contexts, depending on financial and geographic access, and such activities involving commensality may be important in establishing and cementing their social networks (Backett-Milburn et al. 2011). The financial constraints upon low-income families therefore affect children's relations with their peers, with whom they typically engage in processes of 'social comparison' (Festinger 1954). Poverty can make children feel 'different' when they are unable to take part in the types of activities that most of their peers expect to do. For many children, participation in activities outside the home, especially those involving food, is normative and central to feelings of social inclusion. The compromising of participation can create feelings of shame. In such situations, personal reputation may be impugned, affecting children's social status in their peer groups, which in turn affects how they feel about their situation when they compare themselves with others, reducing their self-esteem (Chapters 8 and 10).

Notes

1. ERC grant agreement no. 337977.
2. The research team comprised, in the UK: Rebecca O'Connell, Julia Brannen, Laura Hamilton, Abigail Knight, Charlie Owen and Antonia Simon (Thomas Coram Research Unit, Institute of Education, UCL); in Portugal: Manuel Abrantes, Fábio Augusto, Sónia Cardoso, Vasco Ramos, Mónica Truninger and Karin Wall (Instituto de Ciências Sociais da Universidade de Lisboa); in Norway: Silje Skuland and Anine Frisland (Consumption Research Norway, Oslo Metropolitan University). Penny Mellor and Cécile Brémont provided administrative support.
3. The 'nutrition transition' model was developed by researcher Barry Popkin in 1993. The term is commonly used by researchers to refer to the shift from 'traditional' diets towards foods higher in fats, meats and sugar, together with the rise in sedentary lifestyles as countries become more industrialised. These changes in diet and lifestyle are driven by several interlinked factors, including the process of urbanisation, increases in average per capita income, the growth of supermarkets, market liberalisation, foreign direct investment and food marketing. High-income countries generally began a shift towards diets high in oils, sugar and processed food around the time of the industrial revolution (starting in the late nineteenth century). Most low- and middle-income countries, in contrast, didn't begin that dietary shift until the 1980s to 1990s. See Foodsource (foodsource.org.uk), Popkin (1993) and Hawkes et al. (2017).
4. 'Globalization … generates an opposite trend: a global stage on which food identities – national, ethnic and regional – are declared, elaborated and commercialised' (Colas et al. 2018, 134). Diasporas play a role in shaping 'national' cuisines; for example, the rise in popularity of pizza in Italy coincided with its popularity in the wider world, a trend centring on the United States following Italian migration in the 1970s (Colas et al. 2018). Similarly, the 'Mediterranean diet' that is popularly associated with Southern Europe, including Portugal, was classified by the UN Educational, Scientific and Cultural Organisation (UNESCO) in 2013 as 'intangible world cultural heritage after it was initially identified by dietary and medical researchers, then marketing organizations, including the Olive Oil Council' (Colas et al. 2018). Setting aside regional and ethnic variation, national cuisines and ritualised meals, such as Thanksgiving, are understood to be 'invented traditions' (Hobsbawm and Ranger 1983) that provide a shared identity for 'imagined communities' (Anderson 1983, 6); 'members of even the smallest nation will never know most of their fellow members, meet them or even hear of them, yet in the mind of each lives the image of their communion' (see Guptill et al. 2017).

3
The study

In this research, our understanding of food poverty in families is underpinned by a realist ontological stance. From this perspective, the world is constituted by the empirical (what is experienced and observed), the actual (the conditions that shape everyday experiences and behaviours) and the real (the powerful causes that lie behind observable patterns) (Archer 1995; Sayer 2001). In contrast to (strong) social constructionist approaches that see qualitative research as merely 'giving voice' to research participants' subjective perspectives, we see our job as critical researchers as being to describe, understand and contextualise the multilayered realities of people's everyday lives – not only how people see the world but the social conditions and causes that shape their experiences.

In order to examine how experiences of food poverty are shaped by social contexts and social positionings, we adopted a mixed-method embedded case study design (Yin 2003). As Chicago sociologist Vivien Palmer argued in 1928, 'fundamental to the case study method is the effort to view the different aspects of the problem as an organised, interrelated whole' (Palmer 1928, 20) so that through full description we can extract and make inferences from 'the vital processes' of social phenomena. Low-income families, including young people and their parents, were studied with reference to three intersecting but distinct analytic levels:

- The macro level of the nation: the social structures and national discourses and policies related to poverty, food and nutrition
- The meso level of the locality: its characteristics in terms of population, employment opportunities, housing, schools, shopping amenities, and other local services
- The individual/household level of everyday family life including accessing resources, everyday intra-household negotiations and practices, and support from social networks.

In the quantitative part of the study the UK team (led by Charlie Owen with Antonia Simon) carried out secondary analysis of several large-scale datasets: the EU Survey of Income and Living Conditions (EU-SILC), Health Behaviour in School-Aged Children (HBSC) and Living Costs and Food Survey (LCFS) (see below). In the qualitative part of the study, in which we collected new data in each country, we adopted a case-based approach. As the case study literature suggests, cases must be 'cases of something' (Brannen and Nilsen 2011). Given the multi-layered design, the households we studied are understood to be cases of different types of families experiencing food poverty, located in particular places (communities and cities) and in particular societies (national policies, cultures and institutions). This approach permits explanations that are specific to a set of social conditions for a specific person or household in a particular context and location that may not be typical of a country pattern (Brannen 2005). The aim is not to extrapolate from the individual or household to the country or nation. Instead, cases are treated as *emblematic* of particular social characteristics, conditions and structural contexts (Thomson 2009).

Central to a case-based methodology is its power to make comparisons. Comparative research permits us 'to compare systematically the manifestations of phenomena in more than one temporal or spatial socio-cultural setting' (Hantrais 2009, 15). In so far as comparisons relate to cross-national differences (Przeworski and Teune 1966), Melvin Kohn (1987, 714) suggests, it is important to differentiate between studies that treat the nation as a unit of analysis and those that treat it as a context of study. In this book the nation is only one context of study (see Hantrais 1999). Although comparing and contrasting cases, selected on the basis of apparently similar characteristics in different countries and places, is an important part of comparative research, it does not necessarily guard against 'methodological nationalism'. This term refers to the risk of overemphasising aspects of cultural context in interpreting data within one societal context. There is, furthermore, a second danger that in comparing the same phenomenon we fail to realise that questions or concepts that seem self-evident may have an entirely different meaning in other contexts (Quilgars et al. 2009; Wendt 2019). As Hantrais (2009, 72) suggests, 'concepts cannot be separated from contexts'; each national context has its own demography, cultural expectations and social welfare regime, based in political, cultural and ideological traditions. Because of this we cannot assume a conceptual equivalence or difference between countries. In this book we try to understand the food poverty of families relative to the societies to which they belong, by drawing on budget standards data to examine how the food expenditure of families compares with the cost of diets that meet health and social participation needs determined nationally.[1] We also note difficulties, for example, in comparing lone-parent households across contexts: some lone-parent households in Portugal were embedded in multi-generational families that defied conventional definitions of lone parenthood and were possibly miscoded in large-scale international datasets. In the qualitative research, too, we could not always assume equivalence. For example, the team in Portugal found it difficult to translate terms from the UK team's list of 'coping strategies' that formed part of the interview; for example, one strategy termed 'cooking from scratch' in English had no synonym in common Portuguese parlance.

The macro level: documentary and secondary analysis of international data

The first phase of the research included documentary analysis. We examined national policies and programmes, alongside relevant official statistics, relating to families, food and poverty and analysed newspaper reports on families, poverty and food (Knight et al. 2018). This part of the research contextualised food poverty by taking into account the different histories of the three countries and their welfare states (see Chapter 1).

We also examined public discourses around poverty and, in particular, food poverty (Chapter 1). In Britain, we found that the dominant ideology of neoliberalism was used to justify so-called austerity measures so that people living in poverty were blamed for their plight and regarded in derogatory terms, for example, as 'scroungers', 'sponging' off the state, 'frauds', unwilling to work and making the 'wrong choices' (Knight et al. 2018). In Portugal, in part perhaps because the Troika imposed fiscal measures upon the country following the global financial crisis, discourses of 'shameful' poverty were accompanied by ones of social solidarity as characteristic of Portugal and of being Portuguese (Cardoso et al. 2017). In Norway, Walker and Chase (2014, 11) found that the language used to describe those in poverty was 'more muted' than in other countries, despite participants in their research feeling that they were regarded as 'work-shy' and, in some cases, as 'exploiting' the generous benefit system 'to support an alternative lifestyle'.

To identify the types of families most at risk of food poverty across the three countries, we carried out secondary analysis of the EU-SILC and HBSC (Simon et al. 2018). The findings of this analysis are reported in Chapter 4. Analyses were also carried out on the UK's LCFS (O'Connell et al. 2019a).

The meso level: the areas where the families live

We decided to recruit from both urban and non-urban areas in order to capture differences in housing, employment opportunities, transport and shopping facilities. Around two-thirds of the families in the study lived in the capital cities of the three countries – London, Lisbon and Oslo – and the remaining third was recruited from the surrounding suburbs and rural areas.[2]

Thirty of the families in the UK lived in an inner London borough and 15 lived in a coastal town in the South East of England. Both areas have been undergoing gentrification, though more recently in the coastal area, which became run down during the 1970s when British seaside resorts went out of fashion (Figure 3.1). The two areas differ in key respects. The inner London area is ethnically diverse, it has more jobs and transport for young people is free. Its school system is also more varied and there is a range of local and national supermarkets and shops as well as street markets where fresh food is readily available. In the coastal area, by contrast, employment opportunities are poor, transport is expensive, the education system segregated and the population less ethnically diverse. The coastal town has a limited range of mainly low-budget food shops and outlets.

In Portugal, 30 of the study families lived in two urban/suburban areas covering the outer area of Lisbon and bordering municipalities (31 children) and 15 families in the rural/transitional area further away from Lisbon. The two urban areas are among the most densely populated and impoverished in Lisbon, with high unemployment rates and large numbers of foreign-born or descendants of migrants from Portugal's former African colonies (Truninger et al. 2018). Housing is relatively low cost and one area has large swathes of social housing (Figure 3.2). Both areas are well served by transport, contain large numbers of charitable organisations (state, non-profit and church) and are well provided with supermarkets and a municipal street market that sources food from local farmers and larger suppliers. The areas have few fast food shops and no cafés or restaurants. The rural area, by contrast, is largely populated by white Portuguese; its population is dispersed and unemployment lower

(a)

(b)

Figure 3.1 The UK study areas: (a) an inner London borough; (b) a coastal town in South East England (Source: Abigail Knight).

than in the urban study areas. Some families cultivate the land. The area's shopping facilities consist of small shops and supermarkets that are dispersed too.

In Norway, 28 of the study families (29 children) were from several urban areas in Oslo and 15 families (19 children) were from rural

(a)

(b)

Figure 3.2 The Portuguese study areas: (a) urban and suburban areas of Lisbon (Source: public domain); (b) a rural area (Source: Vasco Ramos).

or semi-rural areas in non-urban Eastern Norway (Figure 3.3). Most of the urban families in Oslo were found in its eastern suburbs. Like London, Oslo has long seen a persistent social divide between its western and much poorer eastern districts. In recent years the eastern suburbs have experienced a larger growth in the population of immigrants and

(a)

(b)

Figure 3.3 The Norwegian study areas: (a) central eastern Oslo;
(b) eastern suburbs (Source: Silje Skuland).

Norwegian-born children with immigrant parents than in other areas of
Oslo (Blom 2002). In 2016, almost one in four children (23.2 per cent)
who lived in Oslo's eastern districts belonged to a household below the
poverty line (60 per cent of median income). The families recruited in
less urbanised areas also lived in Eastern Norway but in an area that has
traditionally depended on primary industries that are now in decline and
where housing costs are much lower than in Oslo (Skuland 2018). The
area has undergone considerable resettlement from smaller municipalities to larger semi-urban centres.

The micro level: the parents and children

At the heart of this book are the cases of parents and young people in low-income families. In-depth interviews and other methods of study were carried out with 145 children and young people, aged 11–16 years, and 133 parents or carers, mostly mothers, in a total of 133 families: 45 families in the UK (51 children), 45 families in Portugal (46 children) and 43 families in Norway (48 children).

Selecting the families

The sampling strategy was purposive; we did not set out to obtain a sample that was statistically representative of a wider population. The families were recruited to the study on the basis of their own definitions of low income – that their income was below what they needed (Gordon 2006; Bradshaw and Mayhew 2011).[3] However, we hoped to recruit families from a range of family types (a mix of lone-parent and couple households) and an array of ethnicities and other characteristics through the organisations we approached to help us find the families and the different fieldwork sites we chose. We also hoped to include families experiencing chronic low income as well as households in acute financial crises. As the achieved samples demonstrate, families in poverty are very diverse.

We decided to focus on the 11–15 age group of children for a number of reasons, namely that young people in their early teenage years are: (a) likely to be better able to articulate their experiences and perspectives than younger children, (b) known to take on more responsibilities in some families, (c) increasingly involved in their own social networks and (d) potentially susceptible targets of consumerism via advertising, marketing and peer groups. We felt that these last two factors might be important influences on young people's experiences of relative disadvantage and social exclusion (Chapter 8). We aimed to include a mix of boys and girls.

We anticipated that recruitment would take a long time and it did: around two years in total in the UK and Norway. We think there are two main reasons for this. First, we were asking a lot of families, in terms both of time and of what we were asking them to reveal about themselves. Second, we were looking for children in a specific age range who were also willing to talk to us. Recruitment took less time in Portugal for several reasons: a larger research team, higher poverty rates and, arguably,

Table 3.1 How the families were recruited in each of the countries.

	UK	Portugal	Norway
Schools	19	19	9
Social and youth services, local organisations supporting disadvantaged families	16	17	8
Food aid organisations	3	4	6
Churches and other charities	–	4	2
Snowballing	6	1	10
Personal contact	1	–	–
Facebook	–	–	8
Total	45	45	43

less stigma around being poor and discussing poverty than in the UK and Norway (Walker 2014). Recruitment and the negotiation of access required diligence, tact and, in some cases, grit.

We used a range of methods to recruit families. Initially, we approached families through schools in the study areas – two or three schools in each, focusing on children in the target age group. Self-completion screening questionnaires that asked about subjective income adequacy and different dimensions of food poverty were sent home to parents of children in the relevant year groups. More families were contacted through local organisations, including social services, charities and food banks, and through Facebook (Table 3.1). In the inner London area we tried but failed to recruit participants through urban growing schemes. We also used snowballing: asking those who had agreed to take part to pass on our details to others who might fit the criteria and be interested in taking part. Differences in recruitment methods are reflected in the samples obtained. As shown in Table 3.1, few participants were recruited from food aid organisations. In Norway, recruitment through schools yielded fewer cases,[4] and a greater range of alternative methods of recruitment had to be employed.

The qualitative methods

A 'multiple perspectives' approach (Ribbens McCarthy et al. 2003) was used to build a rich and complex picture of the everyday practices constituting family life (Harden et al. 2010) and the place of food within it. This involved interviewing a parent (usually the mother) and one or more young persons in the household who met our age criteria. A range of methods were employed, including semi-structured interviews, questionnaires and visual methods.

Where possible, and subject to their informed consent, children and young people were interviewed separately from parents. We did this for several reasons. First, although it may not always be possible to interview young children without parents being present, this is preferable for older young people in that it affords them confidentiality (Brannen 2015; Backett-Milburn et al. 2011). On the one hand, there is some evidence that in research on children's and parents' experiences in the context of disadvantage parents may wish to protect their children from knowing more about, or feeling ashamed of, their difficulties (Ridge 2002, 8). On the other hand, as we found in some instances, children may be aware of constraints and provide a 'united front' with their parents to the researcher. Another reason for seeking to interview young people and parents separately concerns the subject matter of food: given that eating is highly moralised (Coveney 2006) and that children and young people, as well as their parents, may engage in non-normative food practices, they may prefer not to discuss these in front of other family members. In practice, however, it was not always possible to interview children and parents separately. There was a lack of space in some participants' homes, and some parents and children chose to be interviewed together. In some cases, children acted as language brokers for their parents (Crafter and Iqbal 2018).

The qualitative interviews and activities were designed to elicit detailed information on income and outgoings, money spent on food and other items, and how income and expenditure changed at different times of the month and year. Parents were asked about their daily routines and experiences and their methods of 'domestic food provisioning' – procurement, preparation, planning and consumption (DeVault 1991) – in the context of low household income. The research also examined changes in the experience of living and eating on a low income, and the formal and informal sources of support the parents had recourse to and drew on. They were asked to give brief life histories where possible and to compare current circumstances with those in the past.

In order to capture everyday food practices, adults and children were asked to recall the last school and non-school day and the foods and meals eaten on these days. Although eliciting information about food and eating in this way does not completely avoid normative responses, for example, about the foods people 'usually' or 'ideally' buy and eat, it can reduce them (O'Connell and Brannen 2016). Questions were also asked about eating with others inside and outside the home and the participants' feelings about not being able to socialise – either to offer or to accept hospitality. In addition, parents and children were asked who or what they thought was responsible for ensuring that families and children had enough decent food to eat and what they thought the future held in store for them and for families in general.

With some children, where the researchers considered it appropriate and helpful, 'vignettes' were used to elicit conversation about difficult topics such as being left out of eating with friends because of lack of money, or finding there was no food to eat at home, or queuing for food in a food bank (an example of looking in an empty cupboard appears in Figure 3.4). Other sections of the interview asked children, inter alia, about having money of their own, about helping with shopping and other household tasks, and about food at school and outside the home and school.

Most parents and young people also completed questionnaires in the course of the fieldwork visits. The adult questionnaire was designed to collect information and prompt discussion about 'food coping strategies' elucidated from the literature – ways of getting by on a low income,

Figure 3.4 Vignette of a young person looking in an empty cupboard, used as a prompt for discussion in some interviews (Source: authors, 2021).

such as shopping around, making meals that were filling rather than nutritious and turning down invitations to eat out. The children completed a questionnaire that included a 'food habits module', based on the one used in the HBSC study, and two questions, also based on that survey, about going to school or bed hungry owing to a lack of food at home.

To complement the interview material and to gain a deeper understanding of some of the taken-for-granted and everyday experiences of food and eating in families, a subsample of households (10 in each country) participated in additional visits involving photo-elicitation interviews, a method in which participants took photographs of their everyday lives and discussed them with the researchers at a later visit (O'Connell 2013).[5] Visual and other methods can be useful in food research with children and adults to help bring routine and habitual practices to light, or to the level of discourse (Power 2003; Sweetman 2009; Martens 2018), and to bring the findings to life for different audiences.

Interviews were carried out in English in the UK, Portuguese in Portugal and Norwegian in Norway. Because there was insufficient funding for translation of the Portuguese and Norwegian interviews, only the interview 'case summaries' and field notes were translated into English. The interviews were, in nearly all cases and with participants' permission, recorded and transcribed in full in the language of each country.

The families

Although 'low income' was defined subjectively as an income below what the family needed, most household incomes of the families we recruited to the study corresponded with the relative low-income measure that is widely employed as a poverty threshold in Europe, that is, their equivalised household incomes were below 60 per cent of the national median. Table 3.2 shows the distribution of the cases compared with the national distribution in terms of income quintiles. The comparison is illustrative, since income was calculated differently (either before housing costs [BHC] or after housing costs [AHC]), depending on the national data available for comparison with the qualitative sample.[6]

Most of the families in the UK and Portugal were in the bottom two income quintiles of the national distribution and in Portugal a larger proportion of the families included in the study were in the bottom quintile than of those in the UK (Table 3.2). In Norway most of the families were in quintiles 2 and 3, with around a third of families in quintile 4 and a few in quintile 5, according to the method of equivalisation and the

Table 3.2 Equivalised household income compared with the national distribution in each country sample in quintiles: qualitative study.

	UK (AHC compared with HBAI)	Portugal (BHC compared with HBS)	Norway (BHC compared with SN)
Quintile 1	21	38	0
Quintile 2	20	6	6
Quintile 3	4	0	19
Quintile 4	0	1	15
Quintile 5	0	0	3
Total	45	45	43

Notes: AHC = after housing costs; BHC = before housing costs; HBAI = households below average income; HBS = Household Budget Survey; SN = Statistics Norway.

national dataset used for comparison. In all three countries some families had incomes that placed them in quintiles 3 and above, that is, incomes above 60 per cent of the national median. Some of these households also had higher costs of living, for example the costs of housing not accounted for in the BHC calculations used for Portugal and Norway, or expenditure to meet particular needs, such as the disability of a parent or child (Sen 1992, 1999;[7] Hill et al. 2015), or high levels of debt that are not accounted for in standard methods of equivalisation.

In all the countries, nearly all of the lone parents were women and most interviews with dual-parent families were also carried out with mothers (Table 3.3). There were three lone fathers in total (one in the UK and two in Portugal) and fathers participated in 12 interviews in dual-parent households and did the interview without the mother in four couple families. The higher number of fathers included in couple interviews in Norway likely reflects the cultural norms and language skills of the relatively high number of migrant families in the study. Grandmothers were the main carers in three cases; in the UK one was a lone parent and two in Portugal lived with a partner. There were no grandparents caring on a full-time basis for children in the study families in Norway.

As noted above, there are differences in the ways that lone parents are defined and identified in different countries and datasets. In the qualitative research we defined 'lone parents' as those who had children under 18 years old and were not living with a partner. This meant we coded as 'lone parents' those who were living with dependent children

Table 3.3 Family type by parent/carer interviewed in the three countries' samples: qualitative study.

Family type	Parent/carer interviewed	UK	Portugal	Norway
Couple	Mother (in couple)	11	20	15
	Mother and father (couple)	4	1	7
	Father (couple)	–	3	1
Lone parent	Lone mother/ grandmother	29	19	20
	Lone father	1	2	–
	Total	45	45	43

Table 3.4 Family type in the three countries' samples: qualitative study.

Family type	UK	Portugal	Norway
Lone parent/carer	30	19	20
Couple	15	26	23
Total	45	45	43

in multi-family households, for example, with a resident grandparent, or who also had children above 18 years old living at home.

As Table 3.4 shows, a greater proportion of the UK families are lone-parent families, reflecting differences in rates of lone parents and poverty between the countries (see Chapter 4). Among the 'lone-parent' families in the UK is one grandmother and, in Portugal, three cases comprise grandmothers who live with their daughters and grandchildren and two are 'couple families' who have grandmothers living with them.

Large families, often defined as those with three or more children under the age of 16 or 18, are, throughout most of Europe, more likely to be in poverty than those with fewer children (Chzhen et al. 2018). This is a consequence of the greater needs of larger families, the characteristics of the parents concerned and the pressure on finances that having more children tends to impose (Bradshaw et al. 2006). However, given that welfare packages vary between countries, benefits can be more, or less, effective in reducing poverty levels among large families; indeed in some countries (such as Russia) welfare support encourages large family size (Sivoplyasova 2019). In the UK, welfare reform has limited the benefits

Table 3.5 Family size in the three countries' samples: qualitative study.

Family type	UK	Portugal	Norway
Small (1 or 2 children)	22	22	18
Large (3+ children)	23	23	25
Total (N = 133)	45	45	43

Table 3.6 Origins of study mothers in the three countries' samples: qualitative study.

UK		Portugal		Norway	
White British, black British and British Asian	26	White Portuguese and second-generation Portuguese from former African colonies	31	White Norwegian	13
West African countries (former British colonies)	9	African countries (former Portuguese colonies)	12	Horn of Africa (Somalia, Eritrea, Ethiopia)	12
Eastern Europe	6	Brazil	2	Middle East (Turkey, Iraq, Syria, Afghanistan)	9
Other Europe	2			Caucasus and Central Asia	5
North Africa and India	2			The Americas	4
Total	45		45		43

a family can receive regardless of how many children they have, severing the link between need and support.[8] In all three countries we recruited a roughly equal number of larger and smaller families (see Table 3.5).

The three countries differ in their history, including of migration. Since mothers are most often responsible for family food work, we examined families' migration status via the mother's biography. Families in which the mother is a first-generation migrant make up just under half of families in the UK sample (including eight from mainland Europe), just under a third of the Portuguese sample and two-thirds of the Norwegian sample (Table 3.6). The large proportion of migrants in the Norwegian sample reflects the distribution of poverty in Norway.

Table 3.7 Ages of the children in the three countries' samples: qualitative study.

Child's age in years	UK	Portugal	Norway	Total
Under 13	20	20	17	57
13 and over	31	26	31	88
Total	51	46	48	145

The origins of the study's mothers reflect the different migration histories of the three countries. A disproportionate number, either first- or second-generation migrants, were black and doubly at risk – of racism as well as poverty. The largest groups of first-generation migrant mothers in the UK and Portugal came from former African colonies. Both the UK and the Portuguese samples also included second-generation black mothers. In Norway, the largest groups of migrants are relatively recent refugees from the Horn of Africa and the Middle East (Table 3.6). A feature of the UK sample of those who had migrated from former African colonies is that their legal status often meant they had 'no recourse to public funds' at the time of interview (Chapter 7).

The gender mix of the young people overall and in each country was roughly equal, with slightly more boys than girls: UK, 21 girls and 30 boys; Portugal, 22 girls and 24 boys; Norway, 22 girls and 26 boys. All the families included at least one child aged 11–15 years (though a few outlying cases included children aged 10 and 16 at the time of their [first] interview). More than one child took part in nine households. As Table 3.7 shows, the sample was skewed towards the older age range (13+ years) in each country and across the sample overall (88 out of 145 children were age 13 and over).

Analysing the data

In the quantitative part of the study, the UK team carried out secondary analysis of several large-scale datasets: the EU-SILC, HBSC and LCFS (see above and Chapter 4).

In the qualitative part of the study, we analysed the data using a case-based approach. In the first stage, 'case summaries' were written up from the transcripts and researchers' field notes in accordance with a standardised template of format and content which was agreed by the research teams in each country. Consistent with a realist approach to analysis, the case summaries provided thick description (Geertz 1973).

Thick description seeks not only to provide a large range of descriptors of a case but to render it comprehensible in relation to the contexts in which it exists and is observed.

A separate summary was written for the parent and child in each family. The parent case summaries covered the following types of data: tables of 'hard data' (main carer's age, ethnicity/nationality, family type, size, employment status and hours, income, main outgoings, food expenditure), 'food coping strategies' based on the self-completion questionnaire, a 'thumbnail sketch' of the case, the researchers' field notes from the interview, the interview themes under a standardised set of headings and a summary of key points in the particular case. In order to evidence the points being made and to elucidate meanings, excerpts from the interviews were included under relevant headings. Child case summaries contained similar information, with the addition of the completed 'food habits module' from the HBSC and questions about whether the children went to school or bed hungry. Each summary included a section enabling us to draw comparisons with the data from other family members who took part, including any contradictions between what parents and children said in the self-completion questionnaires and their interviews. In the UK and Norway, case summaries were written in English, whereas in Portugal, for reasons of time and because the team had more resources, they were written in Portuguese, then translated into English and checked for accuracy by the Portuguese researchers.

The next phase of analysis entailed a process of comparative analysis carried out by the authors of this book. The case summaries, together with the macro-level data, form the basis of a large part of this book. However, invaluable to the comparative process was material from the reports of findings, methodology and context, written to an agreed structure by the country research teams. These reports provided a key interpretive resource for the analysis, together with secondary analysis of large-scale datasets. A large part of the credit for this book belongs to the country teams; any fault is that of the authors alone.

It is also important to mention that, when they met, the team collectively analysed some of the case summaries. By viewing the summaries through 'strangers' eyes' (Schütz 1964) the researchers sought to elicit aspects of context that might otherwise have remained unspoken or invisible, both in the material collected in their own country and in the material collected elsewhere – for example, cultural, local and national features of context which impinged upon the families' lives (Brannen and Nilsen 2011). This discussion and exchange of case summaries across the team at earlier stages of the analysis were especially important because the Portuguese and Norwegian interviews were not translated in full.

In writing this book we have had to select particular cases and ignore others. We have made the selections on the basis of their typicality in relation to the dimensions we are considering. Thick description of the case (a household) provides the potential for a good 'fit' with other similar instances as long as the necessary information is given to make informed judgements about the extent of that fit in particular cases of interest (Schofield 2000).

Ethical considerations

The study was subject to ethical review by committees in each of the three participating institutions and by the ERC ethics team in Brussels. Emphasis was placed upon the appropriate framing of the study and the provision of adequate information to potential participants to enable them to decide whether to participate. An early discussion with the project's international Advisory Group concerned the study's (public-facing) name. Given the shame attached to poverty and being poor, as well as the differential impact of the global crisis and the implementation of austerity in the three countries, it was decided to frame the study in terms of 'hard times', a phrase broad enough to encompass the different contexts and range of experiences and narrow enough to be meaningful to families facing food constraints in particular circumstances. Leaflets about the study were provided to potential participants at the recruitment and screening stage and parents and children were given the opportunity to ask questions. Written consent was sought from parents and children, including to archive anonymised transcripts for potential reuse. Participants' anonymity has been protected by changing or omitting the names of people and places and removing other identifying details where necessary.

There are different views about the appropriateness of providing financial compensation for participation in research (Head 2009). We felt it was important to thank families for their time and all participants were given vouchers both for completing the initial questionnaires sent home to parents via children in schools and for taking part in the interviews and other procedures. Families were not pressurised to participate and many parents who agreed to talk to us said they did so, or seemed to do so, because they wanted to tell their stories and had something to say.

However, it is likely that some took part mainly because they wanted or needed the money.

Understandably, given their financial difficulties and the shame many clearly felt at admitting to going without decent food, some participants got upset at times in their interviews. When this happened, we always gave them the opportunity to pause the interview. The researchers acted with great sensitivity, choosing not to probe on some matters when they felt it would be insensitive to do so, as we note at various points in subsequent chapters.

Most interviews were carried out in participants' homes, and researchers' field notes suggest that the researchers were usually offered something to drink by the participants. In the Norwegian field notes there are many stories of mothers, all migrants, insisting the researchers eat with the family. These included one family from Somalia who served rice with chicken wings, another family from Eritrea who shared spaghetti bolognese and salad, and a third family who were Iraqi Kurds and provided a traditional dish, kubba, a rice dumpling stuffed with meat and sultanas, served with salad, green herbs, olives and bread. A family from Afghanistan offered the researchers tea, chocolate and biscuits but ate none themselves. In the UK and Portugal, in contrast, although some migrant mothers suggested how it was part of their habitus to share food with visitors (Chapter 9), the researchers were rarely offered food. One exception in the UK was an Italian migrant mother who was rehoused after the researcher, Abigail, signposted her to housing advice; she insisted Abigail join her for dinner in her new home when she next visited. In Portugal, Vasco joined a family to eat capucha, a traditional Cape Verdean stew.

Clearly, the shame and stigma attached to poverty, especially in rich societies like the UK and Norway, make it hard to admit to being poor, and, as noted above, shame is a possible reason it took so long to recruit families in these countries. Because low-income families are by definition 'in need', in the UK we took with us information about local services that might be able to provide help and advice. We were aware that such services were stretched and yet we were surprised by what we learned about the thresholds of, for example, social services in the UK (Jolly 2018). In response to families' circumstances, we had at times to overstep the researcher role, especially in cases of urgent need – for example, buying a bag of shopping and providing two young people with sleeping bags so they could join a school trip. By switching off the tape recorder we also afforded participants an opportunity to talk off the record about their worries and concerns (Brannen 1988). It is difficult to overstate the contribution of a highly experienced and sensitive research team to a project of this kind which touches on matters of considerable intimacy and sensitivity concerning family life, poverty and having enough to eat. Interviewing children and young people about such matters also requires an extra degree of sensitivity and skill.

In the next chapter we move on to analysing the data on which the book is based. Chapter 4 reports on the secondary analysis of international data, the European Statistics on Income and Living Conditions, and examines the relationship between low income, food insecurity and family type in the three countries. In the second part of the chapter we look at how food poverty is distributed among the study households according to their sources of income – those in paid work, those reliant on benefits and those who have neither. We also examine the quality of children's diets and their responses to questions about hunger.

Notes

1. We have done this in a standardised way using a Family Food Budget Standard (see Section 2).
2. According to data from the World Bank (2018), in 2018 over three-quarters of the UK's (82 per cent) and Norway's (83 per cent) population lived in regions that are predominantly urban. In Portugal, the proportion was smaller (65 per cent).
3. Subjective measures ask people if they think they are poor and how much income they would need to avoid poverty. 'This approach, to identifying poverty thresholds, is also known as the income proxy method (Veit-Wilson 1987) consensual poverty lines (see Walker 1987, Halleröd 1995) or sociovital minimum income level (SMIL) (Callan et al. 1989)' (Gordon 2006, 51).
4. Seven hundred questionnaires were sent in an envelope that included an invitation to participate, information about the study and an invitation to receive two scratch cards. Eighty-four people responded to the questionnaire, of which sixteen matched our criteria, and nine families responded positively to the researchers' phone calls.
5. In Norway, photos are missing from three children because it was not possible to collect the photographs of two of them and the camera was broken by a younger sibling in the third case. In the UK, one family who were left with a camera could not subsequently be contacted and so the children's photographs were not retrieved.
6. UK: Equivalised household income AHC was calculated and compared with the national distribution in the HBAI statistics for 2016–17 (the fieldwork years). We used the Modified OECD 'Companion' Scale to equivalise AHC results. Portugal: Equivalised household income BHC was calculated and compared with the national distribution in the HBS statistics for 2015/16 (the last available wave at that time). The Modified OECD 'Companion' Scale was used to equivalise BHC results. Norway: Household income BHC was compared with data from Statistics Norway (2018b).
7. Sen (1992, 1999) uses the example of the costs associated with disability to demonstrate how the translation of incomes into capabilities varies between groups. See also Lister (2004, 65).
8. 'The association between poverty and family size was the focus of Eleanor Rathbone's *The disinherited family*, first published in 1924. She recognised that a working-class wage was insufficient to meet the needs of a couple with children, and this was one of the main arguments she used in her campaign for family allowances. Beveridge incorporated family allowances into his scheme for social security and family allowances were eventually introduced for the second and subsequent child in 1946' (Bradshaw et al. 2006, 5).

4

Which types of family are at risk of food insecurity?

Despite different definitions and measures of food insecurity, a consistent finding seems to be that in all three countries in our study, the UK, Portugal and Norway, food insecurity is higher among families with children than in the general population (Chapter 1). However, knowledge about which types of families are most at risk is uneven. The first part of this chapter reports on our secondary analysis of international data, the European Statistics on Income and Living Conditions (EU-SILC). It examines the relationship between low income, food insecurity and family type (lone-parent households versus couple households with children). The second part of the chapter examines food insecurity within the households included in our qualitative research. The households have been analysed by family type and income source. The analysis also examines diet quality in terms of children's reported fruit and vegetable intake.

The international data: European Statistics on Income and Living Conditions

To examine the relationship between family type and household food insecurity and how this changed over time, we analysed repeat cross-sectional data from the EU-SILC (Eurostat 2010).[1] The EU-SILC is the main source of comparative data about the prevalence of lone-parent families in Europe (Bradshaw and Chzhen 2011). Each year, the survey includes, in its material deprivation module, an item that has been used as a proxy for household food insecurity (Loopstra et al. 2016): the inability to afford a meal containing meat, chicken, fish or a vegetarian equivalent (that is, a source of protein) every second day, an amount generally recommended in dietary guidelines across European countries (Carney and Maitre 2012).[2] Although previous comparative research using this variable as a proxy for food insecurity has covered a large number of countries, it has not looked at differences within countries, such as the types of household at risk. Addressing this, we analysed in our three countries the relationship between family type, income poverty and household food insecurity. We also examined change over time – the years 2005 to 2016, a period that includes the global financial crisis of 2008 and the retrenchment of the welfare state in Portugal and in the UK from 2010 (see Chapter 1).

Our analysis concentrated on three indicators: family type (lone parent versus couple with children aged less than 18 years), income poverty (at risk of poverty [AROP] households with an income below 60 per cent of median equivalised income) and food insecurity (inability to afford a meal containing meat, chicken, fish or a vegetarian equivalent every second day).[3] The results of our analysis were modelled statistically using logistic regression (Agresti 2018).[4]

Family type in the UK, Portugal and Norway

The distribution of family type by country (averaged across all years, 2005–16) is shown in Table 4.1. The UK has the highest percentage of lone-parent families (22.4 per cent of all families with children), in Norway the rate is lower (12.5 per cent) and the smallest proportion is in Portugal (10.1 per cent). Portugal has the highest percentage of 'multi-family' households – including more than one family with children in (24 per cent, compared with 9.3 per cent in the UK and 9 per cent in Norway).

Table 4.1 Family type by country, averaged across years.

Family type	United Kingdom N (%)	Portugal N (%)	Norway N (%)	Total N (%)
Lone parent	7,696 (22.4)	2,510 (10.1)	3,479 (12.5)	13,685 (15.7)
Couple	23,401 (68.2)	16,314 (65.9)	21,866 (78.5)	61,581 (70.9)
Multi-family household	3,191 (9.3)	5,945 (24.0)	2,508 (9.0)	11,644 (13.4)
Total	34,288 (100)	24,769 (100)	27,853 (100)	86,910 (100)

Source: EU-SILC, 2005–16.

Because the data on the risk of poverty and food insecurity are collected at the household level, it is not possible to investigate their differential impact on multiple families living within the same household. This means that it may be misleading to assign a lone-parent family the poverty status associated with another family or person living within the same household when resources may not be shared. For that reason, we decided not to include the multi-family households in the analysis. All further analyses and tables in this part of the chapter include only families classified as lone-parent families or couple families with children. In Portugal, this means the analysis is missing a large proportion of lone-parent families (in multi-family households), a fact that should be taken into account in interpreting the findings.

Families at risk of income poverty and food insecurity

Averaged across 12 years, the percentage of households with children at risk of income poverty is lowest in Norway (7.0 per cent). It is highest in Portugal (22.1 per cent) and then the UK (19.0 per cent) (Table 4.2.)

Over time, as Figure 4.1 graph A shows, the proportion of families (households with children aged less than 18 years) at risk of *poverty* varies between 2005 and 2016, although the variation is quite small. Norway (blue line) had a minimum of 6.3 per cent in 2005 and a maximum of 9.1 per cent in 2007, although this latter figure was exceptional, since the next highest was 7.7 per cent in 2016. In Portugal (green line) the minimum was 19.0 per cent in 2007 and the maximum was 23.5 per cent in 2005. For the UK (yellow line) the minimum was 17.3 per cent in 2013 and the maximum was 21.2 per cent in 2018. In both the UK and Portugal there is a spike in poverty levels (on the AROP measure) in 2008, and in all three countries there is a general increase in the proportion of

Table 4.2 Proportions of families at risk of poverty by household type, averaged across years.

Family type	UK (%)	Portugal (%)	Norway (%)
All	19.0	22.1	7.0
Lone parent	32.4	33.3	22.1
Couple	14.6	20.4	4.6

Source: EU-SILC, 2005–16.

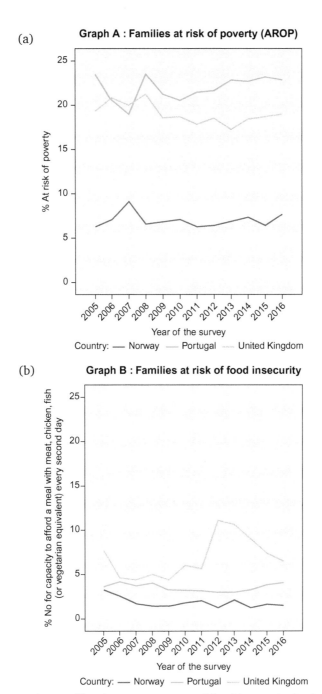

Figure 4.1 Families, income poverty and food insecurity in the three countries: (a) families at risk of poverty; (b) families at risk of food insecurity (Source: EU-SILC, 2005–16).

families at risk of poverty: in Portugal from around 2010, in the UK from around 2013 and in Norway from 2015.

Graph B in Figure 4.1 shows the proportion of families at risk of *food insecurity* (unable to afford a meal with protein every second day) in each country. As the graph shows, the percentage of families at risk of food insecurity varies by country and by year. The country with the lowest level of food insecurity is Norway (blue line), averaging 1.8 per cent over the period 2005–16. Next is Portugal (green line), with 3.5 per cent, almost twice as much as Norway. Finally, the UK (yellow line) stands out with the highest level of food insecurity, at 7.0 per cent, twice the level of Portugal.

What is striking, looking at the graphs side by side, is that although rates of income poverty are generally higher among families in Portugal (graph A), rates of food insecurity are consistently highest among families in the UK (graph B), particularly from 2009 and with a large spike in 2011–12.

As can also clearly be seen from comparing the two graphs in Figure 4.1, the variation over time is more marked for food insecurity (graph B) than for the AROP variable (graph A). Norway (blue line) showed a declining percentage of families at risk of food insecurity, from 3.2 per cent in 2005 to 1.3 per cent in 2012 and 2015. Portugal (green line) had a slight decline then a rise again, with a maximum of 4.1 per cent in 2006 and a minimum of 3.0 per cent in 2013, although the level rose to 4.0 per cent in 2016. The UK (yellow line) showed the largest variation over the period: the maximum was 11.0 per cent in 2012 and the minimum was 4.3 per cent in 2007 and 2009. There was a noticeable spike from 5.6 per cent in 2011 to 11.0 per cent in 2012, gradually falling again to 6.5 per cent in 2016.[5]

Types of family at risk of food insecurity

Turning to the types of family at risk of food insecurity, Table 4.3 shows the variation by lone-parent/couple status, averaged across the 12 years (2005–16).

In all three countries the proportion of lone-parent families at risk of food insecurity is greater than that of couple families. However, the gap is much smaller in Portugal than in Norway and the UK: in these two countries, the proportion of lone-parent families at risk of food insecurity is around three times that of couple families. The table also shows that

Table 4.3 Families at risk of food insecurity,* by family type, in the three countries, averaged across years.

	Proportion of lone parents (%)	Proportion of couples (%)
UK	13.7	4.8
Portugal	5.5	3.2
Norway	5.7	1.2

* Unable to afford a meal containing meat, chicken, fish or a vegetarian equivalent every second day.

Source: EU-SILC, 2005–16.

the proportion of lone-parent families at risk of food insecurity is much higher in the UK – more than twice the proportion in Portugal or Norway.

The relationship between family type, income poverty and food insecurity

The finding that lone-parent families are at higher risk of food insecurity than couple families in all three countries is not surprising, given what is known about the risk of poverty more generally among this group (Bradshaw and Chzhen 2011). As Table 4.2 shows, lone-parent families are more likely to be at risk of poverty (AROP) than couple families in all three countries, though the difference in Portugal is smaller than that in the UK and Norway.

To examine whether family type was related to rates of food insecurity *independently* of income poverty, we analysed the rates of food insecurity for couple and lone-parent families who are at risk of income poverty (less than 60 per cent median equivalised income) in each country, and how this changed over time. Figure 4.2 shows the results for each country. What is clear from the three graphs is that, even after controlling for low income (AROP), lone-parent families (the blue line) in the UK are consistently at much greater risk of food insecurity than couples (green line). The results for Norway also show a widening gap between low-income lone parents and low-income couples since 2013 in terms of the proportion at risk of food insecurity. In Portugal, by contrast, family type makes less difference to whether low-income families experience food insecurity, reflecting the trend for poverty in general (see Table 4.2 graph A).

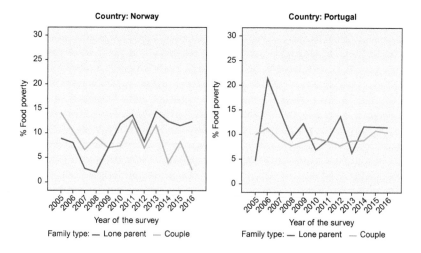

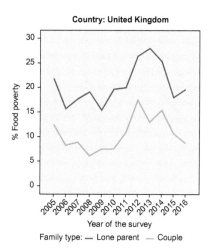

Figure 4.2 Three-way relationship between low income (AROP), food insecurity and family type in the three countries (Source: EU-SILC, 2005–16).

Thus, although we found that in all three countries families in income poverty (AROP) were at greater risk of food insecurity than families who were not (not shown), low income was not a sufficient explanation. Low-income lone parents were at greater risk of food insecurity than low-income couples in the UK and increasingly in Norway. In Portugal, family type made less difference to food insecurity, whether or not families had low incomes.

Discussion

The above analysis finds greater variation over time in rates of food insecurity than in rates of poverty using the AROP measure. Furthermore, particularly in the UK and increasingly in Norway, lone-parent families are more likely than couple families to be food insecure and this is the case after controlling for low income. Given that household food insecurity is tightly aligned with severe material deprivation (Loopstra and Tarasuk 2013), a likely explanation is that the food insecurity indicator is more sensitive to 'absolute poverty' that is hidden by the relative AROP measure (Gaisbauer et al. 2019). The findings likely reflect the depth of poverty among low-income lone-parent families, that is, it is likely that a greater proportion of lone-parent families in the UK and, increasingly in Norway, are not only below the AROP threshold, but a long way below it. As the book discusses, in the UK since 2010 and particularly since 2012 with the Welfare Reform Act, and in Norway since 2013, when the majority centre-left coalition lost office and was replaced by a minority right-wing coalition (Grødem 2017), policies of austerity have impacted on the incomes of low-income lone-parent families in particular. Furthermore, rising food prices across most food goods in Europe from 2005 to 2012 (Eurostat 2016) affected all households, but hit those on the lowest incomes, for whom food is a greater proportion of expenditure, the hardest. Moreover, in some countries, such as the UK, food prices rose more sharply than in other countries.

With regard to the finding of less difference in household food insecurity by family type in Portugal, part of the explanation is likely to be methodological, in that the analysis excludes lone parents living in multi-family households – a significant share of families in this country. In other words, it is possible that, for material and cultural reasons, those most likely to experience food insecurity live in multi-family households and are therefore not included in this analysis. It may also be the case that families in Portugal, a Southern European welfare state, have greater access to non-income resources that protect them against food insecurity than do families in the UK and Norway (Gregorio et al. 2014a; 2014b). However, the families with the lowest incomes in Portugal are likely be those least able to provide and rely on familial support (Wall et al. 2001).

In subsequent chapters we take a case approach and examine the income and other resources to which selected low-income families have access and the conditions that help or hinder their struggle to feed themselves adequately. Chapter 5 is devoted to (non-employed) lone-parent households that, as we have seen, are at great risk of poverty in all three countries and are also more at risk of food poverty, particularly in the UK. Chapter 6 analyses cases of dual-earner families, a growing group suffering in-work poverty, and Chapter 7 focuses on those who lack access to the formal labour market or entitlement to welfare benefits because they are undocumented migrants. Chapter 9 turns to the extra-household resources from charity and from extended family and friends which help families to feed themselves in times of shortage.

Households experiencing food insecurity in the qualitative research

While the EU-SILC data give a useful picture of patterns of food insecurity over time among different types of family across the three countries, they tell us little about the nature or severity of food insecurity (Loopstra et al. 2016), or the experiences of different individuals and families living in the same household. In the qualitative research, we were able to address the invisibility of multi-family households by including some households of this type. We were also able to look at who in the household was most likely to go without adequate food and to address the experiences of children in particular.

As discussed in Chapter 1, the book takes a multi-dimensional approach to defining food poverty. For the purposes of the analysis of food insecurity in this chapter, our discussion relates to one dimension only, that of compromised 'quantity'. We coded families in the qualitative study as 'food insecure' if, at some point in the past year, anyone in the household had skipped meals, eaten less than they felt they should, or gone hungry, owing to a lack of money or other resources. This corresponds with 'very low food insecurity' on the United States Department of Agriculture (USDA) measure (at times during the year eating patterns of one or more household members were disrupted and food intake was reduced because the household lacked money or other means of accessing food) and 'severe food insecurity' on the FAO's Food Insecurity Experience Scale (FIES) measure (reducing quantities, skipping meals, experiencing hunger) (see Chapter 1). This definition differs from the proxy used in the EU-SILC (which is a measure of compromised diet quality [protein deprivation], as employed above).

Across the whole qualitative sample in the three countries, just under two-thirds (85/133) of households were categorised as 'food insecure' (going without enough to eat at times in the past year). In the remaining 48 cases the quantity of food that parents or children ate was not compromised, but parents and/or children experienced other dimensions of food poverty, such as constraints on food purchasing, buying food that is filling rather than nutritious or the inability to participate in social activities such as inviting friends over to eat because of a lack of income.

As described in Chapter 3 (Table 3.4), two-thirds (30/45) of the UK families are headed by lone parents and a third are couple families. In Portugal, the pattern is reversed, with around two-thirds of families (26/45) headed by couples and a third (19/45) by lone parents (6).[6] In Norway, the proportions of lone parents and couples included in the study are about equal (20/43 and 23/43, respectively). As Figure 4.3 shows, although both types of family experience food insecurity in all three countries, a greater proportion of lone-parent families in the UK and Norway (around two-thirds in both) were food insecure, whereas just under half of couple families were classified as such. In Portugal, around the same proportions (four-fifths) of lone-parent and couple families experienced food insecurity. Coincidentally, this pattern is the same as that found in the analysis of the EU-SILC. It should be noted that there

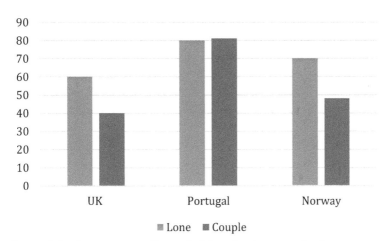

Figure 4.3 Percentages of households in food poverty in the qualitative study by family type and country sample (Source: authors, 2021).

Table 4.4 Households by source of income and country sample.

	UK	Portugal	Norway
At least one adult in paid work	24	26	17
Benefits only	17	19	26
No work, no benefits	4	0	0
Total ($N = 133$)	45	45	43

are differences between countries in how the families were recruited in the qualitative research, as well as in the classification of family type and the definition of food insecurity.[7]

We also looked at the difference paid work made. In the UK, in around half of the families (24/45) one or both parents were in paid employment, whereas just under half (17/45) relied on benefits and a small number (4/45) had no income from either employment or benefits owing to their legal (immigration) status at the time of interview (Table 4.4). In Portugal, also, around half of the families (26/45) had some paid employment and just less than half (19/45) were reliant on benefits only. In the Portuguese sample, all families had access to some income. In Norway, reflecting the economy's demands for high qualifications, just over a third were in paid employment and two-thirds were on benefits only. As in Portugal, there were no families without any paid work or benefits, although one father had no income in his own right (Chapter 7).

When we look at households classified as 'food insecure' there are some clear similarities as well as differences between the country samples. Although some families in paid work were classified as food insecure in all three countries, greater proportions of those who were reliant on benefits or had no income at all were food insecure than of those who had some paid work. In Portugal, however, around two-thirds of the families with paid work were food insecure, compared with around half of working families in Norway and just over a third in the UK. In Portugal, then, it appears that paid work is less effective at protecting families from going without enough to eat than in the UK or Norway, an observation that is discussed in relation to particular cases in Chapter 6. In the UK, but not the other two countries, there is a third group, in which the household had no access at the time of interview to work or benefits. All four of these cases are, as would be expected, food insecure. Chapter 7 focuses on families whose access to paid work and benefits is restricted because of their legal (citizenship) status.

Children and parents going without enough to eat

In times of shortage, parents – usually mothers – are known to sacrifice their food intake to protect their children (Chapter 2), so it is generally only in cases of extreme hardship that children go without enough to eat. In contrast to the EU-SILC dataset, in which the food insecurity variable is collected at the household level, making it impossible to know who in the household goes without adequate food, in the qualitative research we asked about children's and parents' experiences of food poverty.

In some families in all three countries, children go without enough to eat because of their families' lack of resources (Figure 4.4). The families (34/133) in which children go without enough to eat are fairly evenly distributed across the three countries, with 12 cases in the UK and 10 cases each in Norway and Portugal. This distribution contrasts with the food insecurity of adults, which is much higher in Portugal. Relative to adults, then, it appears that children in the sample in Portugal are more protected from food insecurity than their counterparts in the UK and Norway samples. As the case analyses in subsequent chapters, particularly Chapter 10, discuss, it is possible that Portuguese school meals play a part.

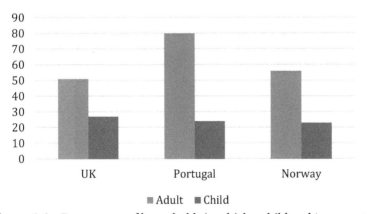

Figure 4.4   Percentages of households in which a child and/or parent goes without enough to eat by country sample in the qualitative study (Source: authors, 2021).

The quality of children's diets

Alongside their interviews, the 145 children (in 133 families) who took part in the qualitative research were asked to fill in a self-completion 'eating habits module' that was adapted from the international Health Behaviour in School-Aged Children (HBSC) study (Chapter 3). Most of the young people completed the questionnaire, but some did not complete it and not all of those who did answered all of the questions. Totals are therefore given for the different questions below.

In the UK, just over half of the children who completed the question about vegetable consumption (26/48) said they ate vegetables at least five or six times a week (Table 4.5). Since we also analysed the HBSC data for England (Simon et al. 2018), we were able to compare the qualitative sample with the national picture. Compared with the national HBSC sample for England (in 2014, the most recent year available at the time of that analysis), the reported consumption of vegetables is slightly below the national average (about 54 per cent compared with 62.7 per cent of all young people nationally who reported eating vegetables at least five or six times a week). The findings for reported consumption of fruit are more stark: a much lower proportion, just over a third of the children in the qualitative sample who completed the question (17/47), reported eating fruit at least five or six times a week, compared with just over half (52.7 per cent) of all young people in the national HBSC sample in 2014 (Simon et al. 2018).

In Portugal, the proportion of children reporting that they eat vegetables at least five or six times a week is around two-thirds (32/46), slightly higher than in the UK. This is likely to be an underestimation, since the module did not ask about soup, which is an important part of many children's diets at school and home. (Other research suggests that

Table 4.5 Self-reported fruit and vegetable intake among the young people.*

	Vegetables		Fruit	
	At least 5–6 times per week	Never or less than once a week	At least 5–6 times per week	Never or less than once a week
UK	26/48	4/46	17/47	8/46
Portugal	32/46	5/46	30/46	2/46
Norway	13/37	2/37	19/37	3/37

* Totals are the number of children who completed each question.

soup makes a significant contribution to vegetable intake in Portugal and should be asked about separately [Araújo 2011])[8] (Chapter 10). About two-thirds (30/46) reported eating fruit at least five or six times per week, which is around twice the proportion of children reporting this in the UK sample.

In Norway, the proportion who say they eat vegetables at least five or six times per week is the lowest in the three countries, being about a third (13/37), while around half of the children reported eating fruit at least five or six times per week (19/37), which is in between the proportions in the UK and Portugal samples. These proportions appear to be similar to those for children in Norway in general. For example, Bere and colleagues (2010, 593) report that 'there has been a large increase in pupils eating fruit at school from 2001 to 2008 in Norway, and the school fruit programmes seem to have been effective. However, a great challenge remains in increasing vegetable intake'. In the Norwegian tradition of having only one hot meal per day, because people eat a sandwich lunch, vegetables are mostly eaten at dinner. The likelihood of Norwegians eating large amounts of vegetables with other meals is low (Wandel 1995).

Overall, the reported intakes generally reflect the findings of the HBSC 2009–10 international research (Currie at al. 2012) that the quality of children's diets – particularly in fruit intake, a more reliable indicator given the methodological difficulty with 'vegetables' noted above – is more strongly related to low 'family affluence' (a proxy for income) in the UK than in either Norway or Portugal.

Discussion

This chapter set out to examine the types of family at risk of food insecurity in the three countries. It has reported on secondary analysis of a large European dataset, the EU-SILC, that examined food insecurity by family type, and has described the spread of the low-income households in the qualitative research by family type, source of household income, adult and child food insecurity and children's diet quality (reported intake of fruit and vegetables).

The analysis of the EU-SILC found that food insecurity was lowest among families in Norway and highest in the UK, despite general poverty rates being higher in Portugal. In the secondary analysis, family type made less difference to rates of food insecurity among families generally, or those on low incomes, in Portugal. However, in both the

UK and Norway, poor lone-parent families were much more likely to be food insecure than poor couple families. One possible explanation for the finding that family type was less important in Portugal was that the analysis missed lone-parent families living in multi-family households. Other interpretations included the depth of poverty among lone-parent families in the UK and Norway and families' potentially better access to non-income resources in 'familialist' Portugal.

Coincidentally, the distribution of household food insecurity in the qualitative research reflected the pattern we found in our analysis of the EU-SILC data: family type made less difference to household food insecurity among low-income families in Portugal than in the UK or Norway samples. It also showed that, among food-insecure families, the largest group in all three countries had no employment per household – that is, the lone parent or both parents were non-employed – and that the largest proportion of families with some paid work who were food insecure was in Portugal. In the UK, there is a group without access to paid work or benefits; unsurprisingly, all of these families were food insecure.

In the analysis of the qualitative material we also examined the distribution of food insecurity between parents and children. We found that although the number of parents going without enough to eat was highest in Portugal, the number of children who reported such an experience was about the same in all three countries, suggesting that children in Portugal were somewhat protected from the direct effects of poverty on their food security. One possible explanation for this lies in the Portuguese school meals system (Chapter 10). The analysis also examined children's self-reported intake of fruit and vegetables. Comparing the children in the research with national data, we found that although vegetable consumption was lowest in Norway, this likely reflected low consumption of vegetables generally, whereas the low consumption of fruit among children in low-income families in the UK reflects a strong social gradient in diet quality, including among young people.

One implication of the finding of a relationship between family type and household food insecurity, in the UK and Norway at least, is the need for social policies to address the particular requirements of different family forms. Comparative analysis has identified a trend in policy-making across Europe, 'away from a family policy perspective focusing on the vulnerability of lone-parent families in general towards seeking to provide social benefits for disadvantaged persons and families' (Letablier and Wall 2018, 50; and see Knijn et al. 2007; Eydoux and Letablier 2009). Jaehrling and colleagues (2015, 88) find that, across countries, a major change is 'the abolition of social security benefits that were specifically aimed at single parents in their roles as mothers (or, much less frequently, fathers) and provided security against inactivity due to parental responsibilities, or their merger with the benefits intended to protect against involuntary unemployment'. However, as we discuss in the next chapter, the particular challenges lone parents face in accessing paid employment, and in feeding their families on social benefits, suggest the importance of a family social policy focus.

Notes

1. This chapter draws on analysis of data from Eurostat, EU-SILC, 2005–16, by Charlie Owen and Antonia Simon. The responsibility for all conclusions drawn from the data lies entirely with the authors. The EU-SILC collates data for countries in the EU based on common guidelines (Eurostat 2017). Data are available for all countries in the EU at that time, including the UK and Portugal, and also for Norway. This is an annual data collection. The sample sizes of households are large enough for different household types to be compared (UK: 7,500; Norway: 3,750; Portugal: 4,500). Data are collected on income, housing type and quality, and material deprivation, including arrears on housing and other payments. The survey is made up of a core component (same content every year) and special modules (which change annually).

2. As noted by Reeves and colleagues (2017, 1415), this measure captures qualitative compromises in food intake owing to constrained financial resources, providing an indication of one dimension of household food insecurity (Radimer et al. 1990). They note that although this measure has never been directly compared with household food insecurity scales used in other countries (for example, the USDA's HFSSM), it has been found to correlate with other indicators of poverty and food hardship in Ireland (Carney and Maitre 2012).

3. The variables are described in GESIS (2016). GESIS is a probabilistic mixed-mode access panel for the social sciences. Household type is contained in the variable *HX060*.

4. This is a method appropriate for a binary outcome variable. In this case the answer to the question about the household's capacity to afford a high-protein meal every second day has the binary response categories Yes or No.

5. Unfortunately, there was a change in the way the data were collected in the UK in 2012. Since 2012 the EU-SILC data have been collected using the Family Resources Survey: 'This led to changes in … most material deprivation questions, causing a break in series' (Guio et al. 2017, 11). However, the changes continued to be implemented in the survey in subsequent years, so if the change in the data collection had been responsible for the sudden rise in measured food poverty then this raised level should have persisted. But it did not: there was a steady drop in the percentage of food poverty after 2012. This gives some confidence that the sudden jump was not an artefact introduced by changes in the survey, but a real increase in food poverty, in the context of the UK government's austerity policy (Alston 2019; Loopstra et al. 2015).

6. As already noted, lone parenthood is 'hidden' in Portugal, where material circumstances and cultural norms mean there is a higher rate of multi-family households (Bradshaw and Chzhen 2011). Among the families in Portugal, as noted in Chapter 3, three have been classified as 'lone parent', referring to either a mother or a grandmother. Two families that are headed by couples also include grandmothers.

7. Only single-family households were included in the quantitative analysis. However, as noted, Southern European norms mean that for cultural and material reasons a number of those we classified in the qualitative study as lone-parent families live in multi-unit households.

8. Although the food habits module asks children to report the frequency of their weekly vegetable consumption, in Portugal, soup makes an important contribution. However, since the local food taxonomy considers 'soup' a distinct category, it is unlikely to be reported by children as part of their vegetable consumption. The first study to assess the food sources of dietary intake in adolescents and in Portugal, by Araújo et al. (2011), a cross-sectional survey of 1,522 13-year-old boys and girls in 2003–4, included 14 different food groups, including separate items for 'vegetables' (cabbage, spinach, broccoli, onion, carrot, lettuce, peppers, tomato or cucumber, among others), legumes (for example, beans, chickpeas or peas) and 'vegetable soup'. The study reported that vegetable soup accounted for 5.2 per cent of the total consumption of vegetables and about 13.2 per cent of fibre intake (Araújo et al. 2011, 1976).

Section 2
Households as resource units

From the 1970s onwards, a focus by feminist sociologists on households as resource units was a means of challenging moral diktats surrounding the normative model of 'the (nuclear) family' headed by a male 'bread-winner'. To some extent this has been successful, although new family forms are not necessarily seen as having equal merit in the mass media and government policy and, as Chapter 5 shows, new stories can target the same culprits.

As part of this theorisation, households came to be understood as sites in which family members engage in the provisioning practices that are central to productive and reproductive processes. Within the household, according to this theorisation, resources were allocated in accordance with the status and benefit of its members, and the value placed upon individuals' labour and time had implications for the work they did in the household and the labour market (Brannen and Wilson 1987; Brannen 2019).

This approach contrasts with models that assume that household 'decisions' are based on economic rationality and with statistical social science that has treated the family/household as a unitary concept in which all members are assumed to share equally the same standard of living. In particular, a focus on intra-household resource distribution highlights that it is those – typically women – whose time is valued less who are likely to have more responsibility for, and to devote more time to, childcare and household work, including 'domestic food provisioning', that is, the often undervalued and 'invisible work' (Daniels 1987) of transforming income and other resources into meals (DeVault 1991). Furthermore, the logic that informs everyday and more strategic action cannot be reduced to economic decisions based on costs and benefits but is grounded in an ethics of care.

When households have to contend with highly constrained financial resources, as Daly (2017, 451) notes, a focus on the ways in which resources that come into a household are distributed 'offers a vital opportunity to develop an account of money as a means of organising everyday lives, articulating relationships and framing worth and meaning for self and social action'. The delicate balance of making ends meet on inadequate budgets involves the exercise of agency in a social and cultural context that may both constrain and enable action (Lister 2004). As Lister goes on to argue, agency is dependent, at one end of a spectrum, on the particular conditions of everyday life encountered by low-income families and, at the other, on the politics of citizenship that determine individual entitlements: the entitlement to enter the labour market and to particular levels and types of benefits provided by the state. As Sen (1981, 155) argues in relation to entitlement to food in famine situations, 'it is the totality of entitlement relations that governs whether a person will have the ability to acquire enough food to avoid starvation, and food supply is only one influence among many affecting his entitlement relations'. According to Lister (2004, 145), 'movements in and out of poverty are a product of both individual actions (taken by poor and non-poor), on the one hand, and economic and social processes and government policies, on the other'.

Low-income families have little room for manoeuvre in negotiating social security and other welfare benefits. Given the changes to which benefits are subject and the precarious nature of many jobs, to speak of 'agency' here may be too strong a word. Conversely, those reliant primarily on benefits express resistance to designations of being 'welfare dependent' through endorsing a strong work ethic (Dean 1998), and some participants in the study emphasise that they see their education and that of the next generation as the main route out of poverty. In understanding how low-income families manage to feed themselves, a dynamic perspective is important. The desire to replicate or avoid one's own early experiences may be a strong motivation or rationalisation of current practices. But, as Atkinson (1998a, 1998b) argues, how people have managed in the past is not necessarily an indicator of how they will manage in the future. Individual trajectories change in relation to wider societal forces: on the one hand, through exclusion from social rights and policies and, on the other, through people acting on their own future.

It is generally women who are the primary 'managers of poverty' in everyday life, as many studies over the decades have shown (Pember Reeves 1913; Spring Rice 1981; Goode at al. 1998; Scott et al. 1999;

Snape et al. 1999; Sung and Bennett 2007; Hanmer and Hearn 1999, 119). Different obligations and entitlements to food attach to different household members and are embedded in, and reproduce, relations of power, including ones that are gendered (Sen 1981). In their every-day lives, mothers living on low incomes 'get by' (Lister 2004), and are expected to get by, in ways that protect their children. One of the chief means is by engaging in 'maternal altruism' or 'sacrifice' (Whitehead 1984): going without food to enable children to have more (Ridge 2009; Dowler and O'Connor 2011, 10). Other methods depend on personal resources, for example, pride in being able to manage, and skills such as shopping carefully and meal planning (Christie et al. 2002). Personal resourcefulness may be bolstered by strong social networks, including kin and local institutions that may offer emotional support, material support in cash or kind, and local infrastructure (Duncan and Edwards 1999). For example, mothers' capacities to manage on a very low food budget may be influenced by the neighbourhood and the types of shops and the cost of the food they offer. At one end of a continuum, some neighbourhoods have a dearth of shops and food is expensive; at the other end, there is a diverse range of food outlets. The cost and ease of transport also varies. Homes are also central resources for food provisioning: some are well equipped for cooking and others lack basic facilities or energy supply.

Because children may be the most affected by adverse family circumstances, owing to their relative immaturity and lack of authority (Boyden and Mann 2005, 3), they have been largely understood as victims of poverty. However, increasing recognition is given to the interdependence of children and parents within families (Thorne 2012), directing attention to multiple perspectives (Ribbens McCarthy et al. 2003). Children may help their families to manage poverty by contributing to household work and by moderating and concealing their own needs, strategies that are 'not without tensions and costs for children themselves' (Ridge 2011, 82). In research on lone parents who are in paid work, Millar and Ridge (2013, 564) coined the idea of 'family-work projects' in which, in order to sustain work and care over time, being a working family must 'become part of the everyday and regular practice of the family, and this actively involves all family members'. Children's contributions to the 'family food work project' may also be vital (O'Connell and Brannen 2016). Yet, although children may feel a sense of responsibility and pride in helping their families, as we discuss, particularly in Chapters 8 and 10, they also experience the stigma that is associated with poverty. This is 'particularly devastating for a child or young person who is developing a sense of her [*sic*] own identity' (Lister 2004, 69) and engaging in processes of 'social comparison' with their peers (Festinger 1954).

In Section 2 of the book we examine the relationship between families' source of income and their experiences of food poverty. In our qualitative research, the most stringent or extreme aspect of food poverty (at least one person in the household sometimes going without enough to eat, owing to a lack of resources) was most often associated with unemployment and reliance on benefits (Table 5.1). Exceptionally, in the UK, some families had access to neither employment nor benefits, all of whom were experiencing food poverty (Chapter 7).

Table 5.1 sets out all the cases according to family type (lone-parent or couple household), employment status of one or more members of the adults in the household, and the proportion of households that are food poor (at least one household member going without enough to eat sometimes in the past year, owing to a lack of resources). It is important to note that in households classified as 'employed', especially in the case of couple families, there is often very low work intensity: in many, only one parent is in employment and in Norway that employment is often part-time. In Portugal, there is a good deal of 'informal' work. Given its irregularity, this has not been included as paid employment.

In Chapters 5, 6 and 7 we have selected specific cases in order to examine low household income and food poverty in different types of families: unemployed lone-parent households, dual-earner households and households in which one parent is an undocumented migrant. Each of these household types has, for different reasons, been the focus of public or policy discourses. Each chapter focuses on three households drawn from each of the three countries. In selecting households for comparison,

Table 5.1 Food poverty by family type, employment status and country sample.

Family type	Employment status*	UK food poor[†]	Portugal food poor	Norway food poor
Lone parent	Unemployed	12/17	9/10	12/15
	Employed	6/13	6/9	2/5
Couple	Unemployed	3/3	8/9	5/11
	Employed	3/12	13/17	6/12
Total		24/45	36/45	25/43

* Employment may be part-time and/or only one parent may be employed.
[†] In the UK there are four households with no source of income, of whom three are lone parents and all are food poor.

we have matched households to the focus of the chapter. In Chapter 5, for example, mother-headed households are selected on the basis of lone parenthood, non-employment and having a teenager and at least one other child. It was not always possible to match characteristics such as type of locality, given the composition of the samples and the specificities of countries' geography.

In analysing and comparing households, we examine the income available, including from state benefits, and how this is spent; the ways in which mothers transform money into food for family members; the quantity and quality of food provided for parents and children; children's accounts of their experiences of their households' insufficient resources; and mothers' and children's orientations to the future. For each family discussed, we have compared actual (reported) food expenditure with the cost of 'food baskets' for a particular family type, calculated using a reference budget approach for each of the three countries. We refer to these amounts as the 'food budget standard' (FBS). This method of comparing reported expenditure with the FBS gives a rough idea of how the spending of a family featured in the book compares with the spending deemed necessary to meet not only health recommendations, but also norms about what is customary in the society to which they belong (Padley and Hirsch 2017). The reference budget approaches in each country differ. The calculations for the UK compare families' reported expenditure with food budgets calculated as part of the Minimum Income Standard (MIS), averaging across different ages of children and including a small amount for the costs of alcohol and celebrating special occasions. Portugal uses a version of the MIS methodology; in the RaP (*Rendimento Adequado em Portugal*) reference budgets are calculated for different family types with an assumption of a 12-year-old or adult child (Pereirinha et al. 2017). The costs of alcohol or celebrating special occasions are calculated separately and we did not include them in the FBS. In Norway, reference budgets are calculated by the National Institute for Consumer Research (SIFO) and the food budgets do not include alcohol or the cost of eating out or celebrating special occasions (SIFO 2015).[1] Thus, the calculation of UK families' spending compared with the FBS is likely to come closer to what families need to participate in social life, whereas the calculations for Norway and Portugal probably underestimate what families will need to spend for the sake of social inclusion, and hence underestimate their underspend.

Chapter 5 features three lone-parent households that are reliant on social benefits. As we found in Chapter 4, the households most at risk of poverty in each country were lone-parent ones, although in Portugal the difference from two-parent households is much smaller. Chapter 6 focuses on dual-parent working families, a group that is increasingly at risk of poverty and food poverty, and Chapter 7 is devoted to households in which one parent is an undocumented migrant who is not legally permitted to participate in the formal labour market and is excluded from entitlement to benefits. As we will show, in all these cases, income from employment and/or benefits is not enough to feed all the members of the families properly, and those without access to either can barely feed themselves at all.

Note

1. In Norway, 'The Standard Budget does not include expenses for housing, electricity and other housing expenses (such as maintenance), tobacco and alcohol, upper secondary school health services, leisure pursuits that require costly equipment, holiday travel, celebration of special occasions, gifts, "clubbing", night life' (Sifo 2015).

5
Three families headed by an unemployed lone mother

The policy focus on lone mothers, in English-speaking countries at least, seems to have abated since the 1990s, in part perhaps because different family forms have become more common, but also because the language has changed to less 'gendered' terminology that renders lone mothers less visible. However, lone-parent families are still overwhelmingly headed by mothers (Bradshaw and Chzhen 2011) and are an interesting 'border case', since they:

> focus some of the most difficult issues faced by modern welfare states in respect of the recognition that is (or, more often, is not) accorded the unpaid work of caring, the ways in which unpaid and paid work are combined, and the responsibilities of the state as opposed to the individual and the family. (Lewis and Hobson 1997, 2)

In many countries, neoliberal policies that promote work as *the* route out of poverty have reduced the length of time that mothers may be supported by the state to care for their children. Such policies and public discourses have also reframed the debate from one that problematises lone motherhood from the perspective of the normative nuclear family, to one that recasts lone mothers as failing according to the moral obligations of the 'social investment state' (Ferrara 2009; Letablier and Wall 2018). In juggling different types of work, lone mothers therefore have to contend not only with material and temporal constraints but also with symbolic violence that blames them for their plight.

In most cases, lone motherhood is the result of relationship dissolution and, less often, the death of a partner; women may also actively choose or defend lone parenthood as a 'promise they can keep' (Edin and Kefalas 2005). Among some groups, for example, some of those with roots in the Caribbean, the living arrangement of 'lone' motherhood is a norm, with fathers providing support and 'visiting' but not co-residing (Fog Olwig 1998). Lone parenthood is a temporary relationship status for many women, though those at the bottom of the income spectrum re-partner less often. The average age at which women become mothers may be important for understanding differences in rates of poverty among them, in combination with the social policy contexts that determine enti-tlement to financial and other types of support, such as childcare.

Lone-parent families are generally defined in the comparative lit-erature as those 'where a parent lives with his/her dependent children, without a spouse/partner, either on their own or in multi-unit households' (Duncan and Edwards 1997 in Letablier and Wall 2018, 30). However, 'the apparent simplicity of this definition conceals a number of problems that are amplified in cross-national comparisons' (Letablier and Wall 2018, 33). Indeed, it has been suggested that difficulties in conceptual-ising and identifying lone-parent families are key reasons for the relative lack of comparative research about this family type (Letablier and Wall 2018). Some lone-parent families are likely to be 'invisible' in household surveys, particularly in Southern European countries (Bradshaw and Chzhen 2011). As noted in Chapter 4, in the EU-SILC international data-set (which may include but not identify lone mothers and their children) the proportion of children living in multi-generational households varies widely – from 1 per cent in the Nordic countries to around 10 per cent in Portugal and 22 per cent in Poland.

In all European countries (except Finland) child poverty rates are highest when lone parents are not employed (although the calculation does not take account of childcare costs) (Bradshaw and Chzhen 2011, 33). The proportion of children living with lone parents not in employ-ment or working less than 16 hours a week is highest in the Netherlands, the UK and Ireland and lowest in Norway, Iceland and Slovakia (Bradshaw and Chzhen 2011, 30).[1] Different countries vary in their generosity and effectiveness in addressing the poverty of lone parents through social transfers such as in-work and out-of-work benefits. Analysing the EU-SILC for 2006, Bradshaw and Chzhen examine the impact of policy on lone-parent families' risk of poverty. Controlling for demographic fac-tors, they find that Norway is significantly more successful in reducing child poverty in lone-parent families than the UK (which they treat as the base case) (Bradshaw and Chzhen 2011, 36). Among our three coun-tries, policies aiming to reduce child poverty in lone-parent families are less successful in Portugal, where social transfers are at least twice as effective for couples as for lone parents.

In our qualitative research the most extreme aspect of food poverty (at least one person in the household sometimes going without enough to eat in the past year, owing to a lack of resources) was most associated with unemployment and reliance on benefits (Table 5.1). Across the samples, lone parents were more likely than not to be reliant on state benefits, except in Portugal, where there is a tradition of women working and where lone-parent families are discriminated against in a benefits system that promotes nuclear family forms (Letablier and Wall 2018). In the UK sample, out of 30 lone-parent households, 17 depended on state benefits for income, of whom 12 were also food poor (according to the definition above in terms of the FBS). In the Portuguese sample, out of 19 lone-parent households, 10 were reliant on social transfers and 9 of these were classified as food poor. In the Norwegian sample, of the 20 lone-parent households, 15 were in receipt of social security benefits, of whom 12 were food poor. Overall, therefore, lone parents reliant on the state for income were likely to be food poor.

In this chapter, the three households headed by an unemployed lone parent that we focus on were experiencing, or had recently experienced, a shortage of food. We examine the similarities and differences in the mothers' and children's material conditions in terms of household income and expenditure. We describe the ways in which lone mothers and their children manage food poverty. We look at the resources available to them to enable them to obtain food, the types of food they are able to procure, whether and how they transform food into adequate nutritious meals, including any contributions made by children, and the consequences in terms of who goes without food. Although we have selected cases where the mothers have gone without enough to eat, this is a strategy practised by mothers across the study, and the cases also include one household in which the children, as well as their mother, go without enough to eat.

Living hand to mouth in a coastal town in the UK: Angela and Bryony

Angela, a white British lone mother, lives with her two teenage children, Bryony (the study child), age 13, and her brother, age 15, in a privately rented maisonette in a Victorian building in the coastal town. Angela has faced many challenges in her life. She described being brought up 'on jam sandwiches' in a mining village and from her mid-teens lived with her grandparents, in whose home, she says, she taught herself to cook. Later, as an adult, she fled from destructive relationships from one coastal town to another with her two children. This led to a breakdown and to close monitoring of her children's welfare by social services. Angela lost her council house when she came to the study town to make 'a fresh start' about nine months before the interview; she has recently been 'cleared' by social services. She now has a new partner who does not live with her.[2] She is keen to get into work and start her own food business but is currently waiting for treatment for several health conditions.

Until recently, Angela depended on ESA. However, she has been moved to Jobseeker's Allowance, a process that left the family with little income for weeks – 'totally skint'. The household is in receipt of around £277 per week, made up of £147 per week Jobseeker's Allowance and £130 per week in tax credits and child benefit. Bryony and her brother receive free school meals. Housing costs are subsidised; Angela pays £88 per month towards them. Gas and electricity are paid by meter, around £15 per week each. The combined cost of all of their mobile phones and the TV/internet is around £100 a month. Angela's family helped with removal expenses to her current flat but she is expected to repay them. Angela also has debts for a TV and a washing machine purchased through instalments from catalogues. She is in arrears on her water bill. The family frequently goes without electricity and resorts to candles.

The family's other expenses include school uniform and clothes. Although sometimes they buy clothing in second-hand shops, Angela doesn't want the children to stand out from their peers. Recalling her own experience as a deprived child, she prioritises branded trainers:

> I won't give them cheap, cheap stuff because they live in a society where it's quite cruel now with kids. So if I send them out in Hi-Tec [cheap brand of trainers], they're coming back crying – I won't even put them in that situation. It's something I experienced as a kid and … so you pay the little bit extra for them.

The family lives hand to mouth. The money Angela has to spend on food varies from £20 to £70 per week, depending on her other expenses: 'If I've got lots of bills going out I can do a shop on 20 quid.'[3] The sum of £20 a week is about a quarter of the FBS for this type of family; £70 is around nine-tenths. However, this money also has to pay for 'toiletries for two teenagers that are the opposite sex, that want hair spray and deodorants and … like you know' and there are animals to feed: 'fish, snakes, spiders, turtles and a guinea pig'.

Angela does not have a car and there is little money for the expensive local public transport; hence, in order to shop they walk everywhere. 'I spend half my life walking. Either walk into town for financial reasons, or walking out of town just to get away from it all.' Angela seeks bargains at big supermarkets such as Morrison's, Aldi and Iceland as well as at smaller independent shops. 'I go out every single day and get dinner.' The large out-of-town shopping centre is 'a good mile and a half, two miles'.

Angela shops at a butcher's sometimes for cheaper meat that she freezes. '[I] can go to a butcher's sometimes to get the trays. If I've got a little bit of extra money I'll get meat trays, freeze the meat, freeze bread, freeze everything.' She also mentions using local 'foreign' shops such as Polish, Sri Lankan and Indian grocers. Shopping is often done in the evening when the fresh food with short sell-by dates is on special offer; this means they eat quite late, at around 7.00–8.00 p.m. To make fish and chips at home, 'we go to Morrison's fish counter and wait for the sale stuff'. Shopping for bargains means having to be flexible, 'because it's whatever's on offer and it's like "Oh that's too good to pass up" so I completely change the menu'.

Good-quality food is more expensive, Angela says. She prefers organic food but tries to eat fresh food if not. 'Just if I've got absolutely no money I'll just buy a big bag of frozen veg, mixed veg.' But the family goes without eggs if Angela can't afford to buy eggs from uncaged hens. They grow some food in the communal garden attached to their block of flats: apples, tomatoes, raspberries, strawberries, fennel and courgettes. Bryony confirms that fruit is generally available at home. In her eating habits questionnaire she reports eating fruit five or six days per week, but vegetables less often, around two to four days per week. Bryony has free school meals but complains that the school does not cater well for vegetarians. Although she says she sometimes buys salad, school meals appear to make little contribution to her vegetable intake (Table 5.2).

Despite severely limited finances, Angela is a creative cook. While growing up she developed a great deal of interest in 'good' food and is proud she can make interesting healthy meals out of whatever is available. Although Angela had hardly any money when she was growing up and lived with her grandparents, she says her 'nan' (grandmother) was a capable cook from whom she learned about food and cooking on a budget. Asked what she learned, she said, 'A bag of flour goes a long way … a long way. As long as you've got a box of eggs and that in the kitchen and some flour and that you'll be all right.'

Table 5.2 Menus for Angela and her daughter Bryony.

	Bryony	Angela
Breakfast	Nothing	Not mentioned
Lunch	Salad *or* wrap, plus biscuit *or* drink	Not mentioned
Dinner	Depends what is on sale: faggots, new potatoes, green beans, with tomato and mushroom gravy	Same as children or water
Snacks	School: nothing Home: fruit if they have it	Not mentioned
Weekend	Fried breakfast with 'reduced' organic pork sausages, bacon, mushrooms	Same as children
Quality and quantity of Bryony's diet	Fruit: five–six days per week. Vegetables: two–four days per week. Ticks 'never' to going hungry to school or bed but admits to going without meals.	

Angela prides herself in being able to make 'something out of nothing'. For example, 'Yesterday … I had three quid before my payday today – I had £3 left, so I was hanging on in there, and I had to cook for … you'd basically say four adults now'. During the 'kitchen tour', Angela showed the researcher (Abigail) her fridge and cupboard (Figure 5.1). Her benefits were due the following day; so the day the photo was taken was 'the toughest' time. However, since Angela shops daily, there is usually 'not a lot' more food than this: 'There'll be a couple of tins of beans, tomatoes, basic things like that's there as a basis and then I've got all my herbs and spices and stuff, and then I can just go out, buy meat and make something little.'

Meals are often unconventional, reflecting the food that is on special offer. The day before the interview, they ate faggots,[4] an unusual dish nowadays that Angela found in a section of the supermarket fridge reserved for 'short life' foods whose price has been reduced. 'My kids will eat anything … anything cos I couldn't afford for them to be fussy.' Bryony speaks enthusiastically about the fruit and vegetables they grow in their shared garden and also seems to do some of the cooking: 'Sometimes I'll take over the kitchen; I'll cook like cakes and stuff by myself. But if it's like meals like as in meat and stuff, I'll help do it with mum.' Bryony is also aware of the benefits of locally sourced food and critical of supermarket promotions, remarking, 'It's like the supermarkets want us to get fat'.

(a)

(b)

Figure 5.1 Fridge (a) and cupboard (b) at Angela's house (Source: Abigail Knight).

Angela used a food bank in the past when her benefits were stopped. The distance to the food bank made this difficult. 'I walked two-and-a-half miles I think to my … to the food bank, walked back with six carrier bags of food – blistering hot day.' As Angela reflects, 'Obviously if you haven't got money for food, you haven't got money for a bus'.

On the one hand, she insists that the children have not gone without food. Perhaps it would be too painful and risky to admit that they have. On the other hand, she says she cannot always give her children as much food as she would like or 'I think than they need sometimes'. However, she herself has gone without:

Angela: It's never longer than a day. Even if I have to go to a food
               bank, it's never longer than a few hours. Like they'll miss a
               lunch but I'll make sure they've got a dinner.
Interviewer: Yeah. But for you, have you missed it more than that?
Angela: Oh gosh yeah, I haven't eaten for days at times.

In her interview, Bryony suggests that she and her brother are protected from the direct effects of food poverty. She ticks 'no' to the questions about going to bed or school hungry but admits to eating cereal rather than meals when there is no money and nothing else to eat. She mentions they ran out of electricity recently and resorted to candles. Furthermore, she is aware of her mother's sacrifice and the indirect effects of this are clearly painful in what she says:

Bryony: If there isn't enough food we'll get it and sometimes Mum
               will go hungry and, and stuff. Even if it's not that much
               food for me and [my brother] it's enough that we've actu-
               ally had something, whereas Mum hasn't, and it gets a bit
               to the point where we'll start feeling guilty because Mum
               hasn't had anything and we've had it.
Angela: I'm a warrior, though. I'm all right.
Bryony: Yeah.

Talking about how she feels about her budget and managing on a low income, Angela says 'it's called surviving I think [laughs]'. Although her laughter appears to make light of their situation, it also reveals a sense of embarrassment. However, her shame turns to feelings of resentment and injustice when she goes on to say:

You see a politician in the paper getting £30,000 a year on taxis cos they need a Mercedes – are you mad? And then there's some days where I'm sat there, I'm starving. Do you know what I mean? And they go, 'Oh well they should have enough money, oh they don't do it for nothing' … I'm a single mum, I've wanted to work, I have tried to work. But there's not as much support and help as they make out there is. There isn't.

Angela would like to get a job, but she is awaiting medical treatment. Further, she feels that the Job Centre is pushing her into work for which she is overqualified and that there is little support for anything more ambitious. This is frustrating, especially because it makes her feel she is not a good role model for her children: 'You know, I teach my kids to have dreams and you go for it – you can do anything you want – and then I'm not being an example of that. But, like I say, a lot of it is to do with the help that's not available.'

Frequent hunger in an extended family in Lisbon: Lala and Goncalo

Lala is a lone mother with four children aged six, eight, 11 and a boy aged 14, Goncalo, the study child. Lala was widowed three years before the interview but, because she was not married, receives no widow's pension. She says she cannot find employment because of discrimination because she is a Roma, but also because she suffers from osteoporosis. She has not worked since she had her first child at 21. Lala's father raised and sold horses and, after his death, the family was forced to abandon their house and the area where they lived. The family has an itinerant past (they used to live in tents) but has been rehoused by the council. However, Lala cannot afford to live in their apartment on the outskirts of Lisbon, not because of the rent, which is extremely low, but because she cannot afford to pay the utility bills. Goncalo also says it is a very bad area with lots of drug-trafficking and he prefers living at his grandmother's home. Most of the time, the family lives at the grandmother's home (in municipal housing) in central Lisbon.

At the end of each month Lala collects €200 in benefits (Social Insertion Income) and, a week before that, child support for her four children which amounts to €140. She also receives €40 per month as a pension related to the death of her husband. The grandmother also has another grandchild living with her, born to one of her sons, for whose care she receives €126 as a carer (he has a learning disability); out of this sum she is expected to pay the rent. Lala spends €14 for Goncalo's bus pass, €30 on household products and €4.19 on rent when she can (though the researcher notes she is probably in rent arrears). Lala spends €150 on medication for herself and three of the children: two have asthma, one has severe short-sightedness (there are no free spectacles and Lala is expected to pay) and the mother and one child have osteo-porosis. Lala charges Goncalo's phone every five months for €10 and her own mobile only when she has money. Goncalo says his mum gives him €2 a month which he saves. In the grandmother's house the gas has been cut off because of debt and they only have TV and electricity because a neighbour splits her cable with them (illegally), for which they pay a small amount. Water charges are €30–40.

Clothes are sought from the church that recently gave them a second-hand sofa. Lala does not like to borrow from neighbours or fam-ily, because she is unable to return the money. She estimates she spends €50 per month on food. This is less than a tenth of the FBS for a family of this type. Now Goncalo is older it is harder, Lala says, because he needs to eat more: 'When he was little we'd put two potatoes on his plate. Now we put three or four.' On the day she gets child support she goes to a big supermarket, Pingo Doce, and spends €50 on meat and, if on offer, eggs, sausages, giblets, liver and bones for soup. The meat is then fro-zen. Lala has a store card; when they have no money they use whatever has accumulated on the card for food. She never buys fish, because meat is cheaper.

For the rest of their food this family is dependent on the food aid organisation, Re-food (Chapter 1), which supplies cooked food, and on the church for a monthly 'food basket' that includes two litres of milk, two packets of biscuits, a can of beans and vegetable oil. Because both the mother and grandmother depend on food aid, they combine their resources and everyone eats together. The variety of food the food bank provides is very limited. The mother does little cooking and the family often has to survive on what they are given by Re-food. Re-food tends to be open only late in the evening and frequently there are long queues. By the time they get back from Re-food with the food for the meal the chil-dren are often asleep, Lala says, having gone to bed hungry.

The family eats better the week after the receipt of child support, having meals made with meat or sausage with pasta or rice. They eat few vegetables, except for lettuce, which they get in abundance from Re-food.

Sometimes the food they are given is rotten. It tends to include a lot of pastries and food the children don't like, such as Chinese food. Goncalo says he rarely eats fruit and never eats vegetables. He does not help much at home except to make a snack for himself or to look after his younger siblings when he is asked.

The week before Lala receives her social security is the most difficult, financially, for the family. At these times, Lala goes without food, buys cheap meat and cake and relies on food charity and the free school lunch that is provided for her children. Sometimes she asks the neighbours for a little milk but, as a Roma, she is fearful of doing this because it is seen as 'begging'. Another time of constraint is weekends, when Re-food is closed. Then the family lives on one meal a day, which is usually soup and/or bread and butter, and any yoghurts or fruit they have left from those given by Re-food during the week. On the day of the interview, Lala had only eaten a chicken pasty. She often lives on bread and butter and saves any meat for the children. These strategies do not always prevent the children from going hungry. The children rarely have breakfast and often cry for food. Lala gives an example of visiting the hospital with one of her younger children; the child started begging for something to eat until a stranger offered her a sandwich. School meals are a lifeline for the children in this family (see Table 5.3). They include soup, a drink, a main course and a dessert (Chapter 10). However, because the children are not used to eating fish at home they often reject it at school.

Lala finds going to the food bank an unpleasant experience. She feels ill-treated by some of the volunteers and is made to feel ashamed. A central theme of Lala's interview is 'dreaming' or wishful thinking, about what she would spend money on if she had any: simple things like taking a child to McDonald's, or buying the children some clothes in the supermarket or some shampoo, or giving the children snacks to take to school – a ham sandwich, bread and butter or a yogurt, milk or fruit – 'things that are good for children'. Another wish is to cook fish instead of 'always meat' and to give the children something before they go to bed, 'which doesn't happen'. She says, 'We know what's good, but we do not have it; it's different.'

Goncalo is aware of there being little money, especially at the time of greatest shortage – the end of the month. He says he would like to eat a healthier diet and has taken the initiative to lose weight. However, he does not worry about running out of food: 'I know my mother will always manage something, that my mother will go to church when there is little money. And the church will give her some.'

Table 5.3 Menus for Lala and her son Goncalo.

	Goncalo	Lala
Breakfast	Usually nothing; but at grandmother's gets cereal, yogurt and pastry	Not mentioned
Lunch	Free school lunch, but sometimes comes home	Chicken pasty
Dinner	Bread and butter at grandmother's; bread, butter, ham, chocolate drink at cousin's house; food from Re-food; at home bread and butter if there is any	Whatever they get from Re-food that day or the day before; last meal was pasta
Snacks	School: two doughnuts and a liquid yogurt	Not mentioned
Weekend	Eats one main meal; sandwich and chocolate milk, fruit accumulated during week from Re-food	Not mentioned
Quality and quantity of Goncalo's diet	Fruit: ticks never. Vegetables: ticks less than once a week. Ticks 'sometimes' goes hungry to school and to bed.	

Lala says that the interview has made her think about how different her life could have been if she had studied harder at school. She does not think the family's circumstances or diet will improve in the near future, because she cannot work. However, further into the future, she thinks life will get better, because her children are in school and motivated to 'take a course and be someone in life'.

Using the credit card to buy food in a migrant family in Oslo: Faduma and Sadia

The third case in this chapter is a lone mother, Faduma, who migrated to Norway from Somalia in 2000 to join her then husband, a taxi driver. The couple divorced four years ago and she now lives with her four children, aged eight to 16 years, including a 14-year-old girl, Sadia, the study child. They live in public housing, a three-bedroom apartment on the ninth floor of a social housing block in Oslo. Faduma says she doesn't like the apartment building because of the 'noise … the families and the drug addicts in the same building. They urinate in the lift, they sell drugs here and I don't like it. But I have no chance at paying the rent [anywhere else].' The younger children are afraid, and all of them have trouble sleeping because of the loud music.

When she first came to Norway, Faduma was a 'housewife', caring for her small children. They had enough money; her husband had a job and she received benefits. Faduma attended the Introduction Programme and afterwards was granted Qualification Support for a year. However, since her divorce, Faduma has been struggling to become financially independent. Until recently, she received 'transitional support' (one of several benefits for lone parents). However, this benefit ceased when her child reached eight years old.[5] Faduma's plan is to finish the Norwegian course, which she attends four days a week, since she believes that will make it easier for her to get a job. At the time of the interview she is living on the child support paid by her ex-husband and child benefit.

For the past four months she and her children have lived on around NOK 12,000 a month (NOK 7,075 in child support from the children's father plus NOK 4,850 in child benefit). Faduma's 16-year-old son receives a scholarship of NOK 2,700 per month, which the social security organisation, NAV, considers to be his own money. This means that Faduma doesn't have to pay for his clothes, football practice, or travel (underground pass).

Although housing costs are paid by NAV, the family's other outgoings amount to NOK 10,212. They include NOK 1,500 per month for electricity, NOK 1,100 per month for after-school club, NOK 690 per month for transport and debt repayments. Faduma also says she has to pay for her 16-year-old's asthma medicine, which used to be subsidised. She says it costs her NOK 1,000 and that the medicine lasts for two to four months depending on how sick he is.[6] She also pays NOK 600 for internet and NOK 450 for telephone.

Faduma is left with around NOK 1,800 for food and other expenses. She spends around NOK 600 every weekend on food at the local shops and NOK 3,000 every month on more food across the border in Sweden. Her food expenditure is just under two-thirds of the FBS for a family of this type, around NOK 5,400 per month. Faduma considers their food expenditure too high, given her income and expenditure on other living costs. As a consequence, Faduma uses her credit card to pay for food and some other expenses. Given the high cost of food in Norway (owing to the protectionism of the historical red–green political alliance), the monthly shopping trip to Sweden is her chief strategy for getting by. She takes advantage of the free bus to get there. 'I buy lamb meat, chicken, hamburgers, sausages, drinks. It is a bit cheaper in Sweden, the food there.' At the weekends, she travels 'downtown' to the 'foreign shops' where fruit and vegetables are a lot cheaper than in the supermarket. For example, a lettuce at the supermarket, Kiwi, costs NOK 22.90, Faduma notes, whereas at the foreign shop it costs NOK 12. Bread for the children's packed lunches is a big expense. Faduma finds it cheaper to bake bread herself, though she does not always manage this. 'We [are on] social benefits. I don't work. It is very hard, but I have to buy bread.'

The quality of the family's diet does not seem to be affected by their low income, because Faduma invests time in shopping around and cooking (see Table 5.4). She cooks daily from fresh ingredients, as demonstrated by her food routines on a typical day. On a school day, Faduma gets up at 6.00 a.m. and prepares three packed lunches for the children. 'There are many different spreads ... Some take cheese or goat cheese; some have salami or sausages, or eggs, boiled eggs.' Faduma takes a packed lunch to her Norwegian class. 'Sometimes I fry ... Sometimes omelette, sometimes boiled eggs, sometimes salad and bread, different spreads.' After she gets home she checks whether 'the children have eaten their packed lunch, and maybe [they can have] some ice cream. [Then] I will cook.' Yesterday, she made 'rice and chicken' with salad; other times, pasta and minced meat, lasagne, fish and potatoes. Sometimes she cooks Somalian food. The children usually have a 'very good breakfast' at weekends, when Faduma gets up early to make 'Somali breakfast, like chapatti with

Table 5.4 Menus for Faduma and her daughter Sadia.

	Sadia	Faduma
Breakfast	Bread with spreads	Not mentioned
Lunch	Bread, salami, eggs or cheese, or noodles from the canteen	Packed lunch: omelette, boiled eggs, salad, bread, spread
Dinner	Rice and chicken with salad	Same as children
Snacks	Ice cream, bananas, milk	Not mentioned
Weekend	Somali breakfast: chapatti with vegetables; sweets	Same as children
Quality and quantity of Sadia's diet	Fruit: every day, more than once. Vegetables: two–four days per week. Ticks 'never' to going hungry to school or bed but admits to running out of food.	

vegetables'. On Sundays, too, Faduma cooks. On Fridays the children are permitted to eat sweets for a treat. Faduma uses the Norwegian expression 'kose', which means something in between having a good time and indulging in food. The children visit their father's house at weekends and during the school holidays; so some of their meals are eaten there.

Sadia gives her mother a lot of help at home. She does the vacuuming when she comes home from school, 'It's a habit,' Sadia says. 'I like to wash the floors and organise at home, kinda.' Perhaps, being a young Somalian girl, Sadia underplays the gendered inequality demonstrated in her brothers' lesser contribution to housework:

> It [housework] works better that I do it. People say that it is girls that study, but boys should also study. That's what my mum says. But my brothers have their own rooms, and they clean their rooms. They don't do a lot, but if my mother asks, 'Can you pick up your brother?' and stuff like that [or] 'I come home late; can you go and buy a pizza?' one of them will go and buy pizza.

Asked whether she ever runs out of food, Faduma says it sometimes happens. 'When I shop in Sweden I have extra food, but in Norway very little.' Money gets tight twice a month and if there is nothing left Faduma borrows from her friends but always tries to repay them. She claims that the children have 'not been hungry, but almost'. Although they never skip meals, Faduma sometimes eats less than she would like. Sadia ticks 'never' in response to the questionnaire questions about going to school or bed hungry and says in response to the vignette showing an empty food cupboard that this has never happened at home. 'If I am hungry, I'll eat what I find.' Although Sadia may not suffer from hunger, Faduma's struggle to feed the children a varied diet is not helped by the lack of meal provision in schools (Chapter 10). Faduma is critical of the Norwegian system: 'I have a friend in Sweden. The children eat food at school. When the children come home to eat at four o'clock, [they are] always full. In Norway, packed lunch at school. When they come home, always hungry.' The lack of money for sufficient food makes Faduma say 'no' to her children when they ask to invite friends to their home for dinner (see Chapter 8).

Asked what it is like to live on benefits, Faduma says it is a matter of survival: 'Social benefits is just living and not dying. It is very difficult on social benefits.' In the past she has had to resort to the food bank and is aware she may need to do so again, but she feels ashamed. 'They are very kind and give us food, but I think it is embarrassing to go and get food and they say, "oh, they are so poor."'

Given she has four children to support, Faduma worries a lot about money. In her interview Sadia shows that she is aware of the burden on her mother and tries to moderate her own needs, saying she tries not to ask for much money for herself. 'When my mother says, "Here you have 200," I say, "It is fine, I can surely have a little bit less."' Sadia does not compare her situation with that of her friends who 'have a lot of expensive things'. Instead, she thinks about those who are worse off than herself: 'I also think about other people that don't have clothes at all. Why should I have expensive things?' Faduma is concerned about how they will manage in the future: 'How will we live?' For the longer term she is hopeful: 'I plan to get a job and children [will go to] school and work, and [I will be] better at Norwegian and I will work.'

Discussion

The lone-mother households in this chapter are among the most deprived households in their respective country samples. In all three countries, being a sole parent in charge of children may well mean that you have no choice but to rely on benefits (Chapter 4); despite widespread rhetoric about work as a route out of poverty (Chapter 6), households' livelihood strategies are not based on purely 'economic' rationalities (Duncan and Edwards 1999; Narotzky and Besnier 2014). However, lone-parent benefits vary across the countries. In the UK, the lone-parent benefit level is low, and no lone-parent benefits exist in Portugal. In Norway, the benefit is subject to stringent conditions (Chapter 1). As the circumstances of these three mothers illustrate, what they are entitled to from the state differs considerably. Angela's benefits have been reduced by the UK's policies of welfare retrenchment and she is now entitled only to a low-level benefit (Jobseeker's Allowance); under the Welfare Reform Act (2012) her access to ESA for disabled people was curtailed. In Portugal, unemployment support is linked to employment history and there are no specific welfare benefits for lone parents. Lala has never been in paid work and, hence, does not qualify for unemployment benefit and, although she is widowed, she does not receive a widow's pension because she was not married. In Norway, welfare benefits are generous but tightly linked to labour market participation, and lone parents may only claim benefits to stay at home with children up to age eight under stringent conditions. In consequence, Faduma has recently had one of her benefits cut.

The varied relational circumstances of unemployed lone mothers have consequences for the support they can draw upon. The three lone-parent families described here differ in their living arrangements and family form. Lala and her children in Portugal are in effect part of a multi-generational household, although two homes are maintained. Angela in the UK has a new partner who does not live with, or contribute to, the family; neither does her former partner. Only Faduma in Norway receives any help from the children's father.

Although poverty is not a static state, these households are among those most disadvantaged because the mothers have been unemployed for long periods. They have become accustomed to living on low incomes, unlike the dual-earner households in Chapter 6 which have moved into poverty because of the financial crisis, job loss, reduction in work hours, or illness. However, all three of these lone mothers say they want training to help them find 'good jobs'. Angela, the white British mother, has moved house a lot and has health problems that make finding a job difficult; she says she is only offered work for which she is overqualified. Lala, the Portuguese mother, has no qualifications and suffers from osteoporosis and racialised discrimination (as a Roma), all of which mean she is unlikely to find suitable work. Faduma, the migrant mother from Somalia living in Norway, is currently completing a course in Norwegian. However, like many migrants in Norway, she is at risk of continuing unemployment; her lack of educational qualifications make it difficult to find work in the Norwegian labour market, which demands high-level qualifications (OECD 2019).

Differences in national health policies also affect the lives of these mothers and whether they can afford medication and healthcare. Whereas Lala and Faduma both spend quite a large proportion of their income on medication for themselves and their children, Angela has access to free healthcare and prescriptions through the UK's National Health Service (NHS). However, because the NHS has long suffered from underfunding by successive governments (Kmietowicz and Iacobucci 2017), she has to wait in a long queue for the treatment she needs.

Housing policies and the quality of living conditions for those on low incomes vary across countries. Although two of the families discussed in this chapter live in public housing, Angela has been in rented accommodation since she lost her council house. The UK stands out from Norway and Portugal as a country where social housing has declined and poor-quality, privately rented accommodation has expanded, catering to those on low incomes (Croucher et al. 2019). Although Angela's privately rented flat is subsidised, she is in debt, including payments due for a TV and washing machine, and often cannot afford electricity. Lala in Portugal pays minimal rent for municipal housing in a poor suburb but cannot afford to pay for the utilities. Instead, the family spends much of their time in the grandmother's flat; there, too, the gas has been cut off because of arrears and access to TV and electricity is provided by a neighbour who splits her cable with them (illegally). In contrast, Faduma's social housing in Norway is subsidised by the social security agency and comes furnished with a washing machine and cooker.

As well as levels of benefits, changes in benefit policies critically affect low-income, non-employed parents. Although all three mothers in the chapter are accustomed to managing on a low income, there are times when life is particularly difficult. Angela described the effects of being moved on to a lower benefit. Faduma no longer receives benefit for one of her children because the child is over the age of entitlement. Lala finds it particularly difficult to get by at the end of the month when she has spent the meagre benefit she receives.

Informal support available to the mothers is shaped by their particular social networks (see Chapter 9). The Portuguese family pools resources with the grandmother. As a migrant in Norway, Faduma has no family locally but sometimes borrows food and money for food from friends. The three mothers adopt similar strategies to cope with perennial food poverty. All have had recourse to food aid at some time; the Portuguese family is currently dependent on it all the time. Each mother mentions feelings of shame at having to resort to charity.

Also important to families getting by is access to low-cost shopping facilities and how long it takes and how much it costs to reach them. In the UK and Norway, the two mothers invest considerable time and effort in shopping around. Angela travels long distances on foot – walking to shops up to two miles away to find bargains. Faduma travels on a free bus across the border to Sweden to get cheaper food.

Meal provisioning requires mothers to invest effort and time not only in planning and procuring but also in preparing food. Both Angela and Faduma spend a great deal of time cooking meals for their families, with help from their daughters. In contrast, Lala rarely cooks, because Re-food, the charity on which the family relies, only provides cooked food that has to be consumed immediately. The late opening times of Re-food means that families dependent on organisations of this kind eat late and are unable to cater to young children's time schedules. The late-evening timing of bargains in UK supermarkets is a consideration for Angela.

Unsurprisingly, getting by in wealthy Western societies on a very low income is considered more akin to 'surviving' than living. Like others in the study, all three mothers mention the 'shame' of resorting to charity. A strategy common in the literature – of mothers protecting their children from food poverty by sacrificing their own food intake (Attree 2005) – is also evident in the cases described here. All three mothers resort to skipping meals and eating less than they would like so that their children can have more. Some of the children in the study also moderated their own needs to help conserve food.

Poverty intersects with other forms of marginalisation and social exclusion. In all three countries racialised discrimination is widespread and embedded in social institutions (see Heath and Richards 2020; Maeso 2014; Norwegian Ministry of Culture 2020). As members of ethnic minorities, both Lala, the Roma mother in Portugal, and Faduma, the Somalian mother in Norway, are subject to racialised discrimination, despite the countries' legislative efforts to end discrimination and promote integration. Yet, as we find in other families included in the study, these mothers are hopeful for the future and cherish aspirations for their children, considering education a central route out of poverty.

In this chapter we have suggested how low income plays out among non-employed lone mothers in relation to domestic food provisioning. Poverty cuts to the heart of the responsibilities of modern welfare states: the states' role in the provision of types and levels of benefits, housing support and housing conditions, health policies and the local infrastructures of services and facilities. In the context of unemployment and limited support from the state, low-income families must turn for help in buying food to charity, or to relatives, neighbours and friends, who may be as impoverished as themselves. These are subjects to which we return later in the book.

Notes

1. Our three countries are covered in Bradshaw and Chzhen's (2011) analysis of 2006 EU-SILC data. In the UK, the proportion of children living with lone parents who are working full-time is 26.3 per cent, working part-time 20.1 per cent and not participating 53.5 per cent (second only to Ireland, where it is 56.6 per cent). In Portugal, the proportion of children living with lone parents who are working full-time is 66.9 per cent, working part-time 2.5 and not participating (or working under 16 hours a week) 30.6 per cent. In Norway, the proportion whose lone parents are working full-time is 70.2 per cent, working part-time 7.6 per cent and not participating 22.2 per cent (Bradshaw and Chzhen 2011, 30).
2. Lone motherhood is often not a permanent state, though it is more likely to be for those on the very lowest incomes (Bradshaw and Chzhen 2011).
3. 'Quid' is colloquial for 'pounds sterling'.
4. A kind of meatball made with minced offcuts of meat.
5. If a lone parent has children under eight years old, transitional benefit can be received for up to three years. However, the child should not be in daycare. The period of entitlement to transitional benefit may be extended by up to two years until the youngest child is eight if a lone

parent is in 'necessary education'; up to three years until the youngest child is eight if a lone parent is in necessary education and cares for more than two children. The benefit is taxable. Lone parents are also entitled to extended child benefit and infant supplement. https://www.nav.no/en/home/benefits-and-services/relatert-informasjon/transitional-benefit#chapter-3

6. In Norway, although medical treatment is free of charge for children under 16, all citizens aged 16 or over must pay for medical attention and medicine, up to NOK 2,185 per year. When medical bills or medicines exceed this amount, patients become eligible for an exemption card and are automatically repaid. Since this 'benefit' is automatic, Faduma may not be aware that she has been repaid the medicine expenses for her son, or perhaps she has yet to exceed the threshold.

6
Three dual-earner households

Recent years have seen increased public attention given to the working poor, a growing group in Europe generally and in the UK and Portugal in particular.[1] One reason for this prominence is that the phenomenon of 'in-work poverty' is not easily dismissed in terms of neoliberal ideas of individual responsibility; the working poor meet the long-standing criterion of 'deservingness' and disrupt the well-worn ideology of paid work as *the* route out of poverty. Contrary to narratives that blame individuals for their plights, the concept and fact of 'in-work poverty' direct attention to the political and economic contexts and policies that foster inadequate pay, and to the responsibilities of national governments to set wages at levels that ensure adequate incomes. Although only a minority of workers, globally, have ever enjoyed the stability of secure, long-term employment, neoliberal capitalism has eroded the collective bargaining power of trade unions in many countries in the Global North where they once upheld the pay and conditions of (some) workers. The corresponding expansion of the 'gig economy' and 'zero-hours contracts' means that financial risks have been transferred from governments and corporations to individuals, leading to insecurity and precarity that are often marked by increased levels of personal debt. Since domestic food provisioning demands both economic and temporal resources, the combination of low and/or insecure wages with the demands of often unpredictable hours of paid work means the working poor are an important and interesting test case for the study of food poverty.

In the aftermath of the 2008 recession, wage levels in countries affected by economic decline and austerity have stagnated or fallen in real terms. This has led to an increase in the proportion of the population in paid work who are at risk of in-work poverty[2] in the UK (Hick and Lanau 2017) and in Portugal (Eurofound 2017). In-work poverty is highly associated with lone parenthood, low pay, part-time work and temporary contracts. As discussed in Chapter 1, Norway was less affected by the downturn and wage levels there are protected by strong trade unions with the result that levels of in-work poverty are lower. However, there is a mismatch between the skills of some migrant groups and the Norwegian labour market, which means there is considerable underemployment among these groups.

In-work poverty has often been reduced to discussions of low pay, that is, the earnings of an individual worker – typically defined as a worker who receives less than two-thirds of median hourly earnings. However, to understand in-work poverty requires a shift from thinking about workers as individuals to thinking about the household and whether its income is adequate to meet its needs (Gardiner and Millar 2006). Low pay and in-work poverty are not the same (Horemans and Nolan 2016; Halleröd and Larsson 2008; Halleröd et al. 2015, 2; Marx et al. 2012). The concept of in-work poverty encompasses not only the issue of low pay but also low work intensity. Although the latter does apply to individuals, such as those on zero-hours contracts who cannot work as many hours as they need, it may also be understood at the household level.

As dual-earner households have become the norm, single-earner households have become increasingly disadvantaged. A study carried out in the UK for the Joseph Rowntree Foundation shows that a key determinant of the experience of in-work poverty is having only one worker in the household (Hick and Lanau 2017).[3] People living in one-earner households face a very significantly elevated risk of in-work poverty, and account for almost six in ten people in the UK experiencing working poverty, more than double their population share (Hick and Lanau 2017). As some have argued (Goerne 2011, 15), the mechanisms that explain in-work poverty at the household level include: (a) job quality (remuneration levels), (b) job quantity (labour market participation of household members) and (c) household expenditure (cost of dependents). Both job quantity and job quality particularly affect women's access to employment and share of involuntary part-time work (Filandri and Struffolino 2019).

Manual and care work have in most countries been regarded as low-skilled jobs and historically have been badly paid. But a particular feature of the labour market in many countries today is precarity. The relation between employment and poverty therefore needs to be conceptualised in temporal terms; families move in and out of poverty especially when their employment is both insecure and low paid. Hick and Lanau (2017) found that more than half of people who experienced in-work poverty in one year had exited poverty by the following year, while remaining in work. However, respondents who experienced in-work poverty were also more likely to transition into unemployment than those working parents who were not poor. Moreover, a quarter of respondents living in workless households who found work entered in-work poverty.

There has been little research into domestic food provisioning in low-paid working families. However, most studies of food practices among working families find that mothers are overwhelmingly responsible for food work even when they are also in paid employment (for example, O'Connell and Brannen 2016). Paid employment has implications for the time available for food work, which can include the considerable investment of time in shopping around and cooking described by the unemployed mothers in Chapter 5. A whole industry of so-called 'convenience' foods is marketed to busy working families. Although such products may save or shift time for food preparation, more nutritious varieties can be more expensive and out of reach of the budgets of low-income employed families. Furthermore, precarity of work has been linked to rising personal debt (Livanos and Papadopoulos 2019) and the use of 'emergency' food provision (Lightman et al. 2008; Goode 2012).

In lone-parent households, by definition, only one parent is available for work. However, lone parents often do not and cannot work full-time owing to responsibilities for childcare and domestic work. As Table 6.1 shows, most were not in paid work; those who were employed could be divided between those in full-time and those in part-time work. This was the case in all three country samples.

Table 6.1 Employment by family type.

Family type	Employment intensity*	UK	Portugal	Norway
Lone parent	0.0	18/30	10/19	15/20
	0.5	5/30	5/19	3/20
	1.0	7/30	4/19	2/20
Couple	0.0	3/15	9/26	11/23
	0.5	3/15	1/26	8/23
	1.0	5/15	6/26	3/23
	1.5	4/15	4/26	0/23
	2.0	0/15	6/26	1/23

* 1 = full-time (30+ hours per week); 0.5 = part-time (less than 30 hours per week). Informal employment is included only if it is regular.

In dual-worker households, there were a few cases where both parents were in full-time work but, even if their work was officially full-time, their hours were often shorter than they wished, for example through loss of opportunities to do overtime, as in Sonia's case below. Even when a household has two workers, the nature of their jobs – designated as low skilled and hence low paid – can be among the reasons for the family's low income, as we discuss below. In the UK sample, eight of the 12 couple families that were classified as 'working' had only one parent in paid work, in three cases part-time. In the Portuguese sample, 11 of the 17 working families headed by couples had either only one adult in employment or two employed but one working part-time. In Norway, work intensity among our sample of families was very low, only one couple of the 12 working couple families having two parents working full-time, the others having only one parent full-time or one parent part-time. It was striking that low work intensity was common among migrant parents, who were disproportionately represented in the sample, since they belong to the low-income group in the Norwegian population (Chapter 1).

Working couple families reported food shortages as did unemployed couple families, lone-parent working families and unemployed lone-parent households. In the UK sample (Table 5.1), three of the 12 couple families with one or more adults in paid work at the time of interview were food poor. In the Portuguese sample, of the 17 couple families with paid work, 13 were food poor. In Norway, of the 23 couple households, 12 had some paid work and half of these (six) were in food poverty.

In this chapter, we focus on two families in which both parents are in work and one family in Norway where only the father is in employment, a more common pattern in the Norwegian sample. All three couple families are experiencing, or have recently experienced, a shortage of food. The fathers are employed full-time in low-paid, traditionally male manual jobs and the mothers (from the UK and Portugal samples) are employed in jobs that are gendered as female and predominantly done by women – care work and cleaning. In the Norwegian household, the mother is no longer able to work, having been diagnosed three years earlier with a chronic illness, and is in receipt of disability benefit. This case was selected for comparison because, reflecting the better employment conditions, there are no cases among the Norway sample in which both parents are in work and the family lacks enough to eat. In the three households the dynamic nature of poverty is evident. In the UK case, the mother's employment hours and consequently her pay vary, while the two other households have recently suffered job loss or reduced hours.

Low and fluctuating income in a coastal UK town: Sally and Owen

This two-parent family lives in a poor seaside town. Sally has been living with a new partner for the past two years. She is white British and has two children aged 12 and eight years, both boys. Owen, the study child, is 12. He has autism and other emotional and communication difficulties. He is very fussy about food. Sally works in dementia care 25–30 hours a week and has a zero-hours contract; she is not paid for the time spent travelling between care visits. Her partner is a full-time shift worker in a supermarket on a full-time hourly contract (39 hours per week). Compared with when she was a lone working parent, Sally feels better off; in those days, she was left with a lot of debt to pay off from her previous marriage and was reliant on her parents to buy food and clothes for herself and the boys.

The family lives in a privately rented two-bedroom house. It is currently overcrowded because Sally's niece and her baby are also staying while the niece looks for housing. This means Sally, her partner and the two boys are sharing one bedroom. The parents' joint income is approximately £2,400 a month including child benefit and some child maintenance from the children's biological father. Sally tries to fit in her hours around her partner's night shifts, but her work depends on the number of clients needing care, making her income unpredictable (her monthly wages vary between £800 and £1,100) as well as insufficient: 'Last week I had 27 hours and I need at least 30 to be able to, you know, just live.' The family does not qualify for tax credits because their income is slightly over the threshold, and the boys do not qualify for free school meals. The niece does not pay into the household budget but provides childcare for the two boys and thus contributes in kind.

The main monthly outgoings are £715 for housing and council tax (around a third of their income); £160 for utilities; £163 for mobile phones and a Sky (TV) package; £60 for transport; £250 in debt repayments, including car finance; £8 for vet bills; and £20 for Owen as payment for chores. Sally needs a car for her job, which is an additional cost and paid for through a car finance scheme. Sally says she cannot afford after-school care for the children, although currently the niece looks after them.

The family spends around £500 a month on food, which is slightly above the FBS for this type of family and includes catering for Owen's food preferences (see Table 6.2). They shop at the supermarket where Sally's partner works, because he receives a 10 per cent discount. For school lunch, Owen takes £1.50 for a slice of pizza. Sally is concerned

Table 6.2 Menus for Sally and her son Owen.

	Owen	Sally
Breakfast	Chocolate Weetos	Coffee
Lunch	A slice of pizza at school; sometimes Sally tops up his school lunch money	Skips meals or eats on the go, such as pot noodle
Evening meal	Bolognese or roast dinner or meatballs with jar of sauce and pasta, or burger and chips from freezer. Vegetables (frozen) with meals: carrots, broccoli, cauliflower	Toast
Snacks	Crisps and fruit	Not mentioned
Weekends	'Loads of bacon toasties for breakfast and lunch'	Same as children. Sally 'tries' to cook a roast on Sundays
Quality and quantity of Owen's diet	Owen says he eats fruit every day and vegetables two–four days per week. Ticks 'never' to going to school or bed hungry.	

this is not enough: 'I'm worried because I don't know how big the slice of pizza is or … because he's not … in my eyes he's not eating a lot. He's a growing lad; he should be eating a lot more than that.'

At the end of the month the family is usually short of money for food, especially when Sally has not worked as many hours as she wants and when there are unexpected expenses, such as a vet's bill, or a period of high expenditure such as Christmas time. When the dog had to be put down, 'we couldn't even do a [food] shop' and she and her partner were reduced to 'eating toast every evening'. They invested in a large freezer so that they can buy in bulk and stock it up. Towards the end of the month they 'run down the freezer'. However, the family has never resorted to a food bank.

This household experiences a shortage of adequate food but, because the parents sacrifice their own food intake, the children are not affected. When money is short, notably when Sally's hours at work are short, or in December, when it is Owen's birthday as well as Christmas, she says that she and her partner skip meals: 'Birthdays are coming up, Christmas is coming up, we will be back to toast again … The kids will never be affected by it but us adults are.' Although Owen ticks 'never' in answer to the questionnaire question about going hungry, Sally has internalised a habit of going without. 'I go past hunger now.'

Sally says that they always buy food that is cheap. Consequently, the food lacks variety and is sometimes not very nutritious. She cuts back on quality especially when money is tight. For example, she trades down to cheaper meat products 'like a pound for four' beefburgers – 'the really tacky things that are virtually full of fat'. Sally finds frozen food 'cheaper in the long run', including frozen vegetables, which she considers just as good nutritionally as fresh. Generally, Sally buys the cheaper types of fruit like bananas, apples and grapes. 'You don't get the chance to go and have strawberries and pineapples, which I love.' She is careful not to throw food away. She cooks food that is filling and meals that 'stretch' like spaghetti bolognese. She does not compromise on the quality of bread (she prefers brown seeded loaves).

Most of the food work is Sally's responsibility, although her partner does some cooking and other housework. Owen says he helps with vacuuming, tidies the family bedroom, does the dishwasher and makes toasted sandwiches. Because of her unpredictable working hours, Sally is constrained by a lack of time for cooking as well as a lack of money. Unsurprisingly, she sees cooking as a chore. 'I would be doing everything from scratch and I used to love it, but now I'm working, I'm a full-time mum, the finance is a bit low, I'm knackered all the time.' As she says, 'By quarter past five you're going, "I really must do it" … And half past five you go, "There's something from the freezer."'

The variability of Sally's income makes life stressful. She spends a lot of time checking what is coming in and going out of her bank account. She also complains about people on benefits who are better off than her family; she thinks this is unfair given that they are both working. 'I sort of sit there with [her partner] and I'll say, "Do you know what? I'm just going to give up work, because I think we'd be better off," but then I don't want to give up work because I don't want to be classed as one of those, you know, mums that can't be bothered, you know.' Sally's account reflects a wider public discourse that sees paid work as not only materially but morally important for mothers, and an understanding of livelihood 'decisions' that goes beyond narrow economic reasoning.

Low wages and not enough hours in Lisbon: Sonia and Bianca

This two-parent Portuguese family,[4] including a daughter, Bianca, aged 12, lives in a privately rented two-bedroom apartment in what the mother, Sonia, describes as a 'poor part' of the city. Their elder child is

23 years old and no longer lives at home. The father is employed full-time as a lorry driver, and Sonia works in the informal economy, two hours a day, cleaning local shops and carrying groceries for older people in the neighbourhood.[5] They are worse off than in the past: the father used to work regular overtime, but this stopped at the time of the financial crisis, and two years before the interview Sonia lost her full-time job in a grocery when it closed down. Since then she has struggled to find permanent work, the difficulty being exacerbated by her low educational qualifications.

The monthly household income is made up of the father's wages of €509 (plus €100 in lunch vouchers), child benefit of €30 (for one child) and Sonia's occasional cleaning jobs (unknown value). The main expense is their rent, which is €255 per month (around a third of their income). Every month, they also spend €40 on electricity; €21 on gas; €15 on water; €22 on mobile phones; €15 on Bianca's health insurance; €29 on TV and internet; €30 on Sonia's public transport pass; and €22 on Bianca's swimming classes. They don't have a car and instead frequently borrow one from a brother-in-law or use the company car. They have no debts. Sonia manages to save a little towards the annual holiday to her hometown and for Bianca's school books (last time these cost €250), but the end of the month is hard. When there is an unexpected expense (such as when the fridge broke down), Sonia resorts to asking two friends for help. Bianca qualifies for a 50 per cent reduction on school meals which means that the parents only pay half of the cost of the school meals, around 73 cents per day, which Sonia says is a big help (see Chapter 10). Sonia prioritises paying the bills, such as water, electricity and the rent. Only when she has taken care of these does she consider how much there is for food: 'First I pay the electricity and the water bills … the basic expenses one cannot avoid … The house rent also. Rent actually comes first and after comes the food.'

There is usually around €200 left for food for the family for the month, which is around half of the FBS for a family of this size, with the result that both the quality and quantity of food are affected. When she has an extra expense, Sonia starts to cut into the food budget and buys items that are less expensive or uses what is available at home. For example, 'I think, today I would like to buy chicken but, because of the low budget, I make, instead, some salad with tuna that I have at home.' She reports several strategies, such as shopping around, planning meals and cutting back on meat, and has never used a food bank.

There is no shortage of places to buy food locally and Sonia takes advantage of promotions and compares prices between shops, 'They send the advertising leaflet home and so one can see and compare prices. I have Continente on one side and Pingo Doce very close by, so I can combine.' She shops mostly at these two supermarkets and also at the street market and the 'Chinese' – the small grocery in her neighbourhood owned by Asian migrants, where she can get good-quality fruit and vegetables fairly cheaply.

Sonia does almost all of the food work, including planning, managing the budget, shopping and cooking. Bianca says she helps and has done more housework as she has got older, for example, setting the table for meals. She also cleans her own room and sweeps and washes the floor. Sonia is an experienced domestic manager, resilient and resourceful. Her mother died when she was 13 years old, her father was an alcoholic and one of her four siblings was disabled. Because of these experiences, she learned at a young age how to run a house and prepare food on a restricted budget. Before she had children she also worked in the kitchen of a restaurant, where she learned how to cook. She enjoys cooking and takes pride in using her imagination to pay the bills and feed her family in the best possible way. She mainly cooks at the weekend, preparing dishes that are expected to last through to the following week. She puts a considerable emphasis on planning and speaks of 'others' who are less organised:

> It's really strange for me that some people, it's six o'clock in the afternoon and they ask themselves, 'What am I going to make for dinner?' That's not what I call housewives. That's typical of the youth, they don't know what they'll be doing, they've got it all ready-made. A grown-up housewife … this can happen once: 'Oops, I forgot to defrost something. What do I do now?' … and she invents. But as a principle I have it all planned.

Asked about times of shortage, Sonia says that things get more difficult from the middle of the month, especially when the electricity bill is due, every two months. This was the case the month before the interview. By way of illustration, she recounts a story about a visiting neighbour and how she had to tell Bianca not to drink the juice that was in the fridge, otherwise they would have nothing to offer their guest.

Photographs (Figures 6.1 and 6.2) from Sonia's kitchen tour and Bianca's photographs show how Sonia manages. In the fridge is a large pot that contains spinach and chickpea soup she cooked the day before. She explains to the researcher that she cooks soup usually on Sunday or Monday and then it is eaten by all three of them at each main meal on the following weekdays (Figure 6.2; Table 6.3). Another strategy is to restrict

(a)

(b)

Figure 6.1 Fridge (a) and freezer (b) in Sonia's kitchen (Source: Sónia Cardoso).

Figure 6.2 Sonia's homemade soup (Source: 'Bianca').

Table 6.3 Menus for Sonia and her daughter Bianca.

	Bianca	Sonia
Breakfast	Bread with butter or ham, or toast or cereal with yoghurt (does not like milk)	Nothing (The father has fruit)
Lunch	Morning snack: bread and butter School meals (subsidised 50%): meat or fish, soup and fruit. Examples: tuna rice, baked chicken legs, cooked hake with boiled potatoes or rice, pasta with fish	Not mentioned (The father gets meal vouchers from work)
Snacks	Sandwich or cookies	
Evening meal	Soup, fruit (apples and pears)	Soup
Weekends	Chicken legs, duck rice, or pork with potatoes (*carne de porco à alentejana*, a typical Portuguese dish); cake if there is money	Same as Bianca
Quality and quantity of Bianca's diet	Fruit: once a day every day. Vegetables: once a day every day (soup). Bianca ticks 'never' to going to school or bed hungry.	

meat to weekends, trading down to cheaper types of meat, shopping around for cheaper products and stretching food to go further. Most of the meat Sonia buys is chicken and pork (see Figure 6.1), because these are the cheapest, although they eat fish, which is more expensive, on occasion. 'A turkey steak costs six euros while some pork steaks are only three euros and something.' Sonia says she cannot afford more expensive products such as free-range chicken: 'When the two of us worked, we used to buy free-range chicken … Now I have to buy the other one that costs one euro and something per kilo, but the taste it is not very good.' She also makes food 'stretch' to maximise what is available to eat. For instance, 'When I should have two or three *bifanas* [pork steaks], I have only one that I cut it in small pieces and make it with rice.' During the kitchen tour she shows the researcher some frozen chorizo that she has brought back from her hometown and can be used for several meals and added to other pork. She always uses the leftovers: '[I] reuse, keep and freeze' everything.

When the family income does not last until the end of the month, Sonia improvises and makes smaller meals, often compromising quality as well, in order to have enough for everybody. She tries to share the food 'according to the needs of each person', although she does not elaborate on this remark. There are times when both parents eat less so that Bianca can have enough food: 'Sometimes it happens that I need to make smaller meals so everyone can eat.'

Bianca says she has never gone hungry but is aware that her mother makes a great effort to provide enough food for the family. She also says that her mother tries to get more clients in order to increase the family income:

> Even if ... even if my mother is really tight, she never let food run out ... She makes a big effort, works ... tries to find more clients to have food in the house. And sometimes, we don't have certain things, I don't know, products and such, because my mother spends some money on food. She's never let there not be food.

Bianca talks about the 'sacrifices' her mother makes for her children, 'She makes sacrifices for me, she wears old boots, with the sole almost falling off.' Bianca moderates her needs accordingly. When she sees there is less food in the house, she thinks, 'This month I won't ask for much.'

Sonia says feeding her family is a constant source of distress: 'I think about that many times at night.' She complains about the injustice that some people 'take advantage' of benefits when they do not need them while others, who really need help, do not have enough assistance. However, she also mentions being at the receiving end of such judgements: 'For her birthday we made a sacrifice ... to buy the so-called fashion sneakers but there were two or three [people in the school] who think, because I am unemployed, Bianca did not have the right to have those sneakers.'

Although Sonia is pessimistic about the future of the country, she is optimistic that she will find more work. However, on the second visit she reports increasing difficulty in finding work as a cleaner, because people are trying to cut down on their expenses where they can. Consequently, the family's financial situation has further deteriorated.

Disability benefits and one insecure income in the Norwegian countryside: Marit, her two sons, Asgier and Filip, and her daughter, Rebeka

The third case in this chapter is a couple with three children living in a coastal town not far from Oslo. The father is employed full-time as a carpenter, while Marit, who was until a few years ago employed part-time, has been reliant on benefits since being diagnosed with chronic fatigue syndrome (also known as 'ME') in 2013. There are two boys, Asgier aged 12 and Filip aged 11, and a girl, Rebeka, aged 14. Marit is an ethnic Norwegian but has spent much of her life in the US, where the father is from and all the children were born. They decided to move back to Norway early in the financial crisis, in 2009, and after the father's parents died. Compared with their lives in the US, and with life a few years ago when Marit had a job, they have a lower income. However, they are better off than last year when the father was laid off for about eight months and was reliant on unemployment support. Several days per month, two other children live with them because their own family is going through a crisis. The father earns on average NOK 20,000 per month after tax, but his salary depends on how many hours he works. Marit receives Work Assessment Allowance, a benefit given to those on sick leave who are intending to return to work.[6] The family also receives child benefit and additional payments of NOK 14,000 a month for taking care of the two visiting children.

The family lives in a large, traditional house that was inherited from Marit's parents. Because the couple have had to buy out the shares belonging to Marit's siblings, they have taken out a bank loan. Even so, Marit says, their housing costs are low compared with those of other families in Norway. The mortgage is NOK 4,000 per month, which is around 11 per cent of their income. However, living where they do, they need two cars that, including fuel, insurance and a car loan, cost about NOK 3,000 per month. Aside from the loans they obtained to refurbish the house and for the cars, the family is careful never to borrow money or get into debt. They also save money every month for their old age and as a small buffer, for example to go on holiday.

Food is the main expense, in part because the family has many dietary needs. Marit is lactose intolerant, her partner has a tomato allergy and one of the children is very allergic to specific vegetables and fruits. They budget NOK 8,000 a month on food, but Marit thinks they usually spend NOK 8,000–10,000. This is about three-quarters of the FBS for a family of this type. Last year, when the father was out of work, their food budget was less, around NOK 5,000 per month. Since then, Marit says, food prices have increased considerably. However, she has never resorted to food charity.

The house is remote from the village centre, linked by a fast road with no pavement. Marit says she depends upon her car for shopping, because there is little public transport and all other options are very expensive. She usually buys food at the nearby local shop, but, when she feels she has enough energy, she drives to the village centre, which has a better selection of food shops – for instance, to buy rice milk at a much lower price than at the local shop. Or, she drives to another area where there is a supermarket with cheap food brands and special offers on food products that are about to reach their expiry date. 'You get good at it.' She also takes advantage of '10 kronor sales'. Freezing food and buying in bulk are other strategies. It is important, Marit says, to keep regular tabs on how much money they have to spend. However, all this shopping around makes her feel 'dizzy' for the rest of the day, so that she has no energy to do anything but rest.

Nutritious food is prioritised, which means Marit sometimes cuts back on other things, such as clothes. She has also cut down on meat, but this appears to be mainly for health and environmental reasons rather than cost. She prefers to buy better-quality meat, but when her partner was out of work they ate a lot of minced chicken meat, because it is very cheap. However, she is adamant that she would never replace meat with 'starchy food' and would rather they eat more vegetables. Marit talks about eating a 'varied diet' – a lot of fruit and vegetables that she sees as healthy. Although she talks at length about cooking from scratch as a means of providing nutritious meals, there are times when her illness means she has no energy for cooking. However, the children expect, and are expected, to help at home, including with the cooking. There is a rota: a different child washes up each day. During the summer the two oldest also cut the grass every second week and the youngest empties the rubbish every day. The children cook dinners occasionally if they want to, but normally help their mother with chopping the vegetables.

When her husband was laid off from work for eight months the year before, Marit worried that the family would not have enough money for food. At the time of the interview things are not as bad as they were then, but there are still times when Marit eats less than she would like to. In the food habits questionnaire both boys tick that they sometimes go to bed and to school hungry (see Table 6.4). Rebeka says that food is rationed: 'We can't eat whatever we want. No, we can't eat yoghurt if we already have eaten one that day, only when it is our first.' This is confirmed by the fieldworker's (Silje's) observation in her notes that the children's complaints about the scarcity of food at home may have been related to their mother's restrictions: 'the parents are somewhat strict, since children have to ask whenever they want to eat or drink something (except water)'.

Table 6.4 Menus for Marit and her three children.

	Children	Marit
Breakfast	Cheerios or bread	Crispbread and goat cheese
Lunch	Bread with ham and cheese	Baguette with pork and pickled cucumber, shrimps, banana, clementine
Dinner	Fish, rice and vegetables	Same as children
Snacks	Soup after school	Same as children
Weekend	Toasted ham and cheese sandwich, fried chicken, soda, sweets	Same as children plus wine or rum
Quality and quantity of children's diet	Two of the boys say they eat fruit two–four days a week and one says he eats it once a week. Rebeka (study child) says she eats vegetables at least once a day and the boys say they eat them five–six days per week. Rebeka ticks 'never' to going to school or bed hungry, but both boys tick that they 'sometimes' do both.	

Talking about other families 'who seem to afford whatever they want', Marit says that many of them use credit cards, which she regards as dangerous. If the boys ask for clothes and sports equipment such as football kits like those worn by famous players, she says 'no'. The parents also try to educate the children that expensive brands are not necessarily better than cheaper ones. The boys inherit clothes from their cousins, and their sister's clothes are often passed on from Marit's cousin. According to Marit, her children have nothing against wearing clothes passed down from the extended family. Because of this the family manages to spend very little money on clothes and shoes.

However, the boys consider themselves disadvantaged compared with other children in their access to money. Filip says it is annoying that their mother always tells them to wait for a week until something is in the sales, because very often it is not on offer the following week. Rebeka expresses annoyance that other young people she knows can buy whatever they want, but she recognises that there is a trade-off, given that her family get to go on holiday to the US. 'I hear about people who have a computer and sound equipment in their rooms. How can they afford it? However, we travel to the [United] States sometimes, and they perhaps just travel on cheaper vacations.' The children report that they have asked their parents if they are poor, 'since we can't … just buy things'. However, they say they are keener to go on holiday than to have their own computers.

Discussion

Families' access to income is structured by the number of adults in employment, and by occupations, job security and hours of work. Their material fortunes also heavily depend on the gendered positioning of their members not only in the labour market but also in domestic and care responsibilities. The households described in this chapter demonstrate how jobs at the lower end of the labour market remain gendered and the ways in which underemployment falls disproportionately on women. All three households include fathers who are in full-time manual jobs. The work hours of two of the mothers vary; their jobs are in the typically 'female' sectors of care work and cleaning, which are associated with low pay, part-time employment and fluctuating hours. The mother in the UK works long hours but is on a zero-hours contract that does not guarantee a fixed number of hours a week. The mother in Portugal is in ad hoc part-time employment; held back by low qualifications and the effects of the economic crisis, Sonia has no formal work contract. In contrast, the household in Norway currently has only one full-time worker; owing to a long-term illness, Marit receives a disability benefit to assist her return to work which, compared with basic benefits in Norway and other countries, is quite generous. Furthermore, both the families in the UK and Norway have other family/children staying with them some of the time who require feeding and looking after.

This chapter also illustrates how families can fall into poverty and struggle to afford food even when one or both parents are in the labour market. The families described have all gone without enough to eat at some time over the past year. Their lives illustrate the dynamic nature of poverty and the ways in which events can transform them in negative ways. All three households have experienced difficult times in recent years. Sally in the UK is on a zero-hours contract that makes her income unpredictable and so leads to difficulties in budgeting. Yet she sees her situation as better than when she was a single mother. The economic downturn in Portugal led to a reduction in Sonia's husband's working hours and the loss of her own job, and so she sees her family's situation as having markedly worsened. Marit's life changed for the worse after she became ill and could no longer work and following her husband's period of unemployment; the family's situation, she says, was much better when they lived in the US.

This chapter has focused on the ways in which the 'working poor' manage to feed their families and how the burden falls upon mothers in two-parent households. In all three families, mothers are responsible for domestic food provisioning, including planning, shopping and preparation. Both Sally and Sonia describe times in the month when they have less money to spend on food, depending on when they are paid and on unexpected costs that crop up. Fluctuating monthly wages and unexpected outgoings make it difficult for Sally to manage until the end of the month. Low but regular wages combined with long-term experience of managing on a low income means that Sonia places considerable emphasis on planning. However, her children are the only ones, among the three families, to receive subsidised school meals. Although all three mothers take an interest in cooking, only Sonia spends a lot of time on this and enjoys improvising meals. In preparation for the weekdays, Sonia does a lot of cooking at weekends. In contrast, Sally, who works long hours, complains about lack of time for cooking. Marit lacks the energy to cook because of her illness and is the only mother who mentions any significant help from the father or her children.

The core strategies these mothers employ to manage food expenditure and provisioning are similar. They include buying cheaper food, especially frozen foods. Sally makes meals stretch and is careful not to waste food. Similarly, Marit freezes food and seeks products on offer. In contrast to Sally, who sometimes resorts to buying cheap 'fatty' burgers, Marit prioritises better-quality meat over quantity and prefers to use vegetables in her cooking rather than starchy food that is higher in carbohydrates. The children in Marit's household suggest that their access to food is rationed by their parents. Sonia restricts meat consumption to weekends and the family lives on soup during the week. She, too, stretches meals and does not waste leftovers. Unlike the lone-parent households in Chapter 5, none of these working families has applied to charity for food despite their difficulties. Perhaps this is because they see their current economic difficulties as short term; if life was better in the past, then they feel entitled to a better standard of living in the future.

It is notable that all three mothers make comparisons with others: with those more and those less fortunate. They seek to distance themselves from unemployed lone mothers and those reliant on benefits or credit. Comments made by Sally reflect a dominant British discourse that positions benefit recipients as feckless and less deserving, in contrast to her self-presentation as 'someone who works hard'. Sonia in Portugal also mentions people 'who take advantage' of the benefits system but adds that her own family's spending priorities may also be negatively judged by others. In Norway, Marit is critical of those who reach for their credit cards to buy luxuries. Her children compare their circumstances adversely with those of their peers, especially children who have access to the latest consumer products.

That we found a significant number of low-income families in in-work poverty in all three countries speaks to the ways in which capitalism is transforming itself. Despite living in societies where citizenship rights are strongly linked to labour market participation, where most women are in employment and where educational levels are rising, there are increasing numbers of parents in low-paid work who are unable to get by. As the opportunities for 'proper jobs' – permanent full-time work – disappear, the jobs that replace them lack guaranteed hours and permanent contracts, illustrating how capitalism has failed to deliver security for its workers. Beyond social exclusion and inequality, in-work poverty therefore jeopardises a fundamental and essential feature of citizenship: the prospect of a decent life (Ratti 2020).

Notes

1. The debate in the UK has largely focused on poverty among working families – and thus counts both those who are in employment and other family members who may depend on their income (see, for example, Scottish Government 2015; Tinson et al. 2016). This differs from the assumptions of the official EU definition of in-work poverty (Eurofound 2020) and most of the European literature on this subject (for example, Crettaz 2011), where the focus is only on the proportion of *workers* who live in poverty, ignoring non-employed family members (Hick and Lanau 2017). Studies of in-work poverty in Europe have drawn on the well-established literature on poverty, which relies on (more or less restrictive) thresholds of household income ranging from 50 to 66 per cent of the median in a given context (SPC 2014).
2. That is, in Eurostat's definition of the term, the rate of poverty risk among individuals who are 'in work', meaning individuals who were employed for more than half the reference period.
3. In the UK, just 22.2 per cent of working-age adults living in households with a low-paid member experience in-work poverty; almost half of individuals enduring in-work poverty are in households where someone is low paid (48.3 per cent) (Hick and Lanau 2017).
4. This family took part in the visual methods and was visited twice.
5. By the time of the second visit the mother had less paid work and money was therefore tighter, something Sonia attributed to the general downturn in the economy: 'because people are trying to cut down on their expenses where they can'.
6. Work Assessment Allowance ensures income during illness or injury when a person needs assistance from NAV to return to work. Full Work Assessment Allowance is the equivalent of 66 per cent of the income in the year before the recipient's illness or the average of the last three years before the illness. The maximum amount of Work Assessment Allowance is six times the National Insurance basic amount (NOK 581,300 before tax).

7
Three undocumented migrant families

Unlike the households discussed in Chapters 5 and 6, some families are unable to access legally either paid work or benefits. They therefore have insufficient income to feed themselves properly and in order to sustain themselves have no option but to turn to charity and other sources of support. Among the households in the study which are in this situation are those in which the parents are 'undocumented migrants'. According to the International Organization for Migration (Perruchoud and Redpath-Cross 2011), migrants designated 'undocumented' are those who lack legal documentation to enter a country but manage to enter clandestinely; who enter or stay using fraudulent documentation; or who, after entering using legal documentation, have stayed beyond the period authorised. Though not representative of low-income households in general, undocumented migrants are among the groups in Europe who are at greatest risk of extreme poverty, that is, living on very low incomes and experiencing multiple material deprivations (Bradshaw and Movshuk 2019). The period after the 2008 financial crisis and the growth in migrants from war-torn countries trying to reach Europe has been a particularly difficult time for undocumented migrants (O'Connell et al. 2019b). Organisations supporting them report that the austerity measures introduced after the crisis have increased the hardship of undocumented migrants in many European countries (EAPN 2015).

Since the state denies them a legal status, undocumented migrants are largely invisible in international and national population surveys and, until recently, have generally been excluded from social research (Gaisbauer et al. 2019). Research in 2008 estimated the number of irregular immigrants in the 27 EU member states as between 1.9 and 3.8 million (Vogel et al. 2011, 10–11); the figure has not been updated since. It is possible that the population has grown in the past decade, owing to events such as the refugee crisis that, at its peak, in 2015, saw more than one million people arrive in Europe (United Nations High Commission for Refugees [UNHRC] 2015). However, processes of regularisation may mean that the number of undocumented migrants has fallen (Sigona and Hughes 2012, 53).

In the UK, according to Jolly (2018), there are no official data on the numbers of undocumented people; the most widely accepted figures are those estimated by Gordon and colleagues (2009) – 725,000 people in 2007 – and Sigona and Hughes (2012): 120,000 children. The number living in Portugal is also unclear, although it has been noted that tens of thousands of (predominantly Brazilian) immigrants are 'irregular' (Fonseca and McGarrigle 2014), that is, around 1.1 per cent of Portugal's population. The number of irregular immigrants in Portugal is comparatively high among EU countries (Cuadra 2012). In contrast, Norway has a small undocumented migrant population: approximately 15,000 out of a population of about five million (0.3 per cent) (Zhang 2008; Onarheim et al. 2018, 3).

By definition, those migrants without papers in the EU come originally from outside it, from what are termed 'third countries'. Migration to the three study countries needs to be understood in the context of the colonialism and racism that are central to European history (Jonsson 2020; see Chapter 2). Immigration and asylum policies are in part driven by the demands of labour markets at different historical junctures and the politics of human rights and discrimination. Undocumented migrants' trajectories are also shaped by the social and economic conditions of the countries they come from, as well as by the conditions in the countries they come to. Thus, some groups of migrants are more likely to be undocumented than others. The parents in all three families discussed in this chapter came from African countries that were experiencing, or had recently experienced, political instability or war. There is evidence that in Europe black African migrants and their descendants are particularly affected by racism: in citizenship entitlements, employment opportunities, access to services such as healthcare and daily encounters (EU-FRA 2018).

The UK and Portugal have a long history of in-migration and have developed different relationships with their former colonies. In the UK, immigration from former colonies became politicised much earlier than in other former European colonial powers; anti-discrimination legislation started as early as 1965 (Hansen 2003), not long after the Bristol Bus Boycott of 1963 that protested against racial discrimination in housing and employment. However, anti-immigration sentiment and the curtailments of the citizenship rights of migrants from the Commonwealth persisted (Hansen 2003), and a series of immigration acts since the early 1960s have limited the settlement of black and Asian people (Solomos 2003). In the aftermath of the 2008 financial crisis, the time of our research, the UK government made severe cuts to public expenditure. Cuts in support for migrants were the greatest in the EU (along with those in the Netherlands), including large reductions in funding for community cohesion programmes and the Refugee Council, and restrictions on eligibility for ESOL (English for speakers of other languages) programmes (Collett 2011).

Unlike the UK's, Portugal's ties to its former colonies shifted to 'an imagined community of descent' based on Portuguese language and customs, in which citizens of their former colonies (known as 'lusophone' countries) were accorded special rights but also, via special labour agreements, were imported as temporary cheap labour in the context of Portugal's entry to the EU (Horta and White 2008). Although racism has been less visible in Portugal, it does exist, as recent protests about living conditions in Lisbon attest (de Sousa 2019). A 2016 report by the UN Committee on the Elimination of Racial Discrimination criticised the persistence of 'Afrophobia' and 'institutional racism' in the country, including hate crimes against racialised minorities, including Roma (OHCHR 2016).

Historically, Norway has been a country with more emigration than immigration. However, the trend has reversed in recent decades (Cappelen et al. 2011), with migrants admitted on humanitarian grounds because of wars and conflict in their home countries. From the late 1990s, refugees came from Iraq, Somalia and Afghanistan under Norway's refugee quota. In 2017, 41 per cent of migrants in Norway were from the EU/EEA, 32.4 per cent from Asia, the Middle East and Turkey, 13.7 per cent from African countries and 12.7 per cent from other European countries, North America, South America and Australasia (Statistics Norway 2017). Although Scandinavian countries have responded to increasing numbers of refugees through the development of integration programmes (Pyrhönen and Martikainen 2017, 6; Hernes et al. 2019, 20), migrants frequently have to spend long periods in asylum centres, which can create and compound mental health problems, and research suggests they are also subject to racism (Midtbøen and Rogstad 2012).

Conceptually, migrants' practices and experiences require an intersectional approach: they 'crystallise at the intersection of individual biographies, family structures, economic developments, and a plethora of social institutions' (Horvath and Latcheva 2019, 128). In comparing the experiences of migrants, whether documented or undocumented, we therefore need to examine migrants' multiple positionings across different fields (Olwig et al. 2012): immigration and welfare regimes, labour markets, local support from charity, schools, informal networks of friends and family. A gain or loss in one field may be accompanied by a loss or gain in other fields (Erel and Ryan 2019, 250). The interrelatedness of fields becomes evident when change occurs, for example, when immigration policy is tightened with the result that some migrants lose their entitlement to public resources.

To understand the experiences of undocumented migrants in their societal contexts, we need to look at how public policies can lead to social exclusion. Social exclusion takes several forms. Undocumented migrants are usually denied access to the formal labour market. They are also excluded from full entitlement to social assistance (DG Employment and Social Affairs 2014; Regioplan Policy Research 2014), which makes them dependent on charity and informal sources to avoid destitution.

In the UK, current public policy under the Immigration Act 2016 does not permit undocumented migrants access to formal employment. Furthermore, they are subject to the 'no recourse to public funds' (NRPF) rule that restricts entitlement to mainstream social security benefits (UKVI 2016), regardless of whether they have children in the household (Dexter et al. 2016, 16). They have no access to secondary NHS healthcare, local authority assistance or council housing. These and other measures, such as restrictions on opening bank accounts, are intended to deter immigration and create a 'hostile environment'. Under Section 17 of the 1989 Children Act, local authorities in England are required to support 'children in need' in their boroughs by providing housing and subsistence from their budgets, which are not regarded as 'public funds'.[1] However, according to the Children's Society, a UK charity, six out of 10 families with NRPF who applied for Section 17 support in 2015 were denied it and the number refused is increasing (Dexter et al. 2016). As Jolly (2018) notes, thresholds for support have drastically reduced in line with budgets in the context of economic retrenchment, leaving social workers powerless. Schools are not funded to provide free school meals to children whose parents have NRPF and, if they choose to provide them, they must cover the costs out of their own budgets.[2]

In Norway, undocumented migrants are similarly denied access to what is a highly regulated labour market, and integration programmes are not available to them.[3] As in the UK and Portugal, undocumented migrants are ineligible for social assistance, since benefits are restricted to legal residents plus other Nordic citizens (Øien and Sønsterudbraten

2011). They have the right to emergency healthcare only (Kvamme and Ytrehus 2015).[4]

In Portugal there appears to be less regulation of undocumented migrants than in the UK and Norway. Portugal depends on a large informal economy that relies on the exploitation of cheap labour, principally in agriculture and construction (LeVoy et al. 2003). The wages of undocumented migrants are much lower than those of legal migrants or resident workers (Oliveira and Gomes 2016), particularly in the construction industry, where wages are among the lowest in Western Europe (LeVoy et al. 2003, 48–9). Despite the International Labour Organisation (ILO) and UN Conventions and the European Commission's demands for tougher control, the numbers of contractors in the industries that rely on such labour have been difficult to monitor, and the Portuguese regulatory authorities have committed irregularities (Corkill and Eaton 1998, 163). Portugal also has an ongoing regularisation programme that, although difficult to navigate (LeVoy et al. 2003),[5] facilitates migrants' inclusion in mainstream social and legal structures. It is also one of only four European countries (the others are the Netherlands, France and Spain) that give undocumented migrants entitlement to access the same range of health services as nationals (as long as they meet certain preconditions such as proof of identity or residence) (Matlin et al. 2018).

Undocumented migrants in Portugal are ineligible for social assistance, which is low anyway (Wall et al. 2001). All non-contributory means-tested benefits are reserved for Portuguese nationals,[6] resident EU citizens and others to whom a bilateral agreement applies (for example, citizens of some Latin American countries) (Eardley et al. 1996; see Table 3.1). But despite the severe austerity policies the Troika imposed in Portugal following the 2008 financial crisis, the Portuguese government remains committed to policies of integrating migrants, for example, through basic literacy training, social assistance for those in extreme poverty regardless of residency status and allowing immigrants to request extensions of stay while unemployed or in unstable temporary employment (Collett 2011).

As we set out in Chapter 3, the study includes disproportionate numbers of families with a first-generation migrant background. A little less than half of the families in the UK sample (19/45) had a parent who was a first-generation migrant (including eight from mainland Europe); just under a third (14/45) of the Portuguese sample; and two-thirds of the Norwegian sample (30/43; Table 3.6). In the UK sample, four mothers, all from former West African colonies, were without leave to remain when interviewed and had no income from paid work or benefits. In the Portuguese sample, two parents (a father and a mother) were undocumented, while in the Norwegian sample one father had no papers or legal residency.

In this chapter we have selected three families in which a parent was undocumented at the time of interview and who all lived in multi-ethnic areas. We selected the mothers on the basis that all three had migrated from former African colonies and their migrations were fairly typical of the wider migration movements mentioned above: the UK mother was from West Africa and the Portuguese mother from Angola, while the Norwegian mother was a refugee from Somalia under a UN quota programme in the 2000s.

The UK mother migrated to England in 2005. Before her leave to remain expired she worked full-time in the NHS. At the time of interview, her status is being reviewed by the Home Office and so her right to work and benefits have been stopped. The Portuguese mother migrated to Portugal with her family of origin in 2002 when she was 16 years old. She was estranged from her family after she became pregnant and, without the support of her parents, has subsequently been unable to access the paperwork to apply for residency. The Norwegian father arrived in Norway in 2014, to be reunited with his family who had earlier migrated as refugees under the UN quota system. The mother and children have residence permits but the father's application has been turned down. In these three families we see how undocumented migrants' positionings across different fields of public policy and other social institutions affect their lives and severely limit their food-provisioning capacities.

We also show how, as a consequence of barriers to citizenship, the families are subject to experiences of social exclusion that hinder their sense of belonging, as expressed in their identities, practices and social participation (Lister 2007). On an ontological level, migration is an act of hope. However, for those who live in fear of being found out or deported and are subject daily to institutional and interpersonal forms of racism, the future is, and looks, bleak. Uncertainty and precarity are constant features of their lives, and so the struggle to get by in the present depletes their energy and hope for the future.

Destitution and child hunger in a hostile UK: Morowa and her teenage sons, Emmanuel and Gideon

Morowa is a lone parent and has lived in the UK for 11 years. She has four children: two teenage boys, Emmanuel, age 15, and Gideon, age 14, and two younger children. Until a few months ago she worked full-time as a domestic at the local hospital. She is no longer able to work because her 'limited leave to remain' has expired. She has applied to the Home Office for 'indefinite leave to remain' and is awaiting their decision.

Because Morowa is currently undocumented she has NRPF. This means she has lost her right to benefits (child tax credit and child benefit) and the family has no regular income. Her former partner pays some utility bills and buys some food for the children, but Morowa is unwilling to ask him for help too often, since they separated on bad terms. The family lives in a two-bedroom privately rented flat for which they can no longer afford the rent of £1,500 per month. Morowa is being pursued by debt agencies and by her bank for overdraft and credit card payments and is in arrears on her council tax (£75 monthly). 'The last month I couldn't pay and this month I don't know if they're coming to arrest me, I don't know.' The family is facing eviction and possibly deportation.

As a mother of children under the age of 18, Morowa is entitled to apply for support from the local authority, which has a duty to protect all children under Section 17 of the Children Act. However, a local authority 'child in need assessment' decided that Morowa was not eligible for support. As the researcher wrote in her field notes: 'She told me the social worker from [the council] had been round – mother reported that the social worker had said to her that because she has a TV and the internet, the children are fine, and there are others far worse off than her, so there is nothing they can do.'

Morowa and her children are regular churchgoers but she does not seek any support from the church members. 'I don't talk to people about my situation because … there is no help coming from there, and they just spread all your problems outside.' She largely depends on a neighbour she calls 'mother' to help with the younger children and to provide food. She has no food budget right now and was recently referred to a food bank by the doctor, who provided the vital 'voucher' she needed. However, the number of referrals is limited, 'because if you haven't got that yellow slip, how can you go there?'

Although Morowa tries to shop around for cheap food, she has no money to spend on transport and so has to weigh travel costs against buying cheaper products further afield. She substitutes better-quality food with cheaper foods and brands and is careful not to waste food. She cooks African dishes and feeds the children with filling foods such as gari, a type of porridge that is made with cassava flour, which is cheap at £2 a box, and beans. She often goes without in order to prioritise her children and only eats once a day: 'I'm not eating meat; only my children they eat meat.' One of her teenage boys comments on the monotony of their diet, 'keep repeating the same food like over and over and over, just gets boring. ... We mostly eat rice; that's what we mostly eat.'

Morowa receives help from her two older boys, who are expected to take their 'duties' seriously, like doing the washing up. '[It is] compulsory; you have to do it. Like yeah you have to do it like ... basically we switch like. One day, basically, for example, today he cleans the floor and I wash the dishes.' The boys also take care of their younger siblings; they help with homework and 'clean them, bath them, read them stories and everything'.

The two teenagers are no longer entitled to free school meals because of the NRPF clause and have to endure the school day with empty stomachs. Before they leave home they fill up on cornflakes and tinned rice pudding (Table 7.1). Hunger affects their performance at school. As one brother notes:

> So I need to have a good breakfast [inaudible] cos sometimes ... Monday yeah I was doing an English test and all I could hear was my belly rumbling ... it was not enough energy for me to, cos being a test yeah, I was half asleep. Even the tutor came up to me three times saying, 'Do your test, yeah,' and I was so sleepy because ... it's difficult and stuff.

Table 7.1 Menus for Morowa and her sons, Emmanuel and Gideon.

	Emmanuel and Gideon	Morowa
Breakfast	Tinned rice pudding or cornflakes	Nothing
Lunch	Nothing	Nothing
Dinner	Same as mother plus meat for children	Rice, tomatoes, cassava, beans
Snacks	Not mentioned	
Weekend	Not mentioned	
Quality and quantity of the boys' diet	One boy says he never eats fruit and eats vegetables two to four days a week. The other says he eats fruit less than once a week and vegetables once a week. The former says he 'often' goes to school or bed hungry, whereas the other says he 'always' goes to school hungry and 'sometimes' goes to bed hungry owing to a lack of food at home.	

Lack of energy has led to him being excluded from class. 'Sometimes you don't have enough energy; you cannot cope in the classroom so you have to like try and rest a bit. You just put your head on the table and you end up falling asleep in the classroom and you get in trouble for it.'

One of the teenagers describes being forced to watch his friends eating in the canteen, 'and it's embarrassing yeah, you have no money on your card and then you just watch them eat'. Sometimes he goes to the school library and tries to work instead. Asked if anyone has enquired why he is not having school lunch, he says they think he is fasting or dislikes the school food. When asked about his food preferences, one brother refers to dishes that he used to have when he was entitled to free school meals: 'Sometimes I crave for spaghetti bolognese, pasta and cheese, lasagne.'

Both boys describe running to school instead of taking the bus and staying for sports after school despite lacking energy because of hunger. Emmanuel told a story about how he had suffered a severe pain in his stomach:

> I can't remember the date but it was like this year, I was so hungry and that, so ... all of a sudden yeah it was like ... it was like ... it was like I got hit on my belly. ... when I don't eat yeah it comes. Yeah, so I'm scared that it might come back. ... it was like I got stabbed with a knife and it's still there.

Emmanuel and Gideon also miss out socially. Morowa cannot afford the £10 for them to join a football club and they do not have money to join in with friends. For example, when asked if they ever go with friends to the local takeaway shops on their way home from school, a common pastime for young people in the area, Emmanuel describes his sense of exclusion; how he waits outside the shop for a friend to offer him 'a little bit', saying it 'Feels like I'm left out of the fun that happens and stuff. Like it just makes me feel empty ... It makes me feel like what have I done like, what have I done?'

The boys do not talk to their friends about their dire situation. In a poignant end to the interview, it became clear that one of them planned to spend the voucher that we gave him for taking part in the study on buying food for a school camping trip. Every child going on the trip had been asked to bring something to cook:

> I'm going to keep this to buy ... like pasta and stuff for my group, because we need to organise what we're going to buy. And

sometimes when we talk about how much am I going to bring, I say, 'I don't really know how much I'm going to bring.' Yeah, so I'm going to save this, then when it comes, yeah, just go and buy pasta, stuff. Hopefully it doesn't expire.

The future feels bleak: they are facing eviction and deportation. A lawyer is helping Morowa with her case but she is worried what will happen. 'They say I have chance because of my children'. Meanwhile, Morowa clings to her Christian faith to keep going. She prays that she will be able to work again and so take care of the children: 'I just pray to God what things are good for me. I will work hard and take care of my children.'

Surviving in the informal economy in Portugal: Nuria and Tola

Nuria is a lone parent who has a 15-year-old son, Tola. She migrated to Portugal from Angola with her family when she was 16 years old. Her father had worked in the aeronautics industry in Angola. When he received a scholarship to finish college in Portugal, the whole family moved. Soon afterwards, Nuria became pregnant and her father threw her out. She has had no relationship with her immediate family since. A social worker at the local town council initially provided groceries and nappies and tried to help Nuria obtain Portuguese citizenship. Because she was a minor, she needed an adult to claim responsibility for her in order to obtain the necessary documentation. She could not count on help from her family. Recently she had an appointment with the Foreigners and Borders Service to progress her case but missed it and had to rebook.[7] With difficulty she obtained proof of the Portuguese paternity of her son, whose father had migrated to Italy. Her son, Tola, finally received his identity card a year ago.

Because Nuria does not have legal documentation she is unable to obtain formal, contracted, employment despite having completed her school education. 'I've used my qualifications to look for work in so many places and whenever they call me and I tell them I don't have documents they won't accept me.' Instead, she works in the informal sector as a domestic cleaner. To supplement her fluctuating low income, in extremis she turns to social services, food charity and even theft.

A couple of years ago the family's situation worsened when Nuria was tricked into taking a job for a company who said they would resolve her citizenship problems. When it went bankrupt, it emerged it had not paid workers' social security contributions. Nuria took the company to court, but the case is still unresolved. Nuria found this hard to bear. She then applied for social security benefits but was unsuccessful. She got into arrears with her rent and, though her landlord initially overlooked the debt in exchange for some cleaning work, she and her son were eventually evicted. She had difficulty renting a new room, and her new landlord was unwilling to let her share the room with her son, who consequently sleeps at his aunt's house most nights. At that time, Nuria asked a social worker from the local social services for help and began receiving help from the food bank: 'They gave bread and gave butter, which was what we ate for breakfast, and they also gave us lunch and dinner … we had lunch and dinner, it was like that every day.' For some months she and Tola were entirely dependent on food aid, until about a year ago when Nuria found her current domestic cleaning job through some of her friends.

Nuria receives approximately €300 cash at the end of each month from her cleaning work. She is not entitled to any state benefits and receives no child maintenance from Tola's father. Sometimes Nuria manages to get some extra odd jobs and cleaning, which brings in an additional €20–50 a month. Tola receives free breakfast and lunch at school – provided even before he got his identity card, 'because meanwhile we made a request to Social Security. And Social Security in this aspect gives a special help to the kids who don't have documents yet.'

Nuria's major outgoing is her rent: €200 a month, which includes the cost of utilities. She has a travel card that costs about €31 a month. The internet and cellphone are €15 a month. She also pays €20 a month for health insurance. Tola has a travel card for the train, which is paid for by his aunt. When Nuria manages some extra hours' cleaning, she spends €5 having her hair done at the salon and gives Tola €5. Tola says he usually spends it on cakes that he buys at school. Nuria tries to do this, she says, so that Tola doesn't feel different from his peers.

Nuria spends a minimum of around €50 a month on food unless she has earned extra money, when she will spend up to €100. This is about a quarter of the FBS for this type of family. She manages by buying the 'basics', shopping for offers and eating a fairly monotonous diet. For breakfast they have bread and butter, with ham and cheese if they can afford it. As is customary in Portugal, Nuria prepares enough food to cover dinner and lunch the next day, and meals are based on rice or pasta. Snacks consist of bread and butter (Table 7.2).

Table 7.2 Menus for Nuria and her son Tola.

	Tola	Nuria
Breakfast	Says he does not eat breakfast	Bread and butter with ham or cheese and milk – or just bread and butter
Lunch	Free school meal	Chicken/pork with rice/pasta; sometimes salad; fish occasionally
Dinner	Same as mother or eats African food, such as funge, at aunt's	Leftovers from lunch (she makes enough for two meals)
Snacks	Bread and butter, cakes at school	Bread and butter
Weekends	Eats at aunt's	Same as weekdays
Quality and quantity of Tola's diet	Fruit and vegetables once a day. Ticks 'never' to going to school or bed hungry, but admits in his interview to their running out of food at home.	

The hardest time of the month is the week before Nuria receives her wages. She admits to having stolen food in the past. Shortly before she began receiving help from the food bank, she took some cans of tuna from the house of one of her clients:

> At the time I had nothing … I brought it from someone's house, I didn't ask, I took and brought it, because I had nothing. I left someone's house and asked myself, 'I'm going to get home and eat what?!' And since I saw someone who had too much, in my head it was like, 'I think that if I take one or two they won't miss it.' But I came home with weight on my conscience, you don't realize … if that person realizes what I did, then perhaps I'll never set my foot there again … but that shame of asking. You understand?! It's difficult!

Nuria became emotional when she talked about what she did and, though she felt guilty, she seems to suggest that stealing was preferable to the shame of asking for food. Later in the interview, however, she says that now she is unafraid of admitting to financial hardship and is not ashamed to ask for help; she tells her son to do the same when he needs to.

The amount of cooking Nuria does is restricted both by lack of money and by limited access to the shared kitchen. Tola does not do any housework or cooking. Nuria struggles to find customary ingredients for the Angolan food that she likes. She depends on visitors travelling from Angola to bring her the ingredients. This happens rarely, 'then I have to wait, sometimes a year, two years, when someone comes and brings something more'.

Because of the lack of space and money for food, Tola sleeps at his aunt's house and eats many meals there. According to Nuria, the aunt's financial situation is better than her own even though she has five children; she manages to offer Tola the dietary variety that Nuria cannot. Sometimes Nuria also has dinner at the aunt's house. She tries not to do this too often, since she knows the limits to the aunt's resources and does not want to strain her generosity: 'I try to avoid … being there all the time so they don't think I go there to eat meals.'

On weekdays, Tola usually eats dinner with his mother. On the days Nuria arrives late from work, she leaves a meal ready for him in the refrigerator and he heats it in the microwave. Tola says dinner is 'basic' things: tuna with pasta, pasta with sausages, chicken breasts, hamburgers, grilled fish with potatoes. Regarding vegetables, he mentions carrots and peas. But in the holidays (the time of the interview) and at weekends he eats at his aunt's, including 'African' food, such as funge, a type of porridge, typical of Angolan cuisine, made with cassava flour.

Nuria comments that her son is a growing boy and therefore eats a lot. She says he is often hungry and does not think about the need to conserve food for the next day:

> It's one of those annoying things, right?! It's already not much and he … sometimes he forgets that the next day he will also need to eat … And sometimes when it's over, until there's money to buy food again, still takes some time. Then he's always complaining that he's hungry, he's hungry, he's hungry. And I can't do anything.

For his part, Tola is reluctant to admit that he goes without enough to eat. He mentions that he doesn't need to ask before helping himself to food at his aunt's. When he eats at his mother's, he does ask, saying this is because she buys and prepares specific foods for her and for him: 'Since I eat a lot … she splits things.' Asked if there is enough for them both, he replies in the affirmative. Discussing a drawing of an empty pantry, he is non-committal about his own experience. The interviewer's field notes say that Tola seems unwilling to admit that he has experienced going without food at home:

Interviewer: Were there times when, for some reason, you had no food?
Tola: That happened once … no, it never happened.
Interviewer: You were thinking of a situation, you said …
Tola: No, that never happened.

Tola also mentions that when there is no food, it is possible to ask the church for help. However, he distances himself from this support: 'There are several, I've been told, especially for that, for [those] who doesn't have food.' He goes on to say that he has been with his mother to ask for help from the church, but this was in the past, when he was a child.

At school, Tola receives free school meals and two snacks each day. He says sometimes the children with more money buy things for those, like him, who have less money. He mentions that the school food lacks seasoning but does not complain about quantity. Nuria says that, although she always encourages Tola to have a snack to eat at school, he often claims to be hungry when he comes home. Sometimes, according to his mother, Tola has asked the school staff for extra food: 'He was hungry, yes … he said that often he'd get there and the school staff, he'd ask the staff for bread, to get something.' Tola says he receives an allowance of €30 a month in total from his mother and aunt, which he usually spends on clothes or food, sometimes buying juice or cola at school.

Nuria compares the Portuguese state favourably with Angola, praising the support she has received from the local council for Tola's school books and the food aid from the local council. However, she fears that her legal status will not be resolved in the near future. Thus she feels stuck and excluded, 'because when we live illegally in a country, you live imprisoned … It greatly saddens me to think I might have to return to Angola as if I am nothing.' Asked about his future, Tola says he does not like to think about it.

Feeding a large family on state benefits in Norway: Aamina and Jamal

Aamina migrated from Somalia to Norway five years ago and was joined by her husband three years later. The couple have five children: Jamal, a son aged 12 (who was interviewed), two older sons aged 17 and 18, a seven-year-old daughter and a baby who was born in Norway. Aamina and her four of her children arrived first under the UN quota system and have resident permits. The father, who arrived in Norway only in 2014, is 'irregular' and his status is under review following three rejections.

The mother and father were born in Somalia, but lived for many years in Saudi Arabia, where the four eldest children were born. Around five years ago, the whole family returned to Somalia in order to be enrolled in the refugee programme. Somehow, the father was separated from the rest of the family and Aamina and the children had to leave alone. Their journey took them through Dubai and Italy before they arrived in Norway, where they initially lived in asylum centres. After a year, they were granted Norwegian residence permits and were helped to find somewhere to live. They now live in a small town near Oslo.

Aamina has completed the integration programme but, because she has a baby, she is not in employment. In Norway, she has never had a job and therefore fails to qualify for contribution-based benefits. The family depends on the basic level of benefit (financial assistance) and child benefit. The family's total benefits have recently been reduced, but it is not clear why. They receive child benefit for the three youngest children. Together, the child benefit and basic financial assistance amount to NOK 12,603 a month. The father is not allowed to work or claim benefits. Their two-storey three-bedroom house costs NOK 9,500 in rent, but NAV pays almost half, plus electricity and other housing expenses, leaving NOK 4,833 in housing costs for the family to pay. The seven-year-old daughter attends after-school childcare every day, for which the family pays NOK 130 a month. The internet bill is NOK 500 a month. The mother does not receive benefits for the two eldest sons, aged 18 and 17, who have their own incomes from scholarships, which they use for their own expenses. They do not contribute to the cost of accommodation or food at home.

Since Aamina speaks little Norwegian, her eldest son interpreted for her and took part in the interview. He reported that they spend around NOK 110,000 per month on food (three-quarters of the FBS for this type of family). This is more than they have left after paying for housing. Recently, after their benefits were reduced and a debt for a hospital bill had to be paid, they were very short of money. The son reported times when they have not had enough money to buy bread and milk; they had to borrow money from friends and buy food on their credit card.

Interviewer: And you have many stomachs to feed here, so has it ever been that you've run out of food, or have been afraid that you would run out of food?

Eldest son:	Yes. Sometimes we just run out of bread and milk, and that's hard for the children, so mum has to borrow money to give us milk and bread.
Interviewer:	Yeah. And then, is it, like, the cupboard's empty, there's nothing here to prepare a packed lunch from? And you don't have money to buy bread. Has it been like that?
Eldest son:	Yes.
Interviewer:	But then you've had someone who could lend you money?
Eldest son:	Yes.
Interviewer:	But is it like … are you going to pay back that loan, do you think?
Eldest son:	Yes, it has been like that a few times. Like, sometimes we have used credit cards, like Mastercard. We borrow money, and then they are paid back next month.

Rice is bought in bulk at the local 'Asian shops' and, once a month, the father and the two eldest sons travel by bus to Sweden, which costs NOK 900 for the trip for the three of them. There they buy halal meat and other foods that are cheaper across the border or that they are unable to purchase in Norway. They have a large freezer that they fill with halal meat. They also buy basics like 'flour, sugar. Cheese and that kind of stuff. And good stuff, like soda. Spices, too. That's things that we can't find here, that we find in Sweden. Like, what foreigners eat. We can't find it here, and if we do, it's really expensive.' One of the eldest sons has a car and sometimes gives his father lifts to fetch the shopping. In his interview Jamal says he helps out at home.

The family eats a lot of bread. It only takes them a day or two to finish one large loaf, since they very often eat bread for breakfast and lunch and may also have it for dinner when money is especially short. At the end of the month, when there is less money, the family cuts back on protein, using meat more sparingly, and 'if we almost go out of food we have bread and eggs for dinner'.

Schools in Norway do not provide meals, free or otherwise, though they sometimes have canteens on some days of the week (Chapter 10). As there is no canteen at Jamal's school, everyone brings a packed lunch from home. According to Jamal, a lot of the pupils have the traditional Norwegian *matpakke* – open sandwiches with meat or cheese. Having enough money for the children's packed lunches is an overriding concern for Aamina. Recently she had to borrow money to buy fruit, 'Because the children want food for school.'

Table 7.3 Menus for Aamina and her son Jamal.

	Jamal	Aamina
Breakfast	Bread or cornflakes	
Lunch	Bread with cheese and lettuce (occasionally Nutella)	
Dinner	Rice and chicken, bread and eggs	Rice and chicken, bread and eggs
Snacks	Wheat buns, cornflakes	
Weekend	Fast food (McDonald's) on occasion	
Quality and quantity of Jamal's diet	Jamal has fruit once a day every day, vegetables five or six days a week. Jamal ticks 'never' to going to both school and bed hungry, but admits in interview to running out of food at home.	

Jamal says he eats fruit more than once every day and vegetables five or six days per week (Table 7.3). He indicates that he has never gone to school or bed hungry because there is a lack of food in the house. However, when shown the vignette with the empty cupboards, Jamal admits to the researcher that he has experienced that situation:

Jamal:	I can see that the man has no food in his house.
Interviewer:	He's trying to find food, and then there's nothing?
Jamal:	No.
Interviewer:	No. Has that ever happened to anyone you know?
Jamal:	No … no, it hasn't happened to anyone I know. I don't know. I don't think it has happened to anyone in my class. Or anyone I know.
Interviewer:	No. Has it happened to you?
Jamal:	Yes, once. Like, I was home, and then I was kind of hungry, but I couldn't find food, but … I was hungry, and I tried to find something to eat, but I found nothing.

Jamal is aware of having less money than his friends. He does not get an allowance but saves money given to him at Eid. He often spends this on 'food and drinks and stuff' or occasionally a toy. He immediately recognised the experience of the girl in the chicken shop vignette (which shows a group of young people buying food and a girl apparently unable to purchase anything), although he was initially reluctant to admit to having experienced a similar situation. He says 'I think so' when asked if this had happened to him. In contrast, he denied it had happened to his friends, since 'they often have a lot of money with them'.

Given his father's ongoing lack of documentation, the eldest son, who acted as interpreter for Aamina, is pessimistic about the future: 'I think it's going to get worse if it continues like this.' Although he hopes his father will get his residence permit, he is not optimistic: 'It's not certain, though. He's been denied three times'.

Discussion

Migration is an act of hope; it is grounded in the belief that geographical mobility may translate into (upward) social mobility (Narotzky and Besnier 2014, S11). Parents who move from one country to another wittingly sacrifice their immediate material and social needs to give their children the chance of a 'better life', a hope often expressed in strong educational aspirations for their children. In the countries to which they migrate, however, the practical opportunities to make a 'better future' and the capacity to imagine it depend too often on the material and subjective experience of precarity. The possibilities of mobility from the Global South to Europe are generally constrained by immigration laws that are grounded in colonialism and racism.

As the cases of the black African families discussed above demonstrate, there are similarities and differences in the material and symbolic opportunities available to those who have failed to acquire legal status in the three countries. All three undocumented migrant parents were denied the right to social security benefits. However, whereas the mother in the UK and the father in Norway were not permitted access to employment, the Portuguese mother was working in the informal economy. Their children's entitlement to support and healthcare from the state also differed. In Norway, because Aamina was legally resident, she and her children received a basic level of financial assistance. A large proportion of the family's rent and utilities was covered by social security. Aamina's younger children received child benefit and her older children received educational grants. The father, who was undocumented, received no state support.

Even though Nuria's 15-year-old son was born in Portugal, she had only recently managed to get him a national identity card that entitled him to state benefits. Morowa and her children in the UK were the worst off. Because her temporary leave to remain in the UK had expired, Morowa had no recourse to public funds, as well as having lost her right to work. Although she had the right to apply for help from the local authority for her children (under Section 17 of the Children Act), she was turned down. Consequently, the family had no regular income.

The experiences of Morowa and Nuria in grappling with legal systems and processes to try to access support for their children from discretionary sources speak to wider processes of negotiation with 'street level bureaucrats' (Lipsky 2010), whose jobs involve 'everyday bordering' (Yuval-Davis et al. 2017), or policing the boundaries of the nation/welfare state. In seeking to realise her children's right to support, Morowa dealt with social workers who acted as gatekeepers to local authority funding. Nuria, too, negotiated with social workers to access support when she first lost her job and made a request to Social Security, who had the discretion to provide free snacks as well as school meals for those like her son who lacked documentation.

Housing and 'home' are fundamental to a sense of ontological security and stability (Saunders 1990).[8] Along with food, a 'roof over your head' is a central component of what parents expect to be able to provide for their children. The housing situations of both Morowa in the UK and Nuria in Portugal were highly precarious. Morowa and her family were facing eviction from her unaffordable privately rented flat, waiting for that 'knock on the door'. Nuria managed to cover the rent for her family's one room in a shared apartment through her informal cleaning job. However, there was inadequate space for her son to stay with her and he often slept at his aunt's house. By contrast, Aamina's family's house in Norway was spacious and comfortable; it was also affordable in being partly paid for by the state.

Because food is a source of 'comfort' and emotional connection with kin and with place (for example, Ray 2004), for migrants the food of one's country of origin provides a direct link with home. However, the ability to prepare culturally appropriate meals depends on both availability and access (money to afford the food, the cost of travel if it is not available locally). All three mothers lived in culturally diverse areas that included shops selling foods that are customary in a range of cuisines. However, the UK mother was reliant on the woman she called 'mother' to provide money for ingredients, such as cassava, for West African meals, and the Portuguese mother said she only accessed Angolan food when visitors bought it (though her son said he ate funge at his aunt's house). The family in Norway bought rice in bulk at the local 'Asian' supermarket. Although halal meat was locally available, they said it was too expensive; instead, they travelled to Sweden where the food was cheaper and they could stock up. When money was short, they used their credit card for this expedition and made use of their large freezer.

The mothers in the UK and Portugal relied on food from charity, which is usually 'surplus' and rarely meets particular cultural preferences (Thompson et al. 2018b). In Morowa's case there were limits on how many times such provision could be accessed, and a referral was needed. Only the Norwegian family had not resorted to charity to obtain food. Morowa in the UK depended for income and food on whatever support or charity was on offer, although she was loath to ask for help. Consequently, the family went hungry, including her children. Nuria in Portugal had better access to food as well as some income (from employment). She successfully turned to charity and the local council for her son's school books and for food, but in extremis she confessed to having resorted on one occasion to thieving. She appeared to rely on her son eating free meals at school and on an aunt who fed her son and sometimes herself (see Chapter 9). Aamina in Norway said that at times they had been so short of money that they were unable to pay for food or hospital bills and had to resort to a credit card or borrow money from friends. Morowa was receiving a little help with utility bills from the children's father and some financial and emotional help from a neighbour. She was in arrears with her rent, council tax and repayments on a store card. Although Morowa said her church and faith were important to her, she also said she did not want to reveal her circumstances to church members, suggesting that begging violates personal dignity. 'What cannot be counted, compared, or exchanged is often what people consider to be of greatest value and essential to the continuity of the thread of life between past, present, and future' (Narotzky and Besnier 2014, S9).

Among the 'coping strategies' mothers employ in the context of food shortage are padding out meals with carbohydrates and sacrificing their own food intake. As the menus of these families show, meals were based on starch, mainly rice and pasta, and Morowa and her children appeared to lack protein in their daily diet. Both Morowa and Nuria reported going without food regularly in order to get by; Morowa's teenage boys vividly described their experiences of going hungry at school with dire consequences for their ability to do their schoolwork. The children of Nuria and Aamina were reluctant to admit that sometimes they lacked enough to eat, perhaps because they wanted to protect their parents from shame.

Only Nuria's son received free school meals (see Chapter 10); this was despite his lack of legal documentation, Nuria having made a request to the social security office. It is not clear whether Morowa had revealed their circumstances to the school; given her irregular status, she may have been reluctant to do so. For Aamina's large family, the high cost of bread for packed lunches was difficult, given the customary Norwegian packed lunch that children are obliged to bring to school (Chapter 10). However, her older children received scholarships that helped cover their maintenance while at school.

Although the lives of all the families that feature in the book are marked by precarity, the three migrant families in this chapter were living in situations of extreme uncertainty and insecurity. Morowa was in imminent danger and constant fear of being deported, made homeless or summonsed for debt. Nuria was still struggling to get her status regularised, and the family in Norway also expressed doubts about their future, given that the father's application for a residence permit had been turned down several times. The experience of being a migrant is a paradoxical experience especially for those who live on the verge of destitution and deportation. It also affects how time is viewed (Brannen and Nilsen 2002). Making a better life is premised on a constantly deferred future. These migrant families are prisoners of a present (Sennett 1998) in which their energy is exhausted and their imagination sapped in simply 'getting by'.

Notes

1. The Immigration Act 2016 applies important changes in England to local authority support (accommodation and financial assistance) provided to destitute families where the parents have no current immigration permission or have a derivative right to reside under European law as the primary carer of a British (or other EEA national) child (Zambrano carer). Instead of providing accommodation and/or financial support under the Children Act 1989, the Immigration Act sets out a new statutory scheme under paragraph 10A of Schedule 3 Nationality Immigration and Asylum Act 2002 which will enable local authorities to provide accommodation and financial support to these families when specific circumstances apply.
2. In the context of Covid-19, in which we are completing this book, the restrictions on free school meals for most families with NRPF has temporarily been lifted, meaning that children's families are, for the time being, able to claim food or vouchers while schools are closed.
3. In Norway, migrants who have refugee status and have obtained a residence permit undertake the introductory programme under which municipalities offer education in Norwegian language and society, together with an employment internship and other measures. Reflecting the Scandinavian welfare model, the programme aims to encourage employment and is linked to the right to financial assistance and social benefits (Hernes et al. 2019, 20). After someone has completed the course, their motivation to find employment is usually high, not least because a job is necessary to obtain a permit for family reunification, that is for other family members to come to Norway (Blom 2010).
4. Kvamme and Ytrehus (2015, 3) suggest that the links between 'undocumented status and … health problems are complex and multidimensional. Inadequate nutrition and the experience of living in fear and insecurity can create and exacerbate health problems (Hjelde 2009; Øien and Sønsterudbraten 2011).' Healthcare services are generally available to all citizens and residents, including regular medical consultations (subject to a small fee), emergency

treatment and hospitalisation. Excluded services are dentistry and physiotherapy, which are paid for by patients.

5. In Portugal, legalisation is available to those able to present a valid work contract and to show they pay tax. Migrants have frequently reported that employers in Portugal have assisted with obtaining documents (van Meeteren and Pereira 2013, 15).

6. Including family allowance, supplementary allowance for disabled children and young people, nursing allowance, orphans' pension, survivors' grants and social invalidity pension.

7. As LeVoy et al. (2003) note, the 'regularization' by which undocumented migrants achieve protection by the legalisation of their residence status is rarely straightforward.

8. Saunders (1990), following Giddens (1984), was writing about the meaning of home ownership in Britain; others note that ownership is not a necessary condition for possessing a home (for example, Miller 1988; Dupuis and Thorns 2002).

Section 3
The social dimensions of food poverty

It is problematic to separate 'nutrition' from social interaction; the two are 'inextricably intertwined' (Lupton 1996, 8). Beginning in babyhood, 'the experience of satisfying hunger … come[s] to mean much more than the physical sensation of tasting the milk or filling the stomach, but is bound up with the infant's emotional and sensual responses to the person or people who provide the food' (Lupton 1996, 7–8). Furthermore, food is a basis of individual and collective identity, since, through the act of incorporation, 'in which we send a food across the frontier between the world and the self', people 'incorporate all or some of its properties' and are thereby incorporated into particular social groups (Fischler 2011, 279). Food 'tastes' and practices are a fundamental means by which social groups – nations, regions, religious and ethnic groups – enact and express their cohesiveness and their distinctiveness from 'others'.

Of particular importance is the family habitus in which the 'durable dispositions' (Bourdieu 1977) that shape food practices and preferences are formed (Wills et al. 2011). Like 'tastes' more broadly, these are strongly shaped by, and serve as an expression of, social class (Bourdieu 2010; Warde 1997). For Bourdieu, consumption behaviour is 'a means by which social classes display their "cultural capital" and their place in a hierarchical system of social distinction' (Warde 1997, 10). Although there are overlaps between income and social class, defined in terms of education and occupation, the two are not equivalent and may have different impacts on diet (Moreira and Padrão 2004, 7). Indeed, once established, the classed dispositions of the habitus, or 'embodied cultural capital', may be relatively independent of income (Stewart 2013, 56–74).

Food is also 'social' in the sense that 'commensality', the practice of eating with others, is fundamental to establishing and maintaining social relations (Fischler 1988), both in everyday routines and on celebratory occasions. While Durkheim relegated eating to the status of a 'biological fact' (1981; translated in Fischler 2011, 530), subsequent theorists have applied his ideas to understand the 'social significance' of the shared meal (Simmel 1997) and the role of food sharing in social cohesion. Implicit and explicit rules about who eats with whom, on different occasions, vary between social groups and countries and over time (Douglas 1975; Danesi 2018). Sharing meals is in some places regarded as an important part of children's socialisation, for example, in teaching them about 'manners' and turn-taking in conversation (Ochs and Shohet 2006), whereas in other places (and times) children eat separately from adults. Either way, meals acculturate children into customary cuisines as well as establishing gender and generational hierarchies (Grieshaber 1997; Wilk 2010).

In the private sphere of the home, food serves an important social function, not only in the reproduction of 'the family' (DeVault 1991, 39), but also in the reciprocity of hospitality (Mauss 1990; King 1995, 222; Julier 2013). As Townsend notes, 'the reciprocation of small gifts and services, and sharing the enjoyment of them, is one of the most important ways in which an individual recognizes and maintains his social relationships' (2010, 92). When a neighbour or a relative calls, Townsend suggests, a host may offer a welcoming food or drink: 'A cup of tea is a widespread custom in Britain while in other societies he or she may offer coffee or a glass of wine' (2010, 92). People without the means to meet such social obligations may withdraw from social networks to avoid the 'burden of reciprocity' (Offer 2012) or may be actively shunned and excluded from social networks when they cannot reciprocate (Chase and Walker 2013). Exclusion or the threat of exclusion also provokes shame (Walker 2014); people may exclude themselves because of the shame they feel, 'retreat[ing] from social contact to avoid their precarious financial position becoming public knowledge' (Ferragina et al. 2013, 17).

In examining the relation of food poverty to families' capacities for social participation, it is also important to take into account the practice of 'eating out'. Modes of eating out remain a principal form of class distinction in some countries, but less so in others, such as Norway (Warde et al. 2007), despite research suggesting a trend towards eating out becoming less 'special' and more routine (Warde and Martens 1997b; Warde et al. 2019). As Bauman (1998) suggests, a person's ability to make choices in the marketplace and to be integrated into social activities are touchstones of their capacity to participate in consumerised societies, to exhibit social preferences and are a crucial mechanism through which the person establishes and communicates their identity.

Market-driven food consumption applies no less to young people's food practices, especially when, as they get older, they seek to express and enact greater autonomy and venture into their communities with their friends. Summarising cross-cultural comparisons of young people's eating practices, Danesi (2018, 103) suggests that the specificities of the 'food culture' of young people are strongly connected to lifestyles and cultural references that include 'global ways of eating and gathering peers around food'. However, she notes, little attention has been paid to young people's eating practices across countries. Even fewer studies have addressed the question of how young people in different countries socialise over food in the context of poverty and low income (but see Wills and O'Connell 2018; O'Connell et al. 2021).

As discussed in Chapter 2 and Section 2 of this book, we have recognised conceptually that low income does not affect all members of households equally. This applies to children's participation in social activities, such as eating out, or having guests to eat with at home. Young people may place more emphasis than adults on the importance of social activities with their friends and on having fun (Main 2013, 2018; Main and Bradshaw 2018). Recognising this, parents may work hard to prevent their children being seen as 'different' (Pugh 2009), prioritising their children's social needs over their own. As the discussion below and cases in the following chapter demonstrate, this includes enabling children to buy food with their friends when they are out and about as well as inviting their friends home to share food. Extending hospitality to children's friends is central their social inclusion; when children are unable to invite friends to their home, feelings of shame can arise (Ridge 2002; Walker 2014; Knight et al. 2018; O'Connell et al. 2019a).

Compared with the rich body of literature on change and continuity in food practices in circumstances of migration (see Chapter 2), relatively little research has explored the ways in which food and eating change, or play a part in coping with change, in the context of falling (or increasing) income. Poverty is dynamic; people move in and out of low income, often quite quickly. In Europe, the term 'the new poor' refers to people who previously enjoyed a relatively high income but have been affected by economic crisis and austerity and are now struggling financially (Burridge 2012; Queiroz 2013; Serrano 2013; Dagdeviren et al. 2017). There tends to be a lag between income falling and the experience of material deprivation, and, vice versa, a rise in income does not immediately translate into a better standard of living (Saunders 2013). Those experiencing persistent (long-term) poverty are most at risk of pernicious effects on their well-being (for example, Smith and Middleton 2007). In contrast, those whose experience of poverty is sudden and recent may attribute greater significance to the lost opportunities for socialising over food than those long accustomed to living on a low income. Although it has been suggested that 'for the "new poor" higher living standards in the past provide fewer opportunities to equip themselves for dealing with a crisis of hardship' (Dagdeviren et al. 2017, 374), they may have other resources, such as skills and social networks – or, in Bourdieu's terms, cultural and social capital – to help them withstand the loss of income. Another implication of embodied classed dispositions is that the 'new poor' may find it harder to change their habits and reduce their expectations than those whose income has always been low. Conversely, those who experience a significant rise in income may not change their habits and tastes immediately, or indeed at all. The importance of social norms is highlighted by evidence that social comparisons made by those experiencing poverty may be both diachronic (comparisons with previous standards of living) and synchronic (comparisons with others' current standards of living). Depending on the socioeconomic position of the subjects of comparison, these ways of making sense of current circumstances may intensify or dampen feelings of hardship (Dagdeviren et al. 2017, 382).

Finally, some research suggests that, when income is constrained, people reduce spending on social activities (Davis et al. 2012). Analysing UK (Understanding Society) data about the relationship between income and (inter alia) participation in social activities, Ferragina and colleagues (2013, 17) find that people cut back on social participation at a higher level of income than they cut back on material necessities. They offer two possible interpretations of this. One is that 'people may begin to withdraw from social participation before they experience real financial stress and deprivation, perhaps in a deliberate attempt to avoid material deprivation by cutting down on social spending'. The other explanation is that feelings of shame may lead to withdrawal. However, the social activities that Ferragina and colleagues (2013) focus on concern engagement in formal organisations, notably religious and political institutions, rather than less formal and more everyday forms of social participation, such as getting together and eating with others.[1]

In Chapter 8 we have selected cases that exemplify some of the ways in which low income has constrained parents' and children's participation in customary food practices, how they felt about being unable to join in and some of the ways they managed to do so. To demonstrate the dynamic nature of poverty and highlight the importance of social norms, we have chosen six families: three who have been living on low incomes for a long time and three whose incomes have fallen more recently.

Before analysing these cases, we describe the overall pattern from which we have selected them, comparing families in the three countries in terms of what they said about their participation in food-related social activities.

As noted in Chapter 3, the qualitative interviews included a questionnaire, with questions developed from the literature, concerning ways of managing food with a low income. This included some questions, adapted from the UK's Poverty and Social Exclusion survey (Lansley and Mack 2015), about participation in social activities involving food: namely, whether, through a lack of money, parents ever avoided inviting friends to eat at their home, or turned down invitations to go out for something to eat or drink and whether they avoided having their children's friends over for something to eat. Table 8.1 shows the responses of those parents in each country who said they 'often' or 'sometimes' avoided having people over or turned down invitations to go out for something to eat or drink. Not all the respondents completed the questionnaires.

A much larger proportion of parents in the Portugal sample said they avoided having friends to eat at home because they could not afford it than in the UK and Norway (Table 8.1). However, as discussed in Chapter 9, almost half of the families in Portugal regularly provided or partook in meals with extended family: 19 of the 45 families regularly ate with grown-up children, aunts, uncles and grandparents. In the UK sample, eating at home with extended family was mentioned far less frequently, although five children ate at their grandparents' home on a fairly regular basis. More common seemed to be the practice of having friends over for a cup of tea or coffee. Poor housing in the UK also limited the ability to engage in hospitality. Three families were living in temporary (hostel) accommodation in which they were not allowed visitors other than from the authorities or charities. Across all the countries, low income was, in some families, caused by and/or led to physical and

Table 8.1 Avoidance of social activities involving food, because of a lack of resources: numbers of parents reporting this by country sample.

	Portugal	UK	Norway
Avoid having friends home to eat	24	14	11
Turn down invitations to go out for food or drink	33	31	22
Total number responding	42	41	35

mental ill health, as some cases in the book demonstrate. This also constrained how much they wanted or were able to entertain guests.

In the Norway sample, around a third of the families (11/35) avoided inviting friends to their homes to eat, and eating with extended family was less common than in Portugal. This may reflect the fact that a large proportion of the sample are migrants, some of whom have no family living nearby. While six migrant families mentioned having no family in Norway and feeling isolated, a further six reported sharing meals with older children or other family members at least once a month. More frequently, mothers in Norway mentioned having friends over for 'snacks', such as fruit, cake or cookies. Offering food to visitors seemed to be a norm, according to the researchers' field notes from their visits to families (see Chapter 3). As in the other samples, housing and health, too, restricted entertaining guests or going out.

Around two-thirds of the parents in each of the countries said they had to turn down invitations to go out for something to eat or drink because they could not afford it. In Portugal, the majority of parents said this (Table 8.1) but many said they had no regrets and preferred eating at home. Some (six mothers and two fathers) mentioned meeting friends at cafes for coffee and cake, something mentioned much less often in the other two countries.

In the UK, as in Portugal, around two-thirds of parents said they turned down invitations to go out for something to eat or drink because they could not afford it. Some said they could not afford unplanned expenditure, some told their friends they could not afford it and others said they made excuses for being unable to go out. A couple of mothers mentioned going out to drink (alcohol), but not to eat – a way to reduce spending and get drunk more efficiently: 'eating is cheating', in the words of one.

As in the other two countries, around two-thirds of the parents in Norway said they had to turn down invitations to go out for something to eat or drink. Those living in rural areas said they had little opportunity to eat out, since there were few restaurants nearby.

Children's participation in social activities involving food and eating

In all three countries, parents said they prioritised taking children to eat out as a family. This consistently involved the patronage of fast food restaurants: in Portugal a trip to McDonald's; in the UK and Norway it could be McDonald's, Burger King or a pizza or kebab shop.

Having friends over to play and eat is part of children's social inclusion. In the UK and Portugal, around a third of parents (17 parents in the UK and 15 in Portugal) said they avoided inviting their children's friends to the home for something to eat because they could not afford to feed them. The proportion was lower in Norway (eight parents), but more parents did not answer this question (9/43 compared with 3/45 in the UK and 4/45 in Portugal). Between half and two-thirds of parents in all the countries said, conversely, that they never had to avoid having their children's friends over.

Around a quarter of children in Portugal and Norway and about a third of children in the UK did not have any regular pocket money. In Portugal, pocket money was often provided by grandparents. Some children saved the money provided to supplement school meals or for transport to school and others used it to buy food and socialise with friends. Whether or not they had pocket money, most young people in each country engaged in some kind of eating outside the home, despite their families' low income. They spent money, either alone or with friends, on snacks purchased from shops and on 'eating out' in cafes or restaurants 'outside'.

As Table 8.2 shows, unsurprisingly, young people in all three countries were much more likely to engage in 'eating out'[2] if they lived in urban rather than non-urban areas (Lund et al. 2017, 31). In the UK,

Table 8.2 Number of children reporting eating out or buying food, by type of area and country sample.

	UK		Portugal		Norway	
	Inner city/ urban	Coastal	Inner city/sub/ urban	Rural	Urban	Non-urban
Eat out with friends (sit-down and takeaway, e.g. chicken and chips)	15/36	2/15	15/31	3/15	22/29	4/19
Buy snacks (e.g. biscuits, sweets, crisps, drink)	8/36	2/15	6/31	5/15	2/29	2/19
Do not socialise over food	13/36	11/15	10/31	7/15	3/29	5/19
Missing data	0	0	0	0	2/29	8/19
N	51		46		48	

two-thirds of the young people in the coastal area (11/15) did not social-ise over food outside the home (eat out or buy snacks with friends). In Portugal, it was just under half (7/15) and in Norway, around a quarter (5/19). The problems of expensive transport and geographical isolation were mentioned by a few children in all three countries.

Despite lower rates of eating out more generally in Norway (Warde et al. 2007), most young people there, particularly in Oslo, said they ate out, compared with less than half in Lisbon and London (Table 8.2). As Bugge (2011, 71) notes, 'fast food has been a particularly successful innovation in post-war Norwegian cuisine. Young Norwegians eat con-siderably more fast food than the adult population.' The higher frequency of eating out among the Norway sample may be because eating out is a less important mode of social distinction in Norway (Warde et al. 2007) or because the low-income families were better off than those in the UK and Portugal. More likely, it may reflect the heightened importance that migrant parents place on their children's acculturation and inclusion.

Outside the home, the foods young people ate generally (but not exclusively) comprised of unhealthy snacks like biscuits, crisps, cakes and sweets as well as fast food including globalised brands – such as McDonald's and Burger King – and generic 'American'-style foods – such as burgers, fries (or chips) and pizzas. But there were differences between the countries. In Norway, kebabs were mentioned more often, in Portugal, chorizo or *bifana* (a traditional Portuguese bread roll con-taining sliced pork) and in the UK, 'chicken 'n' chips' (Thompson et al. 2018a). 'Gummies' were popular sweets in Portugal.

Young people mentioned eating in cafes, fast food establishments and 'proper' restaurants. Garages (petrol stations) were mentioned a few times in the non-urban areas of both Norway and the UK. Children also purchased foods in shops and cafes adjacent to their schools, reflecting the commercialisation of areas near to schools (Wills et al. 2019). In Portugal, most 'eating out' was at school lunchtimes, around once a week in the cafes close to schools; a practice that some parents tried to support as part of having a 'normal' life (Horta et al. 2013). Otherwise, children in the Portuguese sample tended to emphasise the importance of eating with family, rather than friends.

Young people talked about how they managed to socialise over food with little money. They 'planned ahead' and saved and 'juggled' money given for school lunches and transport; they made use of vouchers and special offers and ordered 'children's'-sized meals. In all countries, they also talked about sharing food and reciprocity. Some 'saved face' by excusing themselves from eating with friends and some mentioned feeling ashamed. In all three countries, children mentioned peers who had more money than them, but it was only in the UK that young people talked explicitly about feeling excluded from the social lives of their peers (O'Connell et al. 2019a, 2020).

Notes

1. The inclusion of participation in religious institutions may partly explain the finding that minority ethnic groups experience greater material deprivation than the white majority and yet their social participation is, on average, higher.
2. Given the difficulty of finding a suitable principle by which to classify types and places of eating out (Warde and Martens 1997a, 149–50), we distinguished between buying 'snacks' – cold foods such as sweets, chocolate and crisps – and 'eating out', that is, eating in cafes, restaurants and so on, or eating hot food 'outside'.

8
Exclusion from sociability and social relationships

This chapter focuses on how low income and associated difficulties constrain families' participation in customary food practices and sociability and contribute to social exclusion. As discussed above, families move in and out of poverty. The qualitative study was designed to address the effects of a major economic crisis on family lives. However, in the UK and Portugal we found households that had experienced low income for much of their lives as well as ones that had been significantly better off before the economic crisis and ensuing austerity measures that brought unemployment and cuts to benefits. Because Norway was relatively unaffected by the financial crisis, none of the families there was directly affected in this way. In some families in all three countries, life events unrelated to the crisis led to large drops in income which affected parents' and children's social lives.

Whether or not the lack of capacity to take part in social activities is recent or established, the failure to offer hospitality to others may breach normative expectations of kinship, friendship and neighbourliness. In most households, parents went to considerable lengths to maintain a sense of 'normality' for children by ensuring they did not totally miss out on the same activities as their peers.

In order to reflect the dynamic nature of poverty and the effects on patterns and expectations of social participation, in this chapter we compare three families who have lived on low incomes for a long time and three who have recently suffered a fall in income. Those who have been on low income for a long time have migrated within or between countries. The second three cases previously enjoyed a middle-class standard of living but, as a result of the economic crisis and austerity, or family breakdown, are struggling to maintain the lifestyle they are accustomed to (Burridge 2012; Queiroz 2013; Dagdeviren et al. 2017). In this analysis we examine the extent to which low income constrains both parents' and children's participation in social activities, especially in relation to food, and how they feel about and manage their lives in these circumstances.

Living permanently on the edge in a deprived part of a UK coastal town: Lauren and Calum

Lauren is a white British lone mother with two sons, Calum aged 12 years (the study child) and a two-year-old. They live in the coastal town. Lauren was born and brought up in a city in the North of England and moved to the area as a teenager. She separated from the father of her oldest son because of domestic violence, and the father of her younger son is in prison. The family lives in a two-bedroom house, owned by Lauren's mother, in an isolated, deprived part of the town that has mainly social housing. Both Lauren and Calum say they are not keen on the area. As Lauren says, 'Lots of idiot kids around, want to be gangsters. I mean I wouldn't send him to the shop once it's dark, cos the teens all hang around the shop.' Lauren cannot afford the high bus fares to take her children into town and so they have to walk.

Lauren has lived on a low income for a long time. She left school with few qualifications and, before having her youngest child, worked for many years in the care sector, most recently on a zero-hours contract. The family currently relies on benefits that amount to around £228 per week, made up of Income Support, child tax credit and child benefit. Lauren does not receive maintenance from Calum's father. She pays £200 per month for the rent (the rest is covered by housing benefit), plus £16.50 per month on council tax and £14 for bus fares for Calum to go to school. She cannot afford to pay £50 per month for the water bill and has been in arrears for years. Lauren spends money visiting the youngest child's father in prison, though she receives some assistance with the cost of this. The little she has is 'not enough money to live on'. Expenditure on food varies but is, on average, around a third of the FBS, at about £30 per week. She has resorted to food banks several times in the last year. The first occasion was when the bank charged her for going overdrawn; the second time was in the run-up to Christmas, when she had another overdraft bill and other financial pressures. Lauren prefers to use the food bank in a neighbouring area; she feels 'embarrassed' about using the one at her local community centre, 'because I know them here'.

Food at home lacks variety and Calum is said mainly to eat toast and sausages, though his mother puts this down to him being a 'fussy' eater. Lauren is practised in the art of managing on a low income, including on special occasions. She took out a loan of £300 last Christmas to pay for Christmas presents for the children and says she is currently paying £40 per month in repayments; she lied to the organisation (the Social Fund[1]) and said the loan was for a new washing machine. The previous year she borrowed from a loan company and ended up repaying much more than she borrowed. This year she would have liked to start saving with a different loan scheme but cannot afford to; she has yet to repay the whole of the loan she took out last Christmas. Coping with the shortage of money and constantly juggling money has made Lauren what she describes as 'moody', 'Cos I'm always robbing Peter and paying Paul.' She takes anti-depressants.

The family's social life is very restricted. Lauren notes, 'I haven't been out for a long time.' She had planned to celebrate her birthday with a friend by going to the local 'pictures' (cinema) but was unable to afford this:

> I wanted to go to the pictures for my birthday in December, and we haven't been yet. Can't even afford to do that. That's the one thing I wanted to do. I said the only thing I want to do is go pictures with [friend] … but when it came down to the day I couldn't afford it.

Lauren regularly turns down invitations to go out, or only accepts if someone else is paying. The conversation with friends commonly follows the same lines: ' "Do you want to go the caf?" – "I can't afford it." – "Do you want to meet for a coffee?" – "Are you paying?" [laughs] That's the usual one. "I'll buy." ' She explains that the choice is between spending money on social activities or buying essential food for the family – 'When you think about "Have I got the money to do that or shall I just keep it for when we need milk and bread?" '

It is also rare to have friends round to the house. Lauren says she used to encourage visits from her friend's children, but now that she is not working and on benefits 'I say no to them if I haven't got the food in … and they understand'. Being unable to provide food for guests conflicts with Lauren's strong northern sense of hospitality:

Lauren: There has been times when I can't even offer them toast. There has been times, of a weekend when I've been like, 'I'm really sorry, I haven't even got toast for you.' I feel like

... I don't know if it's the northern blood in me, but when you cook dinner you cook for everyone in the house.

Interviewer: Yeah.

Lauren: But if you haven't got the food you feel rude, you know. I would be like, 'I haven't got enough food for you, but do you want some toast?' you know.

Lauren likes the new art gallery and cafes in the gentrified part of the 'old town', unlike some other families on low incomes in the area. But the prices of the cafes and shops are out of Lauren's reach and she feels frustrated and saddened:

It's frustrating ... yeah it does [make me feel bad], because basically I'd love to go down and enjoy this area the way it should be enjoyed. You know, go down to the old town, sit around, let the kids go into the shops, the old shops. 'Do you remember that time we went into the sweet shop down there?' And he goes to me, 'Mum, please, please, can we get these sweets?' and it was £4.50 for some bamboozled jellybeans.

Lauren wishes she could go out and buy the children an ice cream but instead they are mostly at home. Their one social outlet is the local community centre. 'I had money and I could take the kids out ... just out down the seafront, get a bag of chips and walk along the seafront – them sort of things, you know. At the moment I'm just sat indoors all the time, or at the centre here, you know.' Given how isolated they are, Lauren finds the local community centre a 'lifesaver' for herself and the children:

I've been coming to the centre ... I used to use the centre when [oldest son] was little, cos it was a lifesaver really. You know if they didn't have the centres personally me, I'd be really depressed in my house. I have to get out. I have to get the kids out.

The centre offers a range of services including help with debt repayments and a food bank. Sometimes she shares the food with a friend who does not qualify for a food parcel. She says the other mothers at the centre are in similar circumstances: 'I think we're all in the same boat.'

Calum's social life is also curtailed. He attends the young people's club but rarely goes out with friends otherwise, giving the excuse that he does not like getting buses, the cost of which is very expensive. Although

Calum says he has friends to his house 'sometimes', he says he 'forgets' to offer them a drink or anything, commenting, 'I'm so used to living by myself I forget people want stuff.' When asked whether this is an issue, he replied, 'Sometimes,' but when asked to elaborate, failed to do so. Calum admits that not having money is 'sometimes' a problem but then adds that he doesn't need money because he doesn't often go to the shop or to McDonald's, again giving an excuse: 'No, I don't like going that way.' He also plays down not having the money to travel on the bus to school: 'I always miss my stop.'

Being unable to forge friendships in a Lisbon suburb: Helia and Mattis

Helia, a lone mother, has three children, including Mattis, a boy aged 14, and two older children, who live elsewhere, one of whom she supports. Helia also pays for her granddaughter's childcare and food. Originally from Cape Verde, Helia migrated at the age of 21. She used to live in one of Lisbon's shanty towns, but when her house was demolished during the slum clearances, she used the compensation from the municipality to buy a two-bedroom flat in a suburb of Lisbon. She has been living on a low income for much of her life.

Helia is currently awaiting a back operation and is signed off work. Because for the last 10 years she has been self-employed as a domestic cleaner, she is not entitled to sickness benefits that depend on making contributions. She is therefore reliant on child benefit, some savings and any undeclared cleaning work: 'I get nothing on leave. [How] can I eat with a child, with expenses to pay at home? I had to [do] hidden work.' Through working she is at risk of further damaging her health: 'You can't imagine my state when I get up … I don't touch the floor with my feet. I can't put a sock on my cold foot. I can't put on my shoes.' Helia receives €42 in family benefit plus €50 'bonus' because Mattis is hyperactive. Mattis's father is unemployed and does not contribute to expenses, despite the court having decreed he pay alimony. With the cleaning work bringing in €295, Helia's income amounts to about €387 each month.

Because Helia bought the flat outright, she has no housing costs. The cost of utilities includes €27 a month for electricity and €27 for water. She pays €78 for internet/TV and mobile phones and €93 for transport. She has used most of her savings and has taken on a small amount of debt to furnish the new house. Mattis is an accomplished footballer and sought by several teams. His training, €20 per month, plus clothing and equipment, is a big expense but a priority for Helia. She spends only around a fifth of the FBS on food, about €50 per month.

Helia takes pride in being a good domestic manager and her children do not go without enough to eat; 'With the little I make I feel proud because I make it last.' Food is central to 'doing family' (Morgan 2011) both routinely and in the celebration of special occasions in this household. However, despite her low income she prioritises not only her son but also her two older children who live elsewhere and her grandchild; by cooking for them she is able to show that she cares for them: 'I like to cook these things. But it's for them. For me sometimes I cook or don't eat; it's more for them when they come.'

Celebrating Christmas and birthdays with the wider family is important, but Helia says it is only possible if they pool resources. Before her mother died last year, Helia joined her sisters and brothers at her mother's house for Christmas. They did the food shopping together and Helia's younger sister cooked under the matriarch's supervision. However, there were times when Helia did not take part because she could not afford to contribute and so she and her children spent Christmas by themselves. On Mattis's last birthday, Helia had no money to buy special foods to celebrate. She asked Mattis's father for help, but he refused. 'I said, "I'll never ask you for money again." I never asked him again.' Instead, she asked her older daughter for help to buy the birthday cake.

Helia is unable to offer hospitality to guests, because of low income and ill health. 'I don't have money.' Given her limited budget, she and Mattis eat out very rarely: 'Instead of spending at the coffee shop, what I unnecessarily spend at the coffee shop, I have at home … the same I drink there I can drink at home.' It is not that she would not like to go out for a coffee, a typical thing to do in Portugal, but she has to prioritise:

> My children come first. First are my expenses. My house. If I had [better] conditions, if there is some money left over, but what I have is not enough, I cannot. I cannot take a step longer than my leg. I cannot. It's not that I do not like it; I like it [eating out].

Helia's pride means she will not let others pay for her and she makes excuses for not joining in. But this means that she does not make many friends:

> If go, I also like to pay. And sometimes I can't pay. What I have is not much for my, for my house, for my family, so I won't go …

Sometimes I'm invited and I say, 'I won't go because I don't feel like it, I have no time.'... That's why I don't make many friends.

Being unable to participate in eating out makes Helia feel sad and leads to social exclusion:

> Not being able makes me sad. Sometimes when I see many sitting in the coffee shop, I would also like to. I even say, 'I too want to be in the coffee shop eating and drinking.' How does she find that money? I can't manage to go there. I think, am sad of course, I'm sad.

According to Helia, Mattis would also like to eat out with his friends when they get together in local cafes: 'These ideas are from school; he sees many children. Now one eats in the street, hamburger, French fries, they buy it in the coffee shop, those hamburgers and breaded steak and these things. And he sees these things and also asks me for money to go eat.'

But she has to say there is no money for eating out and instead buys food to cook at home:

> My son will say, 'Oh, mum, come on.' What will we eat? 'Oh, mother, buy me a juice. Let's go eat outside.'
>
> 'Son, what will we eat? Son, I don't have, I don't have the money.'
>
> The other day he asked for a slice of pizza, at the shopping mall. I went to buy those from the supermarket. He said, 'That's not the one I want! Mother, I don't want that pizza; it's the one from the mall I want.'
>
> And I said, 'I don't have money for that.'

Mattis does not get pocket money but his mother gives him a euro or two when she can. If his friends eat out, for example at the cafeteria near school, Mattis says he does not join them. Instead, he takes a snack to school. He has not yet had friends to their new house. Although Helia feels bad that she cannot give Mattis money for social activities, Mattis is acutely aware of his mother's situation and, several times in the interview, he says she goes without and gives him what she can:

> Because ... whenever money comes for my mother, there is almost never any money left for her. Because she has expenses ... has to

buy food … Yes … how can I explain it … She has house expenses, right? And the money she receives is almost the money she spends.

Mattis does not complain about his own lack of money but says it upsets him that his mother has to manage with so little: 'It hurts to see my mother want to buy or have things, but she can't because there is never any money left over … there is almost never any money left over.' His aspiration is to become a professional footballer and to provide for his family and the local community.

Prioritising children's social lives in Oslo: Aska and Eylo

This household includes two parents – Aska and her husband – and two children: Eylo, a boy aged 12, and a daughter aged eight. They live in Oslo in a house that they are buying. The father had to flee Iraq at the age of 18 because of his politics. The family became refugees in Turkey and arrived in Norway under the UN refugee quota agreement in 1992. They lived first in a small municipality in Western Norway and moved to Oslo in 1999. After the father found a job as a deliveryman, the family bought their first apartment in 2000 with the help of a communal housing mortgage. He and his wife bought their current home in 2013. About three years ago, the father had a back injury and has not worked since. Aska works one day a week; she cannot find a full-time job. Besides being on a low income, the family is seriously in debt because of the mortgage and other loans. They frequently use their credit card to pay for food.

Eylo's father receives disability benefits of NOK 19,000 per month, and Aska earns between NOK 6,000 and 8,000 per month, depending on whether she is given extra shifts. The family also receives NOK 1,900 in child benefit. They have recently organised an interest-only mortgage, reducing the monthly payment from NOK 11,000 to 5,500, because 'We had it very difficult. We had to stop the instalments.' They pay NOK 1,000 per month for electricity in the summer and NOK 1,500 per month in the winter. The family took on NOK 40,000 in credit card debt to refurbish the house; the father pays off NOK 500 per month but thinks he will probably never pay it off totally. He continues to use the credit card and tries, often unsuccessfully, to avoid paying the additional interest required for not making the minimum payment on time. Maintaining a car is also costly. The family pays fees for Eylo to take part in soccer and the daughter in handball.

Eylo's father says he has little idea how much money the family spends on food: 'Most of the money we have left we spend on food and important things we need.' The researcher calculated that they spend around NOK 3,000 per month, which is about a third of the FBS for a family of this type; the amount they spend varies from month to month, depending on whether they shop in Sweden, which in turn depends on having both time and money: 'Some months we buy across the border. When you shop there it varies. Sometimes, you have no time or can't afford to go across the border. Then it gets a bit difficult. And [we] use less. It is very variable.'

Through his political interests Eylo's father has found friends in Norway and likes to entertain them for dinner with dishes of rice with meat or chicken and vegetables, and wine if the family can afford it. However, the family has had to cut down on entertaining: 'Over the last years, we have not had a lot of visits because of the economy, because of stress. It is dependent upon many things.' The father dismisses the importance of this, saying that technology means it is not necessary to have friends to the house, because 'you can just phone'. They do invite visitors for tea, 'just tea. Regular tea and stuff. Perhaps we had some fruit and stuff.'

On the one hand, Eylo's father cannot remember the last time he ate at a restaurant and says that, although his wife would like to, it is too expensive. On the other hand, he sees it as a priority for his children to be able to eat out. He takes them to McDonald's or Burger King most weekends, using vouchers obtained by completing questionnaires on the companies' websites. Eylo helps him fill in these online surveys. 'The menu you pay 80 for, you get for 50,' Eylo's father says. Although he suspects that Burger King does this to make 'people become addicted', he thinks it is important for his children to participate in 'normal' social activities.

Even so, he believes that his children would like to eat out more frequently than they do. He says that his son feels sad when he has to tell him that he cannot afford it. So Eylo's father often uses the credit card to avoid disappointment: 'But sometimes he doesn't understand, and perhaps he gets sad. I try to fix it, sort of. I think like, they are children and they don't understand that much. … I think like, I'll try to some other ways. Use credit or something else.'

Eylo's father also thinks it is important to give Eylo money (usually NOK 100 per week) so that he can buy himself something to eat and drink when he is out with his friends. He expresses concern at the thought that his son could be the one child without money on these occasions:

He goes with his friends to the shop. He can buy a Coke. I can't manage that he doesn't have anything. That is depressing for children. And we always think like this. We try to give the children money, pocket money [when they are going] out. But at home nobody sees us. We can fix it ourselves in a way. But outside it is different.

It is important for the children, Eylo's father says, to be protected from being seen to be 'poor' by their friends; it matters much less for adults:

We try to give our children everything we can. And that they don't become someone the other talk about, right. That they haven't eaten there, right? We listen and we see. That's why I, we as a family always think, when you outside try not to make the children upset since others eat. We can't afford it. We try to fix it somehow. For me it does not matter to buy a kebab. I eat it or not. I'm an adult. And I don't think much about myself. I think about the children. When they are out [I want] them to be almost the same as their friends.

Eylo confirms that he gets NOK 100 every week from his father and another NOK 50 from his mother and does not even view this as pocket money, 'It is not pocket money, but it is like after-school [money]. ... I usually don't use it, but I buy... hm ... I usually go to Burger King and buy hamburgers.' Eylo sees going to Burger King as so 'normal' that he sometimes goes there by himself to buy hamburgers as well as going with his friends.

Maintaining middle-class social expectations in inner London: Marian and Phoebe

Phoebe, age 16, lives with her white British parents and two siblings in an inner London borough. This formerly well-off family living in a four-bedroom house (which they are buying) is currently on a low income because the father was made redundant two years ago as part of government spending cuts. Officially classed as 'self-employed', he now has to bid for contracts from London boroughs that have outsourced their services, but has so far been unsuccessful. Phoebe's mother, Marian, works part-time for a local charity, helping in the shop, cafe and toddler group. Although the father has had no work for two years, he has not 'signed on' to receive benefits. Marian puts this down to 'pride' and also to the father's hope that his application for the next job will be successful.

(It is likely that they have been ineligible for benefits because they have income from a second property that they let.)

The income of this middle-class family is much less than it used to be: around £1,300 per month, excluding the income from their rental property, which covers the mortgage on their home. They make debt repayments of around £430 per month. The costs of council tax and utilities are just over £200 per month; TV and phone charges are around £130 per month; and childcare costs for the youngest child are £60 per month. They run an old car. They spend just over half of the FBS on food, around £80 per week. Marian cooks mostly from fresh ingredients not only to save money but because this is what she has always done. The family is vegetarian and Phoebe is vegan. Marian says they do not buy takeaways, not only for cost but also health reasons, 'cos I consider that to be a luxury, and also I think the fat and sugar and salt content is probably pretty high'.

Expenditure at celebrations such as Christmas is reduced by visiting other relatives. Last Christmas they went to Marian's brother's house. They also received some parcels of goods and food from the charity where Marian works. The family's social lives are greatly curtailed. Marian explains that they invite her sister in-law and her family to eat with them sometimes, because they 'understand' and eat whatever the family is eating. By contrast, keeping up social expectations means that they cannot afford to entertain less intimate guests: 'It's when I think if you have people to dinner, grown-ups, they expect you to produce wine and, you know, exotic pudding, and I think that the expectation isn't something that I could handle.'

Moreover, it feels awkward to accept invitations when the family cannot reciprocate. Marian says, 'I feel when we're invited, I feel like I need to invite them back, but right now I can't.' Consequently, Marian turns down invitations to eat out, or only joins friends for a drink if they are going to a restaurant: 'If somebody's having a party and it's at a restaurant or something because I feel that's a bit of an extravagance. So sometimes I'll go and have a drink and say happy birthday and then go home.'

Although Marian and her husband accept the constraints on their social life, they go to great lengths to 'normalise' the social life of their children, as Marian says, 'cos there is a lot of expectation from each other's peers'. For example, when asked how they deal with special occasions such as children's birthdays, she says she makes a homemade cake (Figure 8.1) or they do an activity, for example swimming, which is

Figure 8.1 Homemade vegan marble cake for Phoebe's birthday (Source: 'Phoebe').

subsidised for children in their inner London area. Marian then describes how she managed to avoid having to feed the 10 children her son invited to his swimming party. The event was carefully timed to take place between lunch and dinner so she did not need to provide a meal, but they planned to have a birthday cake in the local park before the children went home:

> And then I suddenly thought afterwards, 'Gosh you know we really can't afford to feed them all, specially in [the shopping centre], I mean it's crazy.' So we did it at three o'clock, so it was five o'clock, so it wasn't quite supper time. So I was able to bring ... I made a chocolate brownie and a vegan banana cake, so there was a choice, and candles.

When the rain spoiled their plans, the parents came to an agreement with a restaurant for the use of their outdoor space:

> And then it was pouring with rain and we were meant to go to the playground. And then I was just thinking, 'Oh you know' ... cos you just want your kids to enjoy it. So we found a restaurant called [name] and we went in. My husband said, 'Could I have a coffee, and could we possibly do a cake outside?' And they were like, 'Of course' ... and it wasn't busy, they were lovely ... and it was

sheltered. So we just did it there, and we blew the candles out, gave out the cake. And … cos there's a ritual in birthdays isn't there? There's an expectation of at least a cake … and then they all went home from there.

Marian says the children understand their parents' financial difficulties and try to be helpful by not asking for things, like new school shoes, though this makes Marian feel guilty: 'I feel a bit bad about that.' She also discusses the difficulty of ensuring equity between the children; they could not now afford to pay for a younger child to go on an overseas school trip that their older daughter Phoebe did go on. For her part, Phoebe shows empathy in response to her parents' drop in income and the pressure it places on her mother to feed them all: 'I think my mum does definitely [worry about money] … I think she's got a lot more pressure on her now. She's only working [at the charity], and it's not a lot for five of us who "inhale" food [laughs]. So I'm sure that's difficult'.

Phoebe helps in other ways. She has a job and uses her own money to buy clothes and some food. She also expresses an ethos of frugality, an ethical stance in opposition to the 'profligacy of consumerism' (Evans 2011, 552). She shops in second-hand clothes shops and describes shopping centres as 'too sterile', saying, 'I like getting things from the charity shop a lot because it's just so cheap, and normally you can find amazing things … so that's really good.'

Phoebe also pools resources with friends to buy health foods and fruit, including fair trade bananas (Figure 8.2) bought in bulk at bargain prices, and makes use of special offers to eat out with friends:

> And the amazing thing is … cos I know what I want, and with Wagamama's I more often than not get the same thing, and I think I get like the kid's mini yasai ramen, which is like £5, and it's so filling … and it's really good. And a smoothie … so it's really cheap and good food. So it's not that expensive. And there's a vegetarian buffet in [neighbouring area] – all you can eat buffet, and I think you pay like £5. I haven't been there recently but we were thinking about going there. … I also go to [wholesale fruit and vegetable] market occasionally to get a big box of bananas … cos that's cheaper. So I think I got 160 for a few pounds.

Whereas Marian feels excluded from the social life of her own peers, Phoebe's social life is not greatly affected by the family's reduced financial circumstances, both because she earns her own money and because

Figure 8.2 A fair trade banana (Source: 'Phoebe').

she is frugal and ethical in her shopping habits (Evans 2011). Meanwhile, Marian and her partner draw on their internal resources, including the confidence to negotiate access to a cafe, to provide a fitting celebration for their son's birthday.

Keeping up appearances in Lisbon: Sofia and her children, Miguel and Ana

This white Portuguese two-parent family has three children: two daughters, aged seven and 10, and a son, aged 13. They live in a two-bedroom apartment that they are buying in Lisbon. Ten-year-old Ana and 13-year-old Miguel were both interviewed. Their parents have been unemployed since the financial crisis in 2008. Before this they were in well-paid jobs; the mother in fashion and interiors while the father was employed on higher-than-average pay in a reputable company. Since they lost their jobs, they have struggled. Sofia does occasional cleaning work and the father is employed intermittently in construction. Miguel and Ana used to attend a private school but have since moved to a state school where they receive free meals – a morning snack, lunch and an afternoon snack.

The family's monthly household income is around €570 (the amount of benefit for two adults and three children under the age of 18), plus €109 in child support, and extra money from the parents' occasional unofficial employment. Their outgoings include the mortgage, which is €475, and €56 in council tax. Utility bills add up to around €150 per month; TV, internet and phones to around €75 per month. Two of the children attend football classes that cost €40 per month. In the past year, they were only able to pay three of the 12 mortgage repayments. They have been in debt for months. The family's food spending amounts to about half of the FBS, around €300 per month. They also buy food in small grocery shops on credit. Living under these constraints has put a strain on the father's mental health and the parents' relationship; Sofia says they argue about money.

The researcher, Sónia, noted how well dressed the mother appeared at the interview. Sofia suggests this is an important way in which she 'saves face' (Goffman 1974): 'because whoever looks at me, won't say that in between pay checks I'm strapped ... that my freezer is empty or full'. However, the family relies on family and friends for help with money, food and transport. The photo of the fridge taken during the kitchen tour shows the shelves virtually empty except for some mousses in disposable containers which the grandmother brought during the interview (Figure 8.3). Opening the fridge, Sofia explains, 'This is my

Figure 8.3   Refrigerator contents (Source: Sónia Cardoso).

refrigerator. It has no vegetables. I have to find someone who can get me some … I have a [frozen] pizza here, I have cheese, ham, I bought it yesterday and it's like this, almost empty.'

Sofia has applied to the municipality for some support. But she did not follow this up because she felt she was 'stealing' from those who are worse off and in much greater need:

> I think I need it, although I have … There are people who really have nothing, right?! Hum, hum … but I feel I'm stealing someone's place. Understand? … It's not fear of facing it, it's not shame … but I always feel like I'm stealing someone's position who needs it more than me. Understand? … There are people who'll do that. And have no conscience. And if I criticize, who am I to do this, right?! … And I think that another person, that there are people who have greater hardships than I … who live on the street, or don't have anything to eat or really have nothing to eat … and scrounge in garbage cans and … that's immensely sad, right?!

In this family, food seems to be a means of maintaining some continuity with the past when they were financially better off. It also engenders a sense of 'normality'. Sofia says she tries to cook food the children like. On special occasions, such as birthdays, she does something more expensive – crab pâté or shrimps – or at least food that looks special:

> Then I think you also eat with your eyes, and you play around with appetizers … elaborate! A homemade pâté with crab sticks, with tuna, all those ready-made things. I can say that sometimes I buy a little shrimp when it's on sale. I'm not someone who'll go entirely without, so … a little bit is enough … On those special occasions, if it's the time of the month that will allow for it, everyone is happy, okay! … And even if … there is one shrimp per person … but they love it, they like … or Vietnamese clam, which is cheaper.

Figure 8.4 shows a lunch of fish fingers and salad made with smoked salmon bought by the paternal grandmother when it was on special offer. Another photograph taken by Ana (Figure 8.5) shows some shrimps that her mother served as an appetiser, followed by an ordinary meal of leftover meat with chips, for the First Holy Communion of Ana's younger sister.

Sofia justifies these 'indulgences' as a reward for the children's good behaviour at school and the way they manage the family's

Figure 8.4 Lunch of fish fingers and smoked salmon salad (Source: 'Ana').

Figure 8.5 Fried shrimps in the pan (Source: 'Ana').

difficulties: 'Sometimes a little spoiling is enough, right?! We don't need much, but sometimes we need to indulge.' She also says she likes to take them to McDonald's once a month so they can feel 'normal':

> It's like that in the beginning of the month ... there goes *x* money, 20 or so euros and ... and perhaps we'll miss it, but at that moment we have to think, 'Let's forget for a little bit,' because they also need it [some indulgence]. The children need to feel that ... because they like it.

In order to prevent her children feeling judged by their peers, Sofia also gives them some money to buy food at school:[2]

> Also, so they won't feel, because their mates always have some. They'll say it themselves: 'You know such and such? His mother gives him ... gives him 20 and 30 euros ... way too much, mother! It's awful!' I mean, they'll make that comment ... to see what I'll say or ... or even just to vent. And I'll say, 'Oh son, or oh daughter, it's because they can, they don't give the proper value, or a child shouldn't have so much money ... because later they won't know how to give money its proper value and we don't know what tomorrow will be like.' That's basically what I tell them. And yes sometimes, sometimes I'll give them 50 cents, one euro ... these things.

Miguel, the 13-year-old, confirms his mother's account, saying he does not get an allowance, though occasionally she gives him a euro or two 'to eat something here at school or to pay something'. He rarely has friends over or goes to friends' houses and does not eat out. He says that eating out is something that other kids do, though with their families rather than friends, and that they 'brag' about it:

> Because they're always talking ... bragging ... which I don't think is necessary ... they'll say, 'Oh, yesterday I went to Burger King and had dinner with my grandparents; they bought me a jacket', 'Look, I have a new iPhone' and like that. They're always saying, 'Hey, look here.' So, on purpose!

Miguel does not comment directly on how this makes him feel, though it is clear he is annoyed when his friends 'show off'. When asked if he visits the sweet shop near his school, he says he rarely does that: 'No! Every once in a while I have about 20 cents in my pocket or something like

Figure 8.6 Hamburgers, chips and Coca-Cola (the last given by a friend) (Source: 'Ana').

that.' He mentions a friend who buys for everyone else: 'He's a kid who … he's not greedy about what he has and helps others.' Ana also mentions a friend who buys her food. Talking about the photo of hamburgers (Figure 8.6) that she and her brothers cooked at home, she mentions that the Coca-Cola was given to her by a school friend. She explains that the friend usually buys food at Mini-Preço near the school and gives it to her. Ana brought the Coca-Cola home and shared it with her brothers and her father.

As the eldest of the children, Miguel remembers life before his parents lost their well-paid jobs, and the changes in food and eating: 'Yes, because before we had more things; now it's more basic. When I was little, I don't know, I'm not sure, I'd go to restaurants with my parents and grandparents, more than my sisters now; they don't have conditions to do that again.'

Both children worry about their parents and about losing their home. Miguel says, 'When I think about it … [places a hand on his chest] … They [the parents] avoid talking about it, we shouldn't have to, but it might happen.' He also worries about his sisters not having anything to eat:

I don't care about myself … to have nothing to eat. I do okay without eating. Because the belly aches etc … but I can manage not eating for a day, I don't mind … I was never someone who eats a lot, but my sisters, I worry a lot more if they stay without eating.

Ana also expresses concern, 'Because I know my mother [and my father] face hardships … and I also wanted to be grown up to help them.'

The shame of appearing poor in an area outside Oslo: Carolina and Antonio

Carolina is a lone mother who was born in South America and grew up in Norway. The family lives in a privately rented flat outside Oslo with only one bedroom. Following divorce, Carolina suffered from depression and lost her job. She has been on sick leave for 18 months. She has three children (each from a different relationship) including Antonio, a boy aged 14, and a daughter aged four. Her other son, aged 13, lives with his father because Carolina cannot afford to look after all three children. Since separating from her partner, she has lived in a rented one-bedroom basement flat in a detached house in a rural area 30 minutes' drive out of Oslo. Antonio has the bedroom, while Carolina and her daughter share an alcove with a curtain separating it from the open-plan living room and kitchen.

Since Carolina's sick pay expired, the family income has been made up of work assessment benefit and child benefit that amounts to NOK 20,410. The largest part of the family's outgoings is housing, which costs NOK 9,000 a month, including utilities. Carolina is in debt to a friend (NOK 1,240 a month) and has other debts she is currently unable to repay. Childcare is NOK 15,000, the cost of which is split with her ex-husband. The budget for food is whatever is left after paying all the other bills: around three-quarters of the FBS for a family of this type, between NOK 4,268 and 5,875 per month. To make sure her children can eat, Carolina eats less than she would like, but says that her children are unaware of the severity of the situation.

Carolina says she cannot afford the additional expense of celebrating special occasions. She approached NAV for help with the children's birthdays but was told that only people who have reached rock bottom can apply for financial aid. She felt humiliated and said she never wants to apply to NAV again. Instead, she turns to the children's fathers:

[Antonio] had a birthday and then he invited three mates to a cinema evening with popcorn and Burger King and it was [my daughter's] dad who paid. When [my 13-year-old son] has a birthday, it was his dad who paid. When [my four-year-old daughter] had a birthday, it was her dad that had to pay. I make a birthday party at home with my [own] dad, my mother and my sisters.

Carolina does not invite her friends or the children's friends to their home, since she cannot afford to feed them and, presumably, because there is a lack of space. Her own parents come to eat at her home but have to contribute: 'they have to bring things to make dinner, because I don't have the capacity or can't afford to prepare dinner for everyone on my budget'. Carolina says she asks them to bring specific products. 'If we're going to eat taco they have to bring cheese and minced meat … they are pensioners now. Thus, they aren't that well off either.'

Carolina's and her children's social lives are consequently very restricted socially. This is especially painful because Carolina's friends are 'very affluent or a bit above the average perhaps … Eh, like I used to be.' She says that whenever she meets her friends she is confronted by the feeling of shame about being poor. Sometimes she accepts their generosity, but at other times she makes excuses:

They can afford to go on concerts and dinners and stuff like that … eh … and I always have a headache or bellyache or something like that. Eh … I have been very open with them about my situation and even though they meant well of course, by paying for my concert ticket and the bus and the food afterwards, it has been awful for me to think about that I don't manage it myself. … That someone has to give me that help in order for me to have some fun from time to time.

Carolina cannot afford to go to the kinds of places her friends go to. For example, 'my friends go to sushi restaurants … and stuff … or yeah like expensive restaurants where the least you can right … just the starter costs you NOK 500, right [laughs]. Thus, I usually says no to, I think, 99.9 percent [of the times] I say no.' This is because she has 'a budget' and has to prioritise food, especially milk, for the children. 'If I go over the budget, I can't afford to buy milk every day or to have milk every day for my children and milk is very important in this house.'

On the one hand, Carolina feels ashamed not to be able to give Antonio the opportunity to eat out: 'My child stands there and does not have opportunities like the other children have to get a small gift or to go out and eat and stuff.' On the other hand, the boys 'have two fathers [laughs] who can give them a bit extra sometimes'. She mentions cinema and going to McDonald's. 'They also have a grandpa who also can do a bit of stuff like that with them now and again.' However, she does mention that she gives Antonio NOK 20 to buy chocolate milk at school on Fridays.

Antonio very seldom has friends over for a meal or a snack, because his mother can't afford it. As Carolina explains, 'Er, because at their age they can eat a lot. I have more visits for the little one. Er, because they eat three meatballs and a bit of spaghetti, then they are full.' She goes on: 'But er, no, we haven't had any visits from his mates here for dinner. We've had visits once or twice with popcorn. Popcorn and a movie. And soda. But dinner for his mates, I am unfortunately not able to do this. Because they eat a lot at that age.'

Antonio is in the chess club at school and is a leader at the youth club, which he goes to every Friday and where he hangs out and has a good time with his friends. He does not eat at the fast food outlets and petrol stations where his friends buy food. He declines to give a reason to the researcher: 'I don't know because I am mostly not out with friends.' Discussing the 'chicken shop' vignette (showing a group of children purchasing food, and one apparently unable to do so), he says that his reason for not buying such food is that it is unhealthy. Antonio thereby avoids the embarrassment of admitting he cannot afford it:

Interviewer: No. I would guess that your mates like to go to places like that rather often to buy food?

Antonio: Er yes, I think that [they] think that it is okay, but I think it is nice that they think it is okay. But I don't think that's all right for me, really, because I don't like to go into those kebab shops because the only thing I smell at once is like fried food and everything and think, 'That is very good to smell that smell and eat and stuff.' But it isn't healthy for you, in general.

Interviewer: Yeah, right, but do you try to avoid joining them when they …

Antonio: No, I try to join them, but try to avoid eating.

Asked whether he worries about money, Antonio again decides against admitting he does not have any: 'I don't care much about money for myself and everything. I do care that mum and [sister] have enough for everything.' He then relents a little: 'I would like to have a bit more money sometimes to er ... and I know that I have to earn it myself.' When asked whether he asks his father or stepfather for money, he says, 'I can ask, but I'm not the type who asks for things actually.' Like some other children in the study, Antonio moderates and plays down his needs.

Like other mothers, Carolina does her best to make up for not being able to provide for Antonio's friends, or for not giving him money to eat out. She invents special activities to do with him at home. For example, she has a 'series date' with him every Wednesday, 'with popcorn, even though it is very cheap popcorn', when they watch an episode of a sci-fi film they both like. These activities are clearly designed not only to compensate Antonio for the absence of material things but to create a positive shared sense of well-being; 'then we do as if we have lots of money and stuff and as long as you feel rich it does not matter how poor you are'.

Discussion

All the low-income families discussed in the chapter, and most of the families in the study, described leading restricted social lives, especially in relation to offering food in the home and eating outside the home. Although commensality is part of everyday life, these families could rarely afford to invite friends and extended family to their homes and in many cases felt unable to accept hospitality from others because they could not reciprocate. Mothers were particularly concerned about the ill effects on their children of not being able to invite the children's friends to their home. But they could not afford the cost of the food that, according to societal expectations, they and their children felt they ought to offer. Many parents also said they could not provide their children with sufficient money for them to participate in peer groups that would purchase food when they were out and about in their communities, a normal activity, particularly among the young teenagers who were the focus of our study, especially in Norway and the UK.

In this chapter we have drawn a distinction between families who experience poverty and deprivation as a long-term state and those in which a fall in fortunes has arisen because of a recent and sudden personal, family or societal change. The first three families discussed had lived on low incomes for several years. The parents were accustomed and, to some extent, resigned to not having a social life of their own.

However, they were concerned about their children missing out. Parents who could not offer their children what other parents provided and what their children expected were particularly vulnerable to shame. Lauren, a mother in a UK coastal town, explained how it went against her 'northern blood' to be unable to offer toast to her son's friends when they visited or to buy her children an ice cream when she was out with them. Helia, a mother in Lisbon, was sad she could not afford special food for her son's birthday or meet his desire for a slice of pizza when he asked for one at the shopping centre. Eylo's father in Oslo was particularly concerned, the family having come to Norway as refugees, that his children should not be 'different' from their peers or feel in any way left out or deprived. He took them to McDonald's at weekends, sacrificing his own social life and adding to the debt on the credit card. He said it was less important that he and his wife never ate out and had had to cut back on entertaining adult friends at home.

In the same way, the second set of families who had more recently experienced reductions in their income and living standards were concerned about their children missing out on social life with their peers. However, for these parents, sustaining a social life and customary food practices seemed to be a way of maintaining a semblance of 'normality' for their children that was associated with their former middle-class social status. Although expectations were higher, they were better resourced to withstand shame when they could not afford their customary social participation (Benjamin 2020).

Some parents drew on social and cultural capital connected to their former middle-class status to ensure that their children lived 'normal' lives and were no 'different' from their peers. A striking instance of this is a situation described by Marian, who lives in London and organised a birthday party for her son, who had invited 10 children. She made use of free local facilities, timed the party not to coincide with mealtimes and negotiated with a restaurant to use their space to serve the birthday cake she had made. On a more modest scale, suggesting how small 'pleasures' help people to 'get by' psychologically (Tirado 2014),[3] Sofia in Lisbon sought to compensate her children by indulging them from time to time. She did this by preparing special dishes, for example, at birthdays and other celebrations such as a first holy communion, or by spending money on fast food as a reward for good behaviour. Likewise, Carolina, who lives outside Oslo, tried to make up for not being able to allow her son to invite friends home by arranging special times she would spend with him, for example, watching an episode of a TV series together and eating popcorn.

Many children in the study seemed well aware of the financial constraints on their parents and expressed concern about them. Sofia's two children worried about their parents having to shield them from knowing their problems, about the parents having no money for themselves and about the long-term consequences of their situation, for example, the risk of losing the family home. Miguel described worrying about his parents and sisters rather than himself when there was little money to spend. What is striking is how some children played down or denied that they were missing out themselves. Lauren's son, Calum, supplied a number of 'excuses' for what amounts to the family's social exclusion. Poignantly, he said he 'forgot' to offer friends a drink on the rare occasions that they came to his house. About spending money at the local shop, he said, 'I don't like going that way,' and about not using the bus to go to school, 'I miss my stop.' At the same time, many young people were clearly aware of differences in access to money among their peer groups – between those who had more money to spend or possessed luxurious or fashionable items and others, like themselves, whose parents could not afford such expenditure.

In this section of the book we have examined the effects of low income on families' social participation. For significant numbers of parents and children in all the families, social participation was compromised both inside and outside the home. We have compared families whose fall in income is more recent, and who in the past were accustomed to a higher standard of living, with families for whom poverty has been a long-term condition. In both sets of families there are parents who try to protect children from social exclusion, albeit we have shown how parents who benefit from a middle-class habitus have more resources to draw upon. Going out and socialising with peers is part of the process whereby young people exercise their growing independence. But, as some of the teenagers in this chapter suggest, they moderate their expectations out of a concern for their parents' financial constraints and worries. Although the aim of the chapter has not been to analyse the health effects of a lack of social participation, the effects of social exclusion for parents and children are consequential for mental health, as became clear in several of the cases.

Notes

1. The Social Fund is a government scheme to help people with expenses that are difficult to meet on a low income. Loans or advances for household equipment can be applied for but they have to be repaid.
2. The children did not take photographs at school, because the mother worried the camera might be lost or broken.
3. 'A vivid picture of this strain is painted by Linda Tirado (2014) in her blog and book, *Hand to Mouth*, where she also brings out how the purchase of small pleasures, which might be castigated as imprudent budgeting, contribute to getting by psychologically' (Lister 2015, 148).

Section 4
Formal and informal support

As the previous chapters have shown, the wages and benefits of most families we studied, were insufficient to feed all members of the family properly, and some families received neither form of income and could barely feed themselves at all. Chapter 4 demonstrates that a low income and food insecurity are associated, but the association is neither simple nor universal; there are higher levels of income poverty but lower levels of food insecurity among families in Portugal than in the UK. Among the factors that may mediate the relationship between low income and food poverty are the availability and use of non-income resources. In times of austerity and shrinking state support, help from civil society organisations, family and friends is likely to become more important to low-income households' livelihoods. However, as we shall demonstrate, even where formal and informal support is available, it does not follow that families enjoy a standard of living that, in Western societies, is socially and culturally acceptable. Families remain poor. Indeed, reliance on such support can further stigmatise and marginalise those who are materially deprived.

Although the welfare state in post-war Europe was established to redistribute resources and entitle citizens to a decent standard of living, there has always been a 'mixed economy of welfare' consisting of the state, voluntary action and support from family and social networks (Polanyi 1944; Bradley 2009). Historically, charity has played, and continues to play, an important role in addressing the immediate needs of those in poverty, advocating for their rights and holding governments to account. Portugal's young welfare state and the continued importance of the Catholic Church in this country mean that charitable support coexists alongside, and is to some extent integrated with, state support. In contrast, welfare retrenchment in the UK means that charitable support is increasingly filling gaps in a greatly reduced welfare safety net

(Lambie-Mumford 2017). In both countries, since the financial crisis and implementation of austerity measures, there has been a growth in 'food aid', that is, the direct provision of food to people in need. In Norway, as in other Scandinavian countries, a strong welfare state is accompanied by a discourse that there is no need for food aid (Salonen and Silvasti 2019), but NGOs that feed families in crises do exist, particularly in the cities (Borch and Kjaerness 2016).

The sociologist Talcott Parsons (1943) and some economists have argued that strong welfare states 'crowd out' the more informal support provided by extended family and friends, and that weak welfare provision is compensated for by a society that integrates its members within a logic of reciprocity (Mauss 1990) through informal networks of mutual support. Although this hypothesis is reflected in influential welfare state typologies, it has been challenged by family sociologists and is not supported by sociological research (Motel-Klingebiel et al. 2005). Indeed, the converse has been found; for example, in Scandinavian countries a good deal of intergenerational transfers take place despite their generous welfare states (Albertini et al. 2007). Furthermore, it has been observed that in Portugal, a Mediterranean or family-oriented welfare state in which reciprocity and informal social networks are assumed to be central, welfare provision can reinforce existing social inequalities rather than compensate for them (Wall et al. 2001, 213). Wall and colleagues (2001), who analysed survey data about the importance of informal support networks to families with children in Portugal, conclude that extended kinship does not play a significant role in support. What assistance is provided flows mainly from (mothers') parents. Moreover, they found that needy families with low educational levels and a less favourable class position have the lowest levels of informal support, whereas the wealthier classes benefit from more diversified, sustained and higher volumes of support (Wall et al. 2001, 230).

Nonetheless, although support from family, friends and charities may be of limited use in eradicating low income, and indeed can perpetuate inequalities, families may turn to informal sources of support on occasions of severe need to mitigate its worst effects. Help from social networks can therefore act as 'an important safety net' for low-income families (Shorthouse 2013; Hill et al. 2020, 3). Alternatively, turning to family and friends in a more limited way may be part of everyday practices and patterns of reciprocity. This support can take many forms, including money (gifts and loans), care (child and elder care), resources in kind (food, clothes, etc.) and emotional support (listening and advising) (Gosling 2008; Daly and Kelly 2015, 110). Recent research from the UK suggests the increased importance of this 'resource pool' in a more precarious socioeconomic environment of labour market insecurity and austerity (Hill et al. 2020, 3–4). However, it is also the case that 'maintaining family privacy in the locality or neighbourhood may be paramount in situations of difficulty' (Daly and Kelly 2015, 137), and so some prefer to 'keep themselves to themselves' and seek help outside the immediate family or community to avoid stigma and shame (McKee 1987; Chase and Walker 2012). People may also withdraw from social networks or be excluded from them because they are unable to satisfy the 'burden of reciprocity' (Offer 2012; and see Chapter 8).

One type of support that can directly affect the diets of children in low-income families is free or subsidised school meals. Children spend a large proportion of their lives in school, and children in the UK consume around a third of their food and drink during the school day (Nelson 2004). Though not usually considered part of formal or informal support, school food can make an important contribution to children's overall diet and has the potential to iron out some of the differences among children in what they eat at home (for example, Oostindjer et al. 2017). For families on low incomes, the financial contribution of free and subsidised school meals may be significant (Penne and Goedemé 2020). Furthermore, since schools are public eating places in which group membership is fostered, school meals have the potential to facilitate social inclusion through institutional commensality (Grignon 2001). School meals are therefore the focus of Chapter 10, in which we consider their role in moderating the effects of poverty on children's diets and food practices among our three groups of low-income families in the UK, Portugal and Norway.

Before that, in Chapter 9, we consider how far the parents in the study turned toward a range of sources of support to help them to provide adequate food for their children. We have selected two-parent families from the Portuguese sample, which demonstrates the significance of agriculture for some families' food provisioning. Though not typical of the families in our sample, they represent a contrast to families in the other two countries. The other four cases, in the UK and Norway, exemplify the disproportionate number of lone-mother families in the study; three of these families are migrants, a status that constrains access to support from family networks with respect to food provisioning. Together, the four families demonstrate the ways in which charity, friends and the state comprise ports of call in the process of managing the precarity of getting by.

9
Charity, family and friends

We begin by examining the types of extra-household resources, in kind as well as financial, that families draw upon to help feed themselves. In particular, we consider support provided by charities and assistance given by extended family, friends and neighbours. Six families are then described, with a focus on the circumstances in which the families make use of such support. As the chapter shows, support from these different sources takes different forms (money, food, advice, emotional support) and varies in the circumstances and frequency with which it is provided (ongoing regular support, emergency support in times of crisis).

Table 9.1 shows the types of extra-household resources that families in the study drew on to help feed their families in the 12 months before interview. Formal support includes two types. The first covers 'direct providers' of food assistance and includes food banks as well as organisations that provide meals. The second includes organisations like charities that provide financial and other assistance such as grants for particular items (a washing machine, for example) or occasions (Christmas, Eid, birthdays, crises) as well as advice like debt counselling. In Norway and Portugal, but no longer in the UK, such support may be sought through local authorities (municipalities) and is funded by the welfare state.[1] Two sub-categories of informal support, which are no less substantial, are provided by family and by friends and neighbours.

The Portuguese families are most likely to rely on both formal and informal sources of assistance in feeding their families. Almost two-thirds (26/45) say they turn to a variety of food aid organisations, including ones with a long history of providing food for 'the poor'. A few (6/45) seek other types of formal support, mainly from churches or the local authority or council, to meet additional or unexpected expenses.

It is striking that the Portuguese families report using familial support three times more often (30/45) than they report turning to

Table 9.1 Formal and informal support used by families*: qualitative study.

		Portugal	UK	Norway
Formal	Food banks and other food charities	26	12	17
	Other (non-food) support: money, debt advice or other assistance	6	11	15
Informal	Family (excluding non-resident fathers)	30	20	16
	Friends and neighbours	9	19	14
Total (N = 133)		45	45	43

* Totals exceed the size of the samples: families may draw on multiple sources of support.

neighbours (9/45). This is a clear difference from the cases in the UK and Norway, where it appears to be as common to draw on the support of friends and neighbours as to draw on that of family. In almost half (19/45) of the families in Portugal, providing and partaking in meals with extended family, including grown-up children, aunts, uncles and grandparents, was something that happened regularly. In many families it was common for children to eat at their grandparents' homes (see Figure 9.1), whereas this happened in few cases in the UK and Norway.

What Table 9.1 does not show is that a handful of families in Portugal also rely on foods that they grow themselves in their gardens or glean from agricultural land or are given to them by members of their family or community. In a couple of cases, produce from the land is given as payment in kind by their employers. (One Portuguese family has been selected for discussion in this chapter to demonstrate this pattern.) In the UK[2] just one family relied on fresh vegetables from the grandfather's allotment to supplement their diet. There were no such cases in the Norwegian sample. One family in Oslo admitted to eating foods gleaned from 'dumpster diving', a different form of self-provisioning (Figure 9.2), but this was unusual. During the kitchen tour, Grethe, an ethnic Norwegian lone mother who led an 'alternative lifestyle', explained that the meat in the freezer was 'actually dumpster food, which we received a whole bag of from [former lodger], who lived with us before. They go dumpster diving in the city. Lots of fine food, really.'

In the UK, more families reported occasions when they turned to informal support (39/45), including family and friends, than reported seeking formal support (23/45). Only a minority used food banks (12/45).

(a)

(b)

Figure 9.1 Saturday breakfast (a) and lunch (b) ('chicken with boiled potatoes, green peas and everything else') at Dalila's grandmother's home (Source: 'Dalila').

Figure 9.2 Frozen meat from 'dumpster diving', given by former lodger to Grethe's family (Source: Silje Skuland).

Around the same proportion (11/45) rely on formal support, including help to navigate a complex and changing benefits system and to access debt advice services. About the same number turned to family (20/45) as did to friends and neighbours (19/45).

By contrast, in Norway more than a third of the families (15/43) reported occasions when they turned to the social security office, NAV, for financial help. This included help with debt repayment plans to private companies, and more often for one-off payments to meet unexpected or unusual expenses. They also turned to the local municipality for help with paying for children's and family activities. As in Portugal, these requests could be turned down (15 applied but four said their application was rejected). About the same proportion (17/43) reported having turned to charity for direct food aid in the past year. Given that poverty in Norway is highly related to migrant status (see Chapter 1), it is unsurprising that a minority turned to family (16/43). As in the UK, around the same proportion (14/43) turned to friends and neighbours.

Self-provisioning in an extended family in the countryside outside Lisbon: Jo and Alexis

This white Portuguese family lives in the countryside outside Lisbon and depends for food largely on self-provisioning from the mother's work on the land. The mother, Jo, and the father have an unemployed 20-year-old son and a younger son, Alexis, who is 12. Their house is fronted by a small courtyard that serves the grandmother's house also. The grandmother, a widow, lives on a very low income; she has never been in formal employment or paid taxes. The interview was conducted at a bus stop near their small house, because Jo said that her husband did not want anyone inside.

Around 10 years ago, Jo lost her job in a local quarry when it closed. After that, she worked for a short period as a cleaner, but because she suffers from severe short-sightedness her employers complained about her work and sacked her. Jo now farms local plots of land that belong to neighbours and relatives. In return, the family gets a share of the produce (eggs and vegetables) that Jo sells for extra income. Jo's husband works full time as a mason for the local council. A van picks him up and brings him home each day. On Saturdays, he helps Jo with the heavier farming tasks.

The family budget depends almost entirely on the father's income (around €700 a month, including child benefit). Jo worries a great deal about the lack of money: 'It affects everything – with the nerves, with sadness, with [crying] … with a will to do nothing. Sometimes one gets the wish to walk away and disappear.' The family food budget is very stretched: their expenditure on food is only a quarter of the FBS for a family of this type, around €150 per month. The parents and their children rarely eat meat or fish and cannot afford to spend money on food outside the home. As they live in the countryside and have no car, transport is difficult: they depend on a motorcycle with a trailer which is in poor condition. They find the local village shop too expensive. When Jo goes shopping once a month she has to rely on her husband or eldest son to drive while she hides in the trailer; to travel this way is illegal. They shop around in different communities and supermarkets to find the cheapest products. Jo also described problems with cooking. She has to boil water on an open fire in the yard because only one flame of the cooker is working and she cannot afford a new one.

Besides Jo's own food production, the family is helped by friends supplying second-hand clothes for the boys. The grandmother also plays her part by caring for Alexis in the school holidays when Jo is out working in the fields. Alexis often eats at his grandmother's, but Jo supplies the ingredients; 'She prepares the things for him.' The two households pool their resources at Christmas, Easter and birthdays: they each bring a contribution to the celebratory meals that are held at the grandmother's house. 'One gives the cod fish, the other one the potatoes, the other the olive oil and grandmother does the cooking.' Perhaps the fact that Alexis appreciates the food provided at school says something about food scarcity at home, especially the lack of fish and meat: 'In the canteen there are only good things.' However, he says that he never goes without enough to eat.

Family help and a food bank in a village outside Lisbon: Maria and Tomas

This white Portuguese family consists of two parents, Maria and her husband (at the second interview both were in work), and two children, a boy, Tomas, age 12, who was interviewed, and a girl aged eight. Two years before, they moved to the rural area outside Lisbon in order to find somewhere quieter to live and closer to the father's workplace – the bus garage, where he works full-time shifts as a tour bus driver. They went through a time of hardship when Maria was sick for six months and unable to work. Maria used to do night shifts in a factory. At the second interview (some weeks after the first) she had found a new job in a stationer's. The family live in privately rented housing (taking 30 per cent of their income,

€1,150 a month). Tomas receives free school meals. The family spends half of the FBS for a family of this type on food, around €250 per month.

They regularly interact with their extended family at weekends, often eating together. When Maria was unemployed, they depended on regular support from their parents and also on a food bank. In the school holidays and on weekends the children stay with their grandparents and regularly eat with them, as many of Tomas's photos show. Pride of place is a photo of a special Saturday lunch at his grandparents' (Figure 9.3). Tomas declares that the lunch was given by his grandfather for 'the whole family', the cooking having been done by his grandmother and great-grandmother with a little bit of help from his uncle. The food consisted of 'pizzas, croquettes, rissoles, samoorsas [mispronounced] … chicken, jelly, a thing with tomato and cheese … pies … I think it's watermelon there, no, it's smoked ham rolls, cheese' and a meatloaf as the main dish. 'Everything was prepared inside the house and then carried to the yard where the meal took place.'

The family's food expenditure is just under half of the FBS, around €200–300 a month. During Maria's sick leave the household depended on money and clothes, as well as food, from her mother-in-law. 'My mother-in-law helps in terms of money every month … she gives maybe €50 or so … she buys clothes for [the children] as well because she likes

Figure 9.3 Saturday lunch for the whole family (Source: 'Tomas').

to go to the food market, she likes to bring vegetables on weekends for us and fruit.' Maria also resorts to visiting a food bank once a month.

Maria describes being on a low income as stigmatising, especially after they moved to the new area:

> I think there is a little bit of stigma towards people with low incomes … I have also lived here for a short time. I still don't get along well with all the parents and the people in the area. But I see there are, at least here, that there are little groups of who is better off, who is not.

Although Tomas says he has never gone without enough to eat, he is aware of the family struggles. He usually accompanies his mother to the food bank and helps carry the bags. He also spoke of his feelings about receiving food assistance: 'I'm glad … but perhaps mother and father aren't so glad, because it would be better … although it's a great help, it would be better to have a … hum … how do you say it?! Not having that help … would mean … we didn't need that help so much.' In short, Tomas would prefer not to be 'in need' and yet is glad help is there.

Reciprocity, community and formal intervention in a UK coastal town: Maggie and Jordan

This white British family consists of a lone mother and her 15-year-old son, Jordan, the study child. They are in continual difficulty. They rely on neighbours, whose support they try to reciprocate, as well as on formal services. Originally from a city in the Midlands, Maggie is estranged from her family. They live in a one-bedroom flat in the basement of a large, multi-dwelling Victorian house in the most deprived part of the run-down seaside town. Jordan has the bedroom while Maggie sleeps on the sofa in the open-plan kitchen/living room. Her elder son, aged 17, who suffers from a psychiatric disorder and has violent outbursts, lives in a one-bedroom flat next door. They have lived in this building for about a year.

Maggie is not in employment. She left school at 13 to care for her mother and has no qualifications. She has worked in many different jobs in the past, mainly cleaning for agencies, but her elder son's unpredictable behaviour and her own mental health difficulties make it difficult for her to get into work, though she would like to: 'I can't go nowhere.' She says her caseworker at the Job Centre has been 'lenient' with her, not forcing her into jobs she would find difficult to manage with her home life.

Maggie's income works out as around £350 per month, made up of £119 per fortnight (Jobseeker's Allowance) and £82 every four weeks (child benefit for Jordan). Jordan receives free school meals. He says he gets an allowance of £2.60 per day. Maggie has a lot of debt (around £14,000) for overpayments on one of her benefits and she is paying off fines amounting to more than £1,000 that her eldest son incurred when he was prosecuted for assault. Her expenditure on food is just under half of the FBS at around £30–40 a week to feed the three of them plus the dogs and a cat. It varies depending on what is left after paying for utilities for her flat and her son's next door: 'Gas and electric is like primary, so food always comes after that.' They live hand to mouth. Maggie shops every day at a small grocer's at the top of the road which mostly sells highly processed, long-life food. 'I did used to [do a bigger shop] and then they go through it like the Tasmanian devil, so it's not happening no more.' She says she doesn't bother with 'sell by' dates: 'I've always brought my kids up "if it looks and smells okay, then eat it".' Their meals are generally based on cheap forms of carbohydrate such as pasta and fresh or tinned potatoes, plus donations from neighbours. Jordan says they have 'gone down to beans on toast' at times and that 'we've all just had to make do with what we did have'.

Help from friends and neighbours is critical: 'Sometimes we've gone without and hopefully the neighbours sort it out, because the neighbours help a lot, so … they all help a lot bless them … to be fair the block's kind of like that.' The regularity of this help from her neighbours is underscored by reciprocating in other ways and building goodwill. Maggie does a lot of 'good deeds' such as cleaning, looking after people and popping to the shops for people. She acts as a spokesperson for the other tenants to the landlady when things go wrong in the building. She looks after one little girl and, in return, her mother will 'just top up my electric or she might go and put some gas on or she just does a shop in general and then she'll bring it down for me'. She cleans for another neighbour and says, 'He'll always make sure we've got dinner or gas and electric or … they don't pay me with cash, they just pay me with other … they, like, help me out in life rather than … which is better.' Maggie has learned to accept help, but she always offers to return the favour: 'I'll help them out in any other way that I possibly can.'

Jordan: They [neighbours] just see that we're struggling and think they do so much to help, maybe they need something back.

Interviewer: Yeah, what do you think about that sort of help you get from them?

Jordan: I think it's nice to see people still standing up for each other.

Interviewer: Yeah, it's good.

Jordan: It proves the country ain't gone completely down the drain yet.

Maggie has received a lot of formal support (as well as interventions) from various agencies. She had the 'full six' food parcels last year from a community centre and regularly has lunch at the Salvation Army. She is being helped with a current problem with tax credits by the community centre and the Job Centre and a Families-in-Need officer there. She also has a support worker (at a social housing organisation) who helps her sort out her benefits and housing when she is struggling to get on top of things.

Maggie says she does not feel 'shy or ashamed' to ask for help. 'I've worked all my life and we all … you don't realise how easy it is to get into a position that you can't kind of get out of.'[3] However, Maggie feels judged by social services and angry at their attitude to her situation; she would rather work but can't and says that the benefits she gets are 'a pittance'. Despite the help she receives, she goes without meals and gives her children less to eat than they would like. For his part, Jordan says that his mum is 'a really good cook' but that what they eat depends on whether they have the ingredients: 'My mum can make quite a lot … if she's got what to make it out of.' Asked whether there are times when there isn't enough for an evening meal, Jordan agrees that 'there has been a couple of times like that' and admits to there being times 'when there was no food in the cupboards whatsoever to have anything and you just have to hope, like Mum said'.

Formal support in London's inner city: Makaya and Danisha

Makaya, a black British lone mother, has three children: a daughter, Danisha (the study child), age 11, a five-year-old and a baby of 11 months. They live in the inner London borough. The two youngest are disabled. Makaya has been through a series of major life crises in recent years involving domestic violence, the loss of her job and home, and spiralling debt. When she became depressed she isolated herself and her family until the health and social services intervened. She eventually turned to agencies such as the Citizens Advice Bureau and to her extended family for help.

Makaya is currently not employed. The household income is around £185 per week, made up of Income Support, child tax credit and child benefit. Danisha receives free school meals. The family expenditure on food, around £35 per week, is less than half of the FBS for a family of this type.

A few years ago, Makaya was hospitalised after being violently assaulted by her partner. She and her children had to leave their home and go to a refuge. They lost many of their belongings in the process. Eventually she was allocated the two-bedroom, privately rented flat they now live in; it is too small and there is no bath or floor coverings. Makaya stopped work around the same time. She had been working in a security firm on a proper employment contract but decided to move to a zero-hours contract because it appeared to offer flexibility. However, she did not realise that when she took time off she would not be entitled to sick or holiday pay.

When she stopped work Makaya did not apply for benefits and they lived off her savings. Beginning to worry what would happen when the savings were used up, she sought advice at the Job Centre. This was unhelpful: 'This really killed it for me, like you know enquire about how I can get on benefits ... well, she said, "Well the first thing you need to do is to sell your car." I was at a point in my life where I was, just like, "I can't. I've had enough."' Makaya could not sacrifice her car because she needs it to transport her younger children to their frequent hospital appointments. She also mentions difficulty dealing with the complexity of the benefits system, in particular child tax credit; she was told she had to pay back £2,000 in child tax credit.

In the few years since she stopped work Makaya has accumulated a number of debts: rent arrears, car-parking fines, a Social Fund loan incurred some years ago in order to help her get back to work, and an overpayment of tax credits. When she first got into debt she went to a commercial loan company because the children were hungry and the car had broken down. This loan increased her debt even further. In desperation, she turned to the Citizens Advice Bureau for help, which was able to reduce the weekly debt repayments. When, eventually, Makaya was receiving all the state benefits due to her, she found that she was still having to pay back 'every debt collector you could think about'.

Makaya routinely depends on her 11-year-old daughter, Danisha, who acts as a carer for her younger siblings and who helps with cooking, making up bottles for the baby, washing up, and keeping an eye on the children.

In extremis, when Makaya's youngest was a newborn, she turned to the support of extended family. She tells a story about a time when her depression was bad and there was no food in the house and she had to resort to asking a cousin to take her shopping because she was expecting a visit from the health visitor:

> I said, 'Take me shopping please because I ain't got no food in my house and the health visitor's coming round and I need to at least be able to feed my baby.' She goes, 'How long has this been going …?' This was going on for like two, three months and it just got worse and worse and worse and literally when there was nothing for like two, three weeks it was like, 'Oh God what do I do?' But by then, once the health visitor come in it's like, I spoke to her about certain things and then she got the social worker and … and then everything just started, putting me towards the food bank, the baby bank and then, yeah.

Formal support was then forthcoming and Makaya received help from different charities, including a food bank. The health visitor arranged for Makaya to receive Healthy Start vouchers that she could use to buy milk and fresh fruit and vegetables. Makaya was grateful for the food and the advice she got from the food bank about ways of making food last. However, it has since closed down. Because the youngest child needs to be kept warm, she has recently applied to a charity for money for carpets.

Although Danisha mentions they visited a food bank over the summer, she does not say she has gone without food. She says there have been times when there was not much to eat, playing down the matter: 'I don't really want those things. I was asking for things that weren't here.'

Both of the families we discuss next are new migrants to Norway and have no family members to turn to. The first family relies on the social security agency, NAV, for financial advice and other types of support. The second family turns to a local charity, the Poor House, as it is called, and relies on mutual support with friends.

Help from the social security office in Oslo: Bilan and Elim

This next family's experience illustrates the significance of the Norwegian social security system, NAV, in providing discretionary support to those unable to access the benefits that most Norwegians are entitled to under the universalist welfare system. Bilan is a lone mother who migrated from Somalia 17 years ago. A widow, she lost her husband, an engineer, to cancer three years ago. She has nine children, three of whom were born in Norway. Four of her children are still at home, including Elim, a 14-year-old boy, who was interviewed. Bilan is currently attending a basic Norwegian education course, having left school at a very young age in Somalia to get married. She expects to complete the course in a year. The family live in a three-bedroom apartment in Oslo.

Bilan receives NOK 4,450 per month in a widow's pension and NOK 3,880 in child benefit for three of the children; the eldest son who lives at home is now 19 and no longer eligible for child benefit. Rent for the apartment is paid directly by NAV. Bilan also receives around NOK 10,000 in financial support from NAV. Her older children are all in professional jobs, having been helped with their schooling by their father. Bilan mentions help with transport from her grown-up children – for example, an adult daughter who regularly takes her shopping in her car.

Bilan budgets day to day with great care and says she never runs out of money or food. The food budget is just under two-thirds of the FBS for a family of this type, around NOK 5,240 per month. She believes in providing the children with a healthy diet and purchases wholegrain bread and plenty of vegetables and fruit of a superior quality, even though they are expensive. In order to manage within her food budget, Bilan buys meat in bulk and at a low price. Usually she goes to Sweden once a month or every second month or asks a friend to shop there for her. 'I don't like to travel. Sometimes I ask my girlfriend, "Can you buy hamburgers or sausages, salami?"' Besides Halal meat products, Bilan buys spreads for the bread in the Swedish supermarkets. She compares prices between the foreign shop nearby and the Halal butcher in Sweden: 'One kilo of minced meat [costs] 120 or 130, and there [Sweden] it is 60.'

The family is reliant on additional help from NAV and other municipal services. For example, the washing machine was bought by NAV, although Bilan chipped in with NOK 1,000. The family is going on a four-day holiday to a Norwegian summer house organised by the municipality. Although Bilan manages big expenses by applying to NAV for help, she also mentions very occasionally borrowing money from a friend: 'I borrow only a thousand sometimes,' she says.

A central theme in Bilan's interview is the need to conform to NAV's bureaucratic rules, one of which is that housing is allocated on the basis of family size. When her eldest child reached 18, the allowance was reviewed. This is based on the assumption that 18-year-olds move out of the family home and the family finds a smaller apartment. At several points in the interview Bilan expresses concern about the possibility that NAV may stop paying the rent altogether. A problem seems to have arisen because Bilan has not provided all the documentation necessary to demonstrate she is still attending her course. She also notes in passing that she had problems with NAV earlier in the year when she needed some new furniture and was turned down. In the end, her adult son gave her his old sofa. She worries, 'just about the rent or sometimes [I need to buy] a sofa or a problem. I ask and fill out form, and … No!' What upsets her most are all the forms she is required to fill in and the constant worry of rejection.

Her son, Elim, does not say in his interview that he has experienced going without food, but on the questionnaire he ticks that he sometimes goes to school hungry when there is not enough food at home. However, this may have been because the interview was conducted during Ramadan.

Regular food aid in central Oslo: Khava and Madina

The final case in the chapter is a mother who migrated to Norway from the Caucasus. Khava, a lone parent, came to Norway with her husband 15 years ago. Her daughter Madina, the study child, is 16 and has type 1 diabetes. Khava has three other daughters, aged 20, 18 and 12. She is divorced and has been ostracised by her family. This limits the family members she can turn to for help. Since she has little family support to draw on, Khava is dependent on food aid from a charity and some help from friends.

Khava's husband was abusive. She reported him to the police and she and her three youngest daughters went to live with her sister and her family. Her ex-husband has since been imprisoned. The family moved around for a while until Khava and two of her daughters found the small, privately rented two-bedroom apartment in central Oslo where they now live. She and her daughters have had mental health problems as a result of the domestic violence to which they were subjected.

Because of racism and her health problems, Khava has found it hard to get a job. She used to have two part-time jobs, but she has not worked since they moved to Oslo. She is trying to complete a course in healthcare. For the past few months, Khava has received unemployment benefit, which amounts to 66 per cent of the wages she received when she was working. Lone parents in Norway are eligible for child benefit for one more child than they actually have. As a mother of two dependent children (under 18 years old), Khava therefore receives child benefit for three children – the two daughters who are under 18 plus one more. This adds up to NOK 2,900 a month. The father, who is in prison, pays Khava alimony of NOK 2,300 a month. Their total income amounts to NOK 25,000 a month.

The rent is the major outgoing; housing costs are NOK 16,000 a month. There is also expenditure for Madina's schooling (books, travel, extra classes) which amounts to around NOK 1,500 a month. This would normally have been met by a scholarship provided by the state. However, there are problems with the paperwork because of the father's prison status.

Khava has to estimate what she spends on food, saying it varies according to what they have left after paying other bills. Her food expenditure is around NOK 7,540 a month, around three-quarters of the FBS for a family of this type. Khava is mindful of food prices and tries to buy food from the cheapest shops. Halal meat is bought in Sweden. Every so often, Khava and one of the daughters go to a part of Oslo where there are many cheap foreign shops and fill several bags with vegetables like onions and potatoes. Khava says it is 'expensive to eat healthy'. They always have flour, but not always fruit or vegetables: 'But it isn't always that we have ... For example, before school started, I could not afford to buy vegetables and fruit that they wanted and prepare like fresh salad or watermelon.'

Khava says she sometimes borrows food and money from those members of her family she is in touch with and from friends. She has turned to charity for food; she has visited the Poor House several times and gets food from the Salvation Army once a month. She would also like to be able to visit another food bank each week, but this one requires an admission card, which she currently lacks. She is also unsure if she fits the food bank's requirements. The family regularly eats at Khava's sister-in-law's home. Madina mentions that she had found it hard to make friends and to 'fit in', especially since she cannot afford 'cool' clothes like her friends or to join in their activities. She ticks 'sometimes' to the question about going to bed hungry because there is not enough food at home and says she eats vegetables every day, but fruit only two to four days per week.

Discussion

The three countries in which the families live are all modern welfare states, but the mix of support for low-income families they provide reflects their different histories and social policies, including their policy responses to the 2008 global financial crisis. As outlined in Chapter 1, in the UK the retrenchment of the welfare state under the guise of 'austerity' is combined with a highly complex, bureaucratic and impersonal bene-fits regime (Alston 2019), with charities playing a major role in medi-ating between individuals and 'the system' and helping them navigate and access welfare and other support. In Norway and Portugal, the state and the municipality play an important role in the lives of low-income families. Although entitlement to social security is tightly regulated in Norway, access to additional financial support is available through local social security offices. Requests for financial help are subject to strict rules and assessed by officials who exercise their own discretion in the support they make available. Consequently, many people feel ashamed to ask.

In Portugal, the government has given some support to organ-isations providing food assistance in the context of austerity measures imposed on the country by external agencies. In the UK, 'emergency' responses to rising food poverty have been left to a growing food charity sector that overwhelmingly operates independently of the welfare state. In Norway, agencies like the Poor House comprise a residual and inade-quate resource and are regarded to some extent as an invisible stain on the public conscience (Chapter 1).

The process of mutual support between family and friends has been conceptualised as negotiation rather than obligation or duty (Finch 1989; Finch and Mason 1993). Similarly, the search for and acceptance of sup-port needs to be understood as guided rather than determined by social norms; in Bourdieu's terms, a 'feel for the game' rather than conformity to 'rules' (Bourdieu 1990, 64). Moral sensibilities enter into this process; decisions to ask for help are influenced by fear of the reputational risk of being seen to be dependent on others (Finch 1989; McKee 1987). The nature of the need and the amount of help required also influence the decisions of individuals to turn to others.

In many social situations help is provided and reciprocated routinely in the course of everyday life, as we have shown in the cases of the two Portuguese families in this chapter, who eat with members of their extended family and draw upon grandparents' help in feeding their children. In contrast, the migrant families in Norway lacked family networks and the opportunities they provide for everyday social exchanges. Housing relocation is a reason why some families in the UK have no relatives nearby and so have to turn to friends, neighbours, charity or the state.

Extra-household support may also be called upon less routinely, in times of crisis. As Finch and Mason (1993) have argued, people find it easier to call for help in these circumstances when commitments have developed *over time*. Two of the families discussed in this chapter, like other families in the book, have experienced several crises in their lives. That have disrupted their family networks, making it difficult to exchange resources or turn to relatives for help. Some are reluctant to seek help from relatives or friends who are as impoverished as they are. The dire situation of Makaya in the UK is instructive, demonstrating both her reluctance to turn to a relative for help and also the personal reputational risk she fears if she is seen to turn to health and public services for help.

Of all the families discussed in this chapter, those in Portugal rely most on both formal and informal sources to help feed their families. Some depend in part on their own food production or engage in in-kind exchanges with friends and neighbours. One mother, Jo, farms local plots of land that belong to her neighbours and relatives and sells the produce. Tomas and his parents, who also live in the countryside, rely routinely on Tomas's grandparents, with whom they pool their limited resources in order to get by. Although the cases presented here suggest the significance of kin in providing support, the families in Portugal are also more likely to source food from charity than those in the UK and Norway. As noted in Chapter 1, Portugal has a long history of charitable provision, much of which has religious origins, and a variety of local food aid organisations were available to and used by our participants in Portugal.

In the UK, as the families of Maggie and Makaya demonstrate, the state is not a viable source of support for low-income lone-parent families, given the government's explicit policy goals of getting people off benefits, cutting benefits and constant changes to eligibility criteria when parents move in and out of the labour market. Problems with the benefits system are among the top reasons given by users of food banks, which have rapidly expanded in the UK in recent years (for example, Sosenko et al. 2019; and see Chapter 1). However, food banks are used by a minority of people living in poverty in the UK and only accessed by a few participants in our study. Maggie and Makaya have turned more often to family and friends than to charity or the state. One further way of getting by is by going into debt;[4] Makaya, for example, has borrowed from loan sharks. Unsurprisingly, given increasingly high levels of 'problem debt' in the UK (arrears on a household bill or credit commitment [Mahony and Pople 2018]), and given the complexity and changing nature of the UK benefits system, some of the families in the UK have sought legal and financial advice from civil society organisations such as the Citizens Advice Bureau and local community organisations.

In Norway, NAV has the power to make discretionary payments for a variety of requests. It is striking that many of the Norwegian families, especially those who are migrants and lack family in Norway, or family with the resources to help them, expect to turn to the state for financial help, particularly for one-off purchases and unexpected expenses. It is also important to note that most migrants are on a basic level of state benefit because they lack eligibility for Norway's universal benefits, which are underpinned by active labour market policy. Financial assistance is granted on grounds of 'need' not eligibility. The procedures for applying to NAV for benefits and discretionary financial aid are highly bureaucratic and intrusive, as Bilan and Khava suggested. Bilan also notes the sanctions that are imposed by NAV for failing to comply with the rules.

The process of seeking support is also underpinned by public discourses on responsibility for poverty and for children's health and well-being. In the neoliberal UK, a strong narrative of maternal and personal responsibility frames the ways that mothers living in poverty navigate and make sense of their situations. In this context, being unable to manage can create feelings of shame that in turn lead to a withdrawal from social life, constraining the decision to seek help, whether formal or informal, as in the case of Makaya. In Portugal, the discourse of personal responsibility appears to be weaker. Perhaps this is because family ties are stronger and often local, and patterns of everyday mutuality and reciprocity are well established. Alternatively, poverty may be deeper among the families in the sample in Portugal than in the UK and Norway – so they have no choice but to turn to agencies and informal support. Both explanations may hold. In Norway, expectations of the state appear to be higher: families feel entitled to turn to the social security agency not only for benefits but for non-routine purchases when they have no kin to turn to or are unwilling to do so. However, the families also suggest that procedures are bureaucratic and that the discretionary nature of some support means the process can be, and feel, intrusive.

Questions about the support that people draw upon inevitably lead to an overemphasis on what they have access to, rather than what is absent. It is therefore important to bear in mind that food provided by charity, meals shared with family and small exchanges between friends and neighbours do not compensate for, or add up to, a socially and culturally acceptable standard of living in Western societies.

Notes

1. Since such support is not statutory, it is included here, though it can also be regarded as a state benefit.
2. As noted in Chapter 2, in the UK we were aware of urban growing schemes in the inner London area and tried, but failed, to recruit participants through these.
3. The mother's narrative of 'having always worked' is interesting, since, although she used to work as a cleaner, she now can't because she is caring for her older son. He has been assessed as not entitled to Personal Independence Payment (PIP).
4. Many (37/45) of the UK families (those in work and not in work) are in a significant amount of debt. See the figures in TUC (2019).

10
Children's experiences of school meals

Children and young people spend a significant amount of their time in compulsory education. School food environments therefore play an important role in shaping children's food practices, and school meals can make a significant contribution to their overall diet. Free and subsidised school meals are also a form of non-financial support for families, which may be especially important for those on low income (Long 1991). This chapter examines the role of school meals in moderating (or not) the effects of poverty on children's diets and food practices among the low-income families in the UK, Portugal and Norway. It begins with a brief discussion of school meals provision in each country. Seven families (two from Portugal, four from the UK and one from Norway) have been selected to demonstrate some of the variety in policy and practice concerning school meals provision and the experiences of children with different entitlements. The chapter considers the material contribution that school meals make to children's diets and their role in symbolic processes of social inclusion and exclusion.

Means-tested meals in UK secondary schools

For more than a century, British governments have provided free school meals (FSMs) to children whose education might otherwise suffer. FSMs were first introduced nationally in response to a concern that young men volunteering to fight in the Boer War were too undernourished or too ill to fight (Gillard 2003). Since then school meals policy has seen a series of sharp turns on funding, privatisation and nutritional content and quality (Lang et al. 2009). Nutritional standards for school meals were first established in the 1940s in England but were abolished in 1980 when the government headed by Prime Minister Margaret Thatcher obliged local authorities to engage in competitive tendering and outsource school meals to the private sector.

In the 2000s, under the New Labour government, nutritional school food standards became compulsory for the first time in 20 years in England and the devolved administrations of Scotland, Wales and Northern Ireland. These standards have since been replaced in England by the School Food Standards introduced in 2015 following the coalition government's School Food Plan review (Brooks 2014; Jamie Oliver Foundation 2017). New regulations are under consultation in Wales and Northern Ireland and are due to come into force on 8 April 2021 in Scotland.

The School Food Standards in England (where the qualitative research for this book was carried out) comprise rules about the quality and quantity of food served across the school day, including at lunchtimes, and cover meat, poultry and fish, fruit and vegetables, bread, other cereals and potatoes. Schools are barred from serving drinks with added sugar, crisps, chocolate or sweets. Vending machines (previously common in schools) have been abolished and children are not allowed more than two portions of deep-fried, battered or breaded food a week. Although most schools are required to meet the School Food Standards, they are not mandatory for all schools and there is a lack of monitoring. The limited research that has been carried out on the subject suggests patchy implementation as well as contradictions between what children are formally taught about healthy eating in the national curriculum and the availability of nutritious food in schools (Jamie Oliver Foundation 2017).

The ways in which school meals are organised and delivered also varies between schools. Some schools have kitchens and employ staff to prepare meals at lunchtime; others outsource the service or buy in pre-prepared food. Moreover, the way the food is offered to children varies. In the schools attended by the children we interviewed, some had a 'communal' or 'family service' in which no money exchanged hands, the same meal was offered to all children and it was prohibited to bring food from home or to go out of school at lunchtime. Other schools operated a 'contractual' or 'cafeteria-style' approach whereby children could choose from among the options on offer and payment was made at the point of service.

Entitlement to a FSM depends on a child's age and family circumstances. Since 2014, as part of the School Food Plan, state-funded schools in England have been required by law to provide FSMs to all Key

Stage 1 (Reception, Year 1 and Year 2) children with the aim 'to improve academic attainment and save families money' (Dimbleby and Vincent 2013). For older children at state schools, FSM eligibility is linked to the parent (or the young person) being in receipt of certain means-tested benefits.[1] However, it has been calculated that around a third of pupils living below the relative poverty line (living in households earning less than 60 per cent of median income) are not eligible for FSMs because their parents are not on 'out-of-work' benefits (Royston et al. 2012). For example, working tax credit – paid to low-paid workers employed for at least 16 hours a week – is not an eligible benefit. Moreover, because the qualifying benefits for FSMs are public funds, FSMs cannot be claimed by people, notably migrants who lack papers, with 'no recourse to public funds'.

In addition to restrictions on eligibility, research identifies problems with the adequacy and delivery of FSMs (Farthing 2012; Royston et al. 2012). In most secondary schools, children receiving FSMs do not receive a meal but instead get an 'allowance' to spend at the canteen. This was £2.30 per day at the time of the study. However, earlier research found that one in seven young people indicated that their FSM allowance did not allow them to purchase a full meal (Farthing 2012). The research also found that delivery systems could be stigmatising. To be identified as receiving FSMs is to be identified as being 'poor' by peers, leading in some cases to feelings of shame and embarrassment and to bullying. One could be identified by payment systems or by having to queue and eat separately, which meant exclusion from the 'normal' lunchtime experience of 'hanging out' with friends (Farthing 2012). Whereas legislation in Wales and Scotland requires that children cannot be identified by anyone other than an authorised person 'as a pupil who receives a school lunch free of charge',[2] no such legislation exists in England. Although 'cashless' systems introduced in many schools play a part in preventing the identification of children on FSMs, some systems still make these children identifiable and thereby cause them to feel stigmatised. Even though the school may not identify children on FSMs through payment method, these children can be identified by the limited range of food options available to them, as illustrated below.

A three-course communal school meal in Portuguese schools

In Portugal, too, national school health programmes date back to the early twentieth century. Organisations created in 1936 under the auspices of the Ministry for National Education managed the school meal system under the *Estado Novo* (New State) regime until its fall in 1974. Most families experienced food insecurity at this time, owing to high levels of poverty and labour shortage because of men's mobilisation for the colonial wars;[3] children contributed to domestic work, which took them away from school. Therefore, school meals were focused on alleviating the effects of poverty, on bringing children to school and on educating them in accordance with the regime's values (obedience, good manners and discipline). The single menu offered a hot main meal with soup, fruit and a spoonful of cod liver oil.

In the 1970s, food came to play a key role in promoting children's physical well-being and intellectual development. Concern about children's nutrition gained more importance after the 1974 revolution (marking the transition from an authoritarian state to a democratic government) and has become a priority in recent years (Truninger et al. 2013; Gregório et al. 2014b). From the end of the 1990s until the mid-2000s, school meals policies were oriented towards tackling excess weight and obesity among children and young people (Truninger 2013). Nowadays, beyond concerns with hygiene, nutrition, health and food-safety norms, school meals policies are paying attention to seasonality, regional food cultures, commensality, environmental issues (for example, fish should come from sustainable sources), reducing meat consumption and increasing plant-based diets, all encompassed by the general promotion of the Mediterranean diet in schools (Truninger 2013; Cardoso et al. 2019; Pereira and Cunha 2017).

In line with the more 'communal' approach to eating that Fischler (2015)[4] associates with continental countries, all Portuguese schools are required to provide a standard menu which consists of: (1) a fresh vegetable soup (with potatoes, legumes or beans); (2) one portion of meat or fish/seafood with pasta, rice or potatoes and legumes (optional) on alternate days; (3) one piece of brown bread; (4) one plate of vegetable salad (raw or cooked); (5) a dessert consisting of raw seasonal fruit or cooked or baked fruit without sugar (pudding, jelly, ice cream or yoghurt is served twice a month at most); (6) water as the only drink available (Lima 2018) (see Mariana's school lunch in Figure 10.1 for an example). The menu varies every week and is displayed to the school community. Salt reduction has been promoted and the use of aromatic herbs is encouraged as a salt replacement. Some schools have in-house catering services (cooking facilities and staff to serve school meals) while others rely on meals prepared by external catering companies. Some of

Figure 10.1 School lunch in Portugal (Source: 'Mariana').

these companies prepare meals in school kitchens (if cooking facilities are available), and others use a central kitchen and distribute the meals to schools (Cardoso et al. 2019).

Every school-aged child is entitled to school lunch every weekday. Prices are subsidised by the Ministry of Education and local authorities, which in many cases provide or distribute food. Prices are determined by law every year but have remained unchanged for many years. According to the current legislation (see Despacho 8452-A 2015, *Diário da República*, 31 July 2015), the price of a school meal is €1.46 (if the meal is bought in advance or plus 30 cents extra if paid for on the day). School meal prices are set by the Services of School Social Action (*Serviços de Ação Social Escolar* – SASE) to cover three brackets of family income level (A, B and C). Students in brackets A and B have 100 per cent and 50 per cent, respectively, of school food expenses covered by public funds. Those in bracket C pay the full price of their meal. Some schools use their financial resources to provide a food supplement during the morning/afternoon break. These supplements consist of bread (with butter, cheese or ham), sometimes accompanied by milk and fruit (the latter under free fruit schemes such as the EU's school fruit, vegetables and milk scheme).

The Norwegian packed lunch

In Norway a school meal programme for poor children was launched in the 1880s (Lyngø 2001, 117). Later the programme was opened to all children and participation increased in the 1920s because of rising food prices. During the 1920s, nutrition appeared on the political agenda. Three processes were significant. First, with scientific discoveries of the importance of vitamins in the first decade of the twentieth century, and under the influence of the Director of School Medicine, Carl Schiøtz, a new school meal programme was launched based on scientific rationality (Lyngø 2003). The hot meal was replaced by a cold meal consisting of bread, milk and fruit or a vegetable. However, the most important change was not the meal itself, but the state's intention to promote ideas about nutrition to the population. The school meal programme called 'the Oslo breakfast' was launched in 1930, continuing the preventive work of teaching the 'lower strata' about proper hygiene. It aimed to provide nutritious food to all schoolchildren (Lyngø 2003). By 1935, all schools in Oslo offered a school meal (Bjelland 2007) but many municipalities were too poor to offer meals for free.

In 1936 the idea of the 'Sigdal breakfast' was born, which meant that pupils were expected to bring to school the ingredients for their meal. The Sigdal breakfast system became widespread in the 1960s and rapidly transformed into the Norwegian packed lunch, that is, pupils brought their own sandwiches to school (Døving 1999) (see Kombo's sandwich in Figure 10.2). The packed lunch has become such a well-established tradition that Norwegians tend to believe that a cold meal for lunch is 'natural' and that eating something warm for lunch (as well as a warm dinner) would be fattening and unhealthy (Løes 2010).

Figure 10.2   Sandwich school lunch in Norway (Source: 'Kombo').

Over the past two decades, the school packed school lunch has been at the centre of public and political debate. The Socialist Left Party (SV), which governed the Ministry of Education and Research following the 2005 elections (which led to the Red–Green coalition government of 2005–13), emphasised in their election campaign the introduction of a free, complete school meal for all pupils; it estimated the cost to be about €250 million (NOK 2 billion) per year (€2.50 per meal) (Løes 2010, 11). In the 2013 election, the SV lost a significant number of votes and the Red–Green coalition was replaced by a coalition government of the Conservatives and the Progress Party.

School meals for children in low-income families in Portugal and the UK

Since school meals are not provided in Norway generally or for the children in the Norwegian sample, we begin with an overview of the spread of young people entitled to receive free or subsidised school meals in Portugal and the UK. Table 10.1 shows the distribution of secondary school age children according to whether they were entitled to a free or subsidised school meal.[5] It shows that almost all of the children we interviewed in Portugal were entitled to a free or subsidised meal (42/46), compared with only half of those attending secondary school (23/46) in the UK.[6]

The majority of children in the Portuguese sample (35/46) are in bracket A and receive free school meals.[7] Seven children (7/46) are in bracket B (they pay €0.73 per meal) and four pay the full price (€1.46); these paying pupils usually go home for lunch or, less often, eat in the school canteen or local cafes.[8] The main reason for not receiving a FSM in the UK was that a parent was in paid employment, despite this work often being low paid and/or insecure.[9] Since FSMs are paid out of public

Table 10.1 Free and subsidised school meals in the UK and Portugal.

	Portugal	UK
Free meal	35	23
Subsidised meal	7	n/a
No free or subsidised meal	4	23
Total	46	46

funds, in four cases the family's immigration status meant that they had NRPF and so no FSM entitlement.[10]

We now examine the contribution of school meals to families' budgets and children's diets. The two cases selected from the Portuguese sample represent opposite ends of the low-income spectrum in Portugal: an unemployed lone-parent family and a family with two parents in paid work. In the UK, we selected a range of low-income households because of the variation in school meals provision and children's experiences: two unemployed families whose children attend schools with contrasting systems of meal provision, one working family and one family with no source of income (NRPF). From the Norwegian sample we have chosen a case that typifies the large low-income migrant family in which neither parent is in paid work.

Free school meals in Lisbon: Cheila and Aleixo

Cheila is a white Portuguese lone parent with five children including Aleixo (the study child), age 14, her twin sister, a six-year-old brother and three-year-old twin sisters. Cheila has been unemployed for much of the time since her six-year-old son was born, apart from some very part-time work that is unofficial and sporadic. Her sister and her nephew have been living with them for the past seven or eight months, having escaped from domestic violence. They do not contribute to the family budget.

The overall monthly household income is €622, made up of €447 (Social Insertion Income), plus €175 (child allowance, 5 × €35). Cheila also does some cleaning/cooking jobs in private homes; at best, she can earn €20 in a week. At present, she is receiving a lower *Rendimento social de inserção* (RSI – Social Integration Income) because she is repaying social security overpayments. She also owes €600 in rent, which she is paying back in instalments. The cost of rent, utilities, TV, internet, phones and transport add up to around €475. The money Cheila has to spend on food is extremely low, around a tenth of the FBS for a family of this type (€50–60 per month). Food is consequently in short supply at home and she has been reliant on Re-food for about one month and on a food bank for the past two months. She also receives a weekly food basket from the church.

Cheila likes to cook and is sometimes asked to cook by the people whose houses she cleans. Although she says her children prefer her cooking, meals at home are currently ready-prepared meals from Re-food, normally soup and a main course. Cheila says that 'At this moment, not only because I want, but because I can't, I only buy meat about once a week. The rest we get from the food bank. And we get food from Re-food, which is already cooked.' Two of her neighbours, who also receive a weekly basket from the food bank, share food with the family.

Cheila questions the quality of food received from Re-food. She explains that two-thirds of the time the food is unfit for consumption. She cannot choose the type or quantity of food she receives from Re-food. She feels insulted by the small amount of bread provided. Moreover, no account is taken of dietary needs. For example, Cheila's son is allergic to fish. On the days that Re-food provides fish, there is no other option. Cheila finds this distressing and instead has to make an inadequate meal for her children:

> There were some situations when I had to make food the kids didn't accept and ended up hungry … because there was nothing else. There were situations I made only spaghetti … plain. Because we didn't even have some ketchup. To give it some taste, right! There were situations like that, yes!

Cheila recognises that without this help she would be in greater difficulty: 'If it weren't for that help … because even when the kids don't like the food, there is bread.' Food remains a constant concern and she is often anxious that it will run out before she has money to buy more. She is glad that her three-year-old twins still breastfeed, but this is physically draining: 'Even when there is nothing for dinner, I rest assured, because I know they can breastfeed all night. Although that bothers me and doesn't let me rest.'

In this context, free school meals (Figure 10.3) are vital. Aleixo and her twin qualify for SASE bracket A, which entitles them to a free lunch. Cheila says that although the children sometimes complain about the quality of the food at school, she tells them they need to eat it. She is tearful when she says:

> That's why I prefer it, when they have lunch at school, even when they like the food a little less … I ask them to have lunch, because I don't know if I'll have dinner … I ask them to eat, because sometimes I don't know what will come … and sometimes they have to eat toast for dinner and … bread. Drink chocolate milk and such … I mean … and I'm more relaxed if they've had a meal already.

Figure 10.3   Lunch in the school canteen (Source: 'Aleixo').

Cheila also asks the nuns at the school to supply her daughters with snacks:

> If I ask the nuns to fortify their snacks, they go with them to the kitchen alone … and sometimes they give something more. They give them soup at the afternoon and then … I don't worry as much.

Aleixo says she prefers the food her mother cooks, but that the school meals (see Figure 10.3) are better than at her previous school: 'I like [the food] from home more, right?! But … Compared with the other school I attended, the food is quite good.' She mentions in her interview that lunch is a more important meal than dinner.

Cheila does not say whether school holidays are harder when it comes to feeding the older children. This may be because during the summer holidays Aleixo does not spend much time at home, largely because she goes to summer camps, and she eats lunch there.

Subsidised meals in Lisbon: Diana and Sofia

Diana and her husband, white Portuguese, are both working; they have three children, Sofia (the study child), aged 12 years, and two sons aged

10 and two. They live in a rural area outside Lisbon. The house belongs to the maternal grandmother, who lives with them and is sick. Both parents are in full-time employment; the mother works as an assistant in a bakery from 9.00 a.m. to 6.00 p.m. on three weekdays and long hours from 4.30 a.m. until 6.00 p.m. at weekends. The father is a cable installer in the informal economy and frequently works late.

The household income is around €1,583, composed of Diana's wages, about €530 a month, the father's wages, €600–800 a month, Diana's mother's €300 old-age pension and family benefits. The children are eligible for SASE bracket B, meaning that they pay half the cost of the school meal (€0.73). The monthly outgoings include the rent, around €400, and utilities, around €180 per month. They do not pay for TV/internet and the parents' mobile phones are topped up with €10 every other month. Transport costs are high at around €200 per month. Besides low income, the main cause of the family's hardship is the debt they have accrued from modernising the house as well as from the grandmother's care (she has two daily carers), which is not covered by her pension.

The amount Diana says they spend on food is around half of the FBS for a family of this type (€300–440 per month, although this includes toiletries and detergents). Money is frequently tight and Diana often relies on credit at the local shop; 'I gained that friend in the supermarket. She started letting us have a tab.' Diana enjoys cooking but lack of money and broken kitchen appliances make this difficult. Although they have not had to use a food bank recently, Diana said that sometimes she does not eat, or limits herself to soup or a sandwich. To get by they use up leftovers in soup and omelettes. They eat more meat than she would like, instead of fish: 'Fish is very expensive, so we eat more meat.'

Diana tries to ensure their diet is good but is aware she does not always manage this. To supplement the lack of fish at home she tells her children to eat fish when it is served at school (the children like fish):

Diana: I try, but sometimes I know it's not. Sometimes fish is lacking, but they need fish, but sometimes we don't have it because it's too expensive and we don't buy it.
Interviewer: And your children, do you think they have a good diet?
Diana: Because at school they try to eat fish, I say, 'You eat fish at school,' because at home … and they sometimes eat fish at school.

Sofia usually has lunch at the cafeteria at school, except when she has no classes in the afternoon and then she eats at home, and on

Thursdays, when she takes food from home. On that day, she usually takes a bag of potato chips and some croquettes.

Lunch at school includes soup, the main dish (meat or fish) with salad (lettuce, carrots and cabbage) and dessert (normally fruit). Sometimes there is jelly, *arroz doce* (rice pudding) or *aletria* (thin pasta cooked in milk and sprinkled with cinnamon). The cafeteria assistants insist that the students take the soup. Like many other children in the Portuguese sample, Sofia complains about the lack of salt in school food.

Diana says she does not always ask her daughter what she had for lunch but that she always tells her if she doesn't like it. 'When it's food she doesn't like, she'll say, "Look today it was horrible" [laughs].' Diana thinks this happens when the food is vegetarian. '[Sofia] doesn't really like that … it's chickpeas, beans, all mixed up.' Sofia also has an afternoon snack at school, which she usually buys from the school bar. Only occasionally does she bring food from home, and only when Diana cannot afford to put money on her card. In that event, Diana says, Sofia takes bread and butter.

According to Sofia, the students can ask the canteen assistants to serve them larger portions and to give them second servings of the main course. To be given these they have to finish the soup first. Sometimes, Sofia asks for second helpings: 'On the days that, sometimes I don't have time to go to the bar [mid-morning], or sometimes I don't take food from home, because I have money on the card. And then I didn't have time to go to the bar and sometimes I repeat lunch.'

Understandably, Diana says that the school holidays raise problems, not only because more money has to be spent on food, but also because there is more food work:

> It's harder because we have more concerns, have to make lunch, make dinner. In this case, they are having lunch at school, it's one less expense for me, I only have to concern myself with dinner. Only at weekends and holidays do I have to worry about breakfast, lunch, snacks.

Free school meals in London: Chibuzo and Joseph

For some families in the UK, too, free school meals are vital. This family comprises a lone mother, Chibuzo, and her 12-year-old son, Joseph (the study child). They are of West African ethnicity and live in temporary accommodation (a hostel) in inner London. Because they are not allowed visitors in the hostel, the mother and son were interviewed together in a McDonald's.

Chibuzo has lived in the UK for 15 years without any benefits because of her legal status and has largely been financially supported by her church. She was recently granted 'discretionary leave to remain' for two-and-a-half years and currently lives on Jobseeker's Allowance (£136 fortnightly) and child tax credit (£62 weekly), which she has received for the past year. For some reason that was unclear (but seemed to be linked to the renewal of discretionary leave to remain) she is not getting child benefit at the moment. Chibuzo spends a large proportion of her income (£50 per week) on debts incurred to obtain her 'papers' (legal status) as well as £70 per month on her and her son's mobile phones. Because Chibuzo is in receipt of a qualifying benefit, Joseph receives FSMs. As there is often a lack of good food at home, this is vital.

The family food budget is variable, but very low, usually less than half of the FBS for a family of this type (£25 per week), and so there are constraints on the quantity and quality of food. Chibuzo cooks mainly West African food, and some 'British food' for her son, such as spaghetti bolognese and instant noodles. She cuts up fruit so it goes further and Joseph sometimes takes this to school to eat at break time. Chibuzo thinks their diet is reasonably healthy but says that with more money she would buy food that 'would make my boy grow' and 'something that's good for the brain', such as a variety of fruit and oily fish. When food supplies run low they eat potatoes and bread and butter. Chibuzo misses meals or eats less to make sure her son has enough, although Joseph says he is sometimes hungry too. Chibuzo has used food banks in the past. She is critical of them, saying a lot of the food she was given was near or past its expiry date and so was wasted.

Given there is often a lack of good food at home, the free school meal is vital. Though this was a difficult matter to raise in front of his mother (they were interviewed together), Joseph said the school holidays (particularly in the summer) are hard and he gets hungrier then.

Free school meals in London: Mary and Maddy

The experience of Maddy, who lives in the same London borough as Joseph but attends another school, is quite different. Maddy is aged 16 and white British. She lives with her grandmother, Mary, who has brought her up. Mary lost her job as a part-time cleaner and is reliant on

ESA (disability benefit) and child tax credit, which adds up to £520 per month, and child benefit (£80 per month). Maddy worries about lack of money.

The money Mary spends on food is around half the FBS for a family of this type (about £30 a week). Although she is aware of recommendations for a healthy diet, she buys what she calls 'cheap food' in order to manage. She thinks that her granddaughter eats a lot of 'junk food' because 'that's all we can afford'. However, Mary also says she tries to cook one 'decent meal' a week and, as Maddy's photo shows and Maddy confirms, Mary cooks a roast dinner 'every Sunday' (Figure 10.4). The grandmother thinks Maddy 'should eat a little more fruit, cos it's quite cheap, fruit'. However, Maddy says that it can be a waste of money, since it is perishable: 'when I do fancy one it's sort of like dried out or gone off'.

Maddy receives free meals at her school, which has adopted a cafeteria-style approach in which children select from hot and cold foods at a counter and pay at the till. Students can also bring in their own food and some of her friends have a packed lunch. According to Maddy, the food 'isn't great at our school, it's terrible'. She explains that her FSM allowance is £2.20 per day and the school uses a cashless system designed not to identify those on free school meals. However, those receiving free

Figure 10.4 Nan's roast (Source: 'Maddy').

meals are restricted, she says, in terms of which items they are allowed to select, an experience she describes as profoundly humiliating:

> I was really embarrassed actually. Cos we have a finger print where you just put a finger print on and you can top up. And there's two machines and um … what it does, if I put my finger on every lunch time it will say £2, but I haven't topped £2, it's just automatically in my account cos I'm free school meals. And a small baguette is £1.25 and you can get that at free school meals, and you can get like a juice carton – you can only get certain drinks. And a long baguette is £1.75 … um … so then one lunch time I was really hungry, I was like, 'I don't want a small baguette; I want a big baguette.' And it was £1.75 and I was like, 'If I don't get a drink …' I was like, 'It says £2 on my account so surely I have the credit to get this?' So I put my finger on and obviously it tells the canteen lady that I'm free school meals. And the way the canteen's set out, like everyone can see what you're doing and everyone can hear and stuff like that. … So, when she [lunchtime staff at the checkout] was like, 'You can't get that, you're free school meals,' like I was really embarrassed cos people were waiting behind me. I was kind of like, 'Oh my God.' And I was like, 'But I've technically got £2 on my account.' She was like, 'No you can't get that at free school meals.' And it's like you're really restricted to what you can eat with free school meals. And it's like if you're saying £2 is on my balance surely I should be able to get something that's worth less than £2. So that really like got me, so now I just get what I know I'm safe with … so a small baguette and carton of juice.

Mary consequently gives Maddy £2 a day to 'top up' her FSM allowance. Since this is the only money she has, Maddy often saves it to go out with friends, for example, for something to eat or to watch a film at the cinema at weekends.

The holidays are harder and a time when Mary says she eats less because there is less money. It is not only the extra meals but also the need to pay for activities. 'She wants money to go out "cos I want to get an ice cream, all my mates have got one" and wee-wee-wee-wee … "Can't I go swimming?" cos … you know … there's always something.'

Mary has to say no to Maddy sometimes: 'It's not nice, but you know it happens.' She emphasises here that she likes to 'treat' Maddy, since she's a 'good kid': 'I try to always keep a pound in my purse to say yeah I can, if she asks.' In the holidays, Maddy has friends home more often and this is an additional cost; sometimes Mary has to ask them to bring food with them. 'Yeah because she's always got friends here as well and "Can they stay?" – "Well I've got to feed them haven't I, [Maddy] now," you know. I'll get some bits, and I'll make sure they bring some bits with them.' The friends sometimes bring food like 'crisps and rubbish, yeah … chocolates, pop'. Even so, Mary feels the pressure to provide a meal; she says, 'I find something.'

Packed lunch in a UK coastal town: Jenny and Cole

Around half of the children in the UK research were not entitled to FSMs, many of whom lived in families in which one or both parents was in paid work, and this added to the family food expenditure. This white British family comprises a couple with four children, including Cole (the study child), age 14, and three girls aged 12, 10 and seven years. Both parents are employed in low-paid work; the father is a cook and Jenny is a carer in a home for the elderly. Their strategy is to work 24 hours per week between them so they can claim working tax credit.

The household income is around £2,100 per month, including income from employment (about £700 per month), working tax credit (about £1,120 per month) and child benefit (about £280 per month). They also receive housing benefit that covers most of the rent and is paid directly to the landlord. The family's outgoings include repayments on an individual voluntary arrangement (IVA), a form of consolidated debt. For a family of six, their food budget is very small: they spend less than half of the FBS for a family of this type (about £60 per week).

All the members of the family work hard at seeking out bargains, such as by going to Tesco just before the shop closes to pick up reduced items of food. 'What we'll do is when we go to the shops we'll look and we'll think right well this will be for today's dinner and then that's what we're going to make for tomorrow's dinner.' Cole is especially proficient at this. Meals at home consist of what Jenny describes as 'the classics', dishes like pasta bake or sausage and mash and bought pies, depending on 'what's the best deal that we can get and how far we can make it go … the two cheapest meals that I always make for the kids are pasta bakes and sausages'.

Because the parents are not in receipt of benefits that entitle their children to FSMs, they take packed lunches, 'because that's the cheapest thing for us to do'. The children 'have their sandwiches, their crisps, their bit of fruit and their drink and then obviously they'll come home and they have their dinner'. The packed lunches add to the family's food costs, despite their shopping around for bargains: 'We'll go to Aldi for the big bags of crisps. Because we've got four children and their packed lunches it works out cheaper buying it from there than it would do to buy from Tesco.'

Because the children have cold packed lunches, the cost and effort to prepare the hot meal that is deemed necessary each day are considerable, Jenny says:

> If they could have a school dinner it would make it easier for us, because they would've had a hot meal at school. I'm not saying that they couldn't have a hot meal, but it could be something as simple as beans on toast or something, because they would've already had their hot meal at school.

Going hungry in London: Kahina and Amara

This family comprises a lone mother, Kahina, and her daughter, Amara (age 15), who live in a hostel in inner London. Kahina is originally from North Africa and Amara was born in Southern Europe. They recently moved to the UK because Kahina wanted 'to give my daughter education'. After initially living with friends, they were placed in temporary accommodation in one room in a very large hostel. When we interviewed them, they were facing eviction. Kahina is registered at the Job Centre and is seeking work. She is not allowed to claim benefits because, it seems, she has an NRPF clause on her visa, though this is unclear. They rely on help from friends and sometimes Kahina does informal, cash-in-hand work.

Kahina and Amara enjoy, and take pride in, cooking. When they have the money, they cook Mediterranean dishes and are learning 'to cook English'. However, they find that the ingredients for cooking from scratch are more expensive than ready-made meals. Kahina and Amara eat much less meat and fish than they would like. Moreover, the reality of their lives leaves little scope for preparing homemade food. In their one room, they have poor cooking facilities and unhygienic conditions in which to store food (the building is rife with cockroaches).

They live hand to mouth. With no budget for food, Kahina resorted to the food bank but, on the last occasion, was turned down because she had used up her quota of three visits a year. She protested unsuccessfully: 'I said, "Sorry, well, we have to eat. Well, we're [not] eating just three times a year. I'm sorry to say that, I'm sorry. Well, we're eating every day, humans." She said, "This is how it work."'

Both Amara and Kahina act in ways that suggest a great deal of sacrifice and altruism. Each considers the needs of the other and this extends to the limited quantity and quality of food. Kahina says, 'I say, "Well okay, I can struggle, I can starve for my daughter." You understand, I want her to have proper education, proper stuff.' She goes without food during the day and reserves what little there is for the evening when they eat together:

> Sometimes like I don't [eat] nothing, just – I wait for my daughter to come at home and we have sandwich which we have, well, tin of tuna or something like that, you understand? I can starve all day long waiting for her, like, then we can share what we have at home. This is how it is, you understand? … morning I had coffee and that's it really, yeah, soft drinks or something or some toast. This is my day.

Amara says she often goes both to school and to bed feeling hungry. Like her mother, she sacrifices her own food intake, 'I skip meals to share with my mum [inaudible] … for example, I skip my meal to wait for her to come back and at least we can have the same amount of food … [We] starve together through the whole day, so at least we will have had something to eat.'

Because the family has no access to benefits, Amara is not entitled to free school meals. Until recently, she was not eating anything at school: 'I used to starve in school because … well I couldn't manage to make sandwiches at home or take crisps or whatever [inaudible] so I was just starving in school for the whole day.'

This affected her schoolwork but she tries to build resilience: 'When I'm hungry I just can't concentrate; it's really, really hard for me to do that … so I just need to make my mind up and know that I will eat after five hours, seven hours when I get home.'

Kahina eventually spoke to the school, which now provides Amara with free lunches from its discretionary funds. However, the daily allowance, which Amara says is £2, does not go far. For example, 'a small sandwich is like £1.60'. Although she would like to take cheaper food from home, she says, 'When I don't have food at home what am I going to do?'

Packed lunch in Oslo: Mwari and Panya

As discussed above, schools in Norway do not generally provide meals, although a few schools have canteens or provide food on some days. Children are normally expected to take lunch with them, which can be expensive, especially for large families.

This family consists of Mwari and her husband and four children aged under 18 who live at home, including Panya (the study child) aged 16 years, another daughter aged four years and two sons aged eight and 13. Originally from Somalia, the family migrated to Norway in 1994. Before that they had spent time in Syria and the UK. The father worked for the postal service until 2000, when he developed a back problem. He has not been in employment since then but attends a rehabilitation and qualification programme for four hours a day. Mwari attends a Norwegian course for around 4 hours a day. The family is reliant on benefits. The father receives NOK 1,400 in qualification support, and child benefit of NOK 3,700 for the four children. He says they receive little subsidy for the high rent and they only manage to pay NOK 4,000 towards it per month. The social security office, NAV, pays the electricity bill. In total, the father estimates that, after housing and utilities are paid, their income for six people amounts to NOK 16,248. Their food budget is less than a third of the FBS for a family of this type (around NOK 5,200 per month).

Food at home is generally Somalian, but they eat Norwegian food too. The father says that rice is important in Somali food culture and confirms that there is usually more rice on the plate than meat and vegetables. He says that at home 'sometimes we eat like Somali food called *injera* (a type of flatbread) or *kibbeh* (Middle Eastern street food) that Mom makes', as well as Norwegian meals that are usually 'rice and meat, rice with chicken, rice with fish or spaghetti with fish, spaghetti with chicken. Sometimes we prepare potatoes with chicken' (Figure 10.5).

On school days, Mwari prepares packed lunches for her children. As is the norm in Norway, this consists of bread with different toppings and is somewhat different from and more expensive than the food usually eaten at home. As Skuland (2019) reports, children are reluctant to take food to school which is 'different' and may be called 'smelly' by others. However, the cost of food is high, especially the price of bread for packed lunches, as the father explains when he compares their experience in Norway with that in the UK:

Figure 10.5 Curry (a) with potatoes and carrots served with sour porridge (b) at home (Source: 'Panya').

Father:	Everyone who lives in Norway has packed lunch. We lived three years in England. Thus, you needed not to bring packed lunches when they eat at school.
Interviewer:	Yeah, they were served food, right?
Father	Yes.
Interviewer:	But then in the mornings you do have some packed lunches to prepare? And lots of bread slices?
Father:	Slices of bread, we have to … I have to buy two or three [loaves of] bread so we need two–three slices of bread [for each child] or sometimes they have exams and has to have extra …
Interviewer:	Extra?
Father:	Yes, extra.
Interviewer:	And then you need two–three breads?
Father:	Two–three–four breads, right
Interviewer:	Every day?
Father:	Yes.
Interviewer:	That's a lot of bread … And the oldest, do they prepare packed lunches for themselves?
Father:	The oldest, yes! The oldest, yes! Just [name of youngest daughter] and he who is eight and he who is 13 who Mom prepares, but the others manage [them]selves.

The family shops once a month in Sweden, making use of a free bus to buy food in bulk: bread, milk and meat. However, the father says they do not feel they can buy the cheapest bread for the children, so each loaf costs around NOK 35.

Panya wants to be like her friends and buy drinks and food in the school canteen in addition to bringing a packed lunch:

Panya:	Different food like pizza or burgers like fishburgers or … and like fruit, cakes and what is it called again … like bread?
Interviewer:	Baguettes?
Panya:	Yeah!

However, her parents disapprove and she says they tell her to '"stop using your money on nothing, buying drinks" when I have [something to] drink, buying food when I have brought food with me and stuff. "You have food, so eat it. Don't buy anything else. Think about another time when you will need it."'

In contrast to families in the UK and Portugal, who found school holidays hard because these were times of greater food expenditure, Panya's father said that it was easier to save money during the summer vacations, because the children ate Somalian food at home:

> Next month school starts and the children need packed lunches. But when it is summer you can save a bit and you can buy clothes, jackets and stuff. Thus, you can save a bit because you don't do packed lunches … Mostly we cook Somalian homemade food, which doesn't cost much, thus you can save a bit.

Discussion

School is an important environment for shaping the diets and eating practices of young people, since it occupies such a large part of their everyday lives. In all three countries, free school meals were introduced in the late 1800s or early 1900s to address poor nutrition among children in poor families. In Norway, subsequent changes in policy and practice related to changing understandings of nutrition have led to school meals no longer being provided. In the UK, despite national provision and national school food standards, there is variability in the quality of provision and eligibility for FSMs for secondary school age children in England is based on families' receipt of particular means-tested benefits. In Portugal, national rules regarding pricing and the provision of a three-course meal are more uniform and stringent, and means testing is based on household income with a three-tier contribution system.

In this chapter, we have conceptualised school meals as an important resource, both quantitatively and qualitatively, in contributing to children's food intake. We found that almost all of the children in the Portuguese household sample were entitled to a free or subsidised three-course meal at lunchtime. Although some children said they preferred home-cooked meals, parents generally welcomed the provision and indicated their importance in mitigating the effects of poverty on their children's diets. As discussed in Chapter 4, a smaller proportion of children in Portugal than in the UK go without enough to eat. Furthermore, children in Portugal meet more of the WHO dietary reference nutrient intake

(RNI) values than do adults in the same country or children in the UK (Rippin et al. 2017, 2018), and the children we interviewed in Portugal report higher consumption of fruit and vegetables than children in the UK and Norway (Chapter 4). There is a range of possible reasons for this, including the greater availability of fruit and vegetables in Portugal and the centrality of food in Portuguese culture. According to our analysis of the study families, the free or subsidised school meals in Portugal seem to play a part. Furthermore, given the system of universal delivery and communal eating, they do so in a way that fosters social inclusion.

In the UK, by contrast, only around half of the children in the study households are entitled to a FSM. There is variation in the adequacy of the food that is available, especially for teenage children. Those who do not qualify for FSMs sometimes go without food and are socially excluded. Those who do qualify find the allowance insufficient for their needs and unless their parents find the money to supplement the allowance they experience hunger. Norway provides a contrast; given the absence of school meals, most children bring a packed lunch to school, which makes term times expensive, especially for parents with large families, because the cost of food is high. Packed lunches can also act as a form of surveillance that may expose mothers and embarrass children whose food brought from home does not conform to social norms (Skuland 2019).

For families in both the UK and Portugal, school holidays are an expensive time for feeding children. In Portugal, at these times, some children go to grandparents' or other family members' homes to be fed. In Norway, by contrast, term times are expensive because of the cost of providing packed lunches; school holidays, when children can eat home-cooked food, are seen as a time when families can save money.

Although schools can and should mitigate the social inequalities that exist among children from different backgrounds, in the UK in particular they appear to reinforce them, especially when meals delivery systems identify and stigmatise children as 'poor', albeit unwittingly. In Norway, school lunchtimes are one method of acculturating children into the Norwegian tradition of a cold lunch. However, the cost of the normative *mattpakke* components, especially bread, places a burden on poorly resourced families. By contrast, the school meals system in Portugal appears to moderate the effects of poverty on children's diets, and the communal meal, whether children appreciate it or not, serves as a means of social inclusion.

Notes

1. There are differences between the devolved nations in FSM eligibility criteria. In England, the qualifying benefits are: Income Support; income-based Jobseeker's Allowance; income-related ESA; support under Part VI of the Immigration and Asylum Act 1999; the guaranteed element of pension credit; child tax credit (provided there is not also entitlement to working tax credit and the annual gross income is no more than £16,190); working tax credit run-on (paid for four weeks after the recipient stops qualifying for working tax credit); Universal Credit – for those applying on or after 1 April 2018, the household income must be less than £7,400 a year (after tax and not including any benefits). During the coronavirus pandemic, eligibility for FSMs has been extended to include some families with NRPF.
2. Section 7 Healthy Eating in Schools (Wales) Measure 2009; Section 8 Schools (Health promotion and nutrition) (Scotland) Act 2007.
3. Between 1960 and 1974, the 'mobilization of young men to the colonial wars and high levels of emigration caused severe labour shortages' (Tavora and Rubery 2013, 223–4; and see Barreto 2004; Crompton 2006). This crucial period established Portugal's unique position among Southern European countries with respect to its relatively high levels of female and maternal employment.
4. According to Fischler (2015), two dimensions of commensality may be distinguished: a 'communal' dimension – the people having a meal together forming a communion – and an individualised 'contractual' dimension, whereby people spend time together around a meal but what is eaten is a product of negotiation. Fischler links these two dimensions of commensality to different cultural contexts: the communal dimension being found in continental European countries like France and the contractual dimension in the more individualised Anglo-Saxon, Protestant countries, which are more disposed towards individualised dietary practices and a contractual form of commensality.
5. It excludes children in primary school, of which there were five in the UK sample.
6. The 46 secondary school pupils in the UK attended 16 schools: three in the coastal area and 13 in inner London. Almost all the children lived in households in the lowest income category. However, FSMs were received by only half of the children, reflecting the national picture.
7. Less common are cases where children receive the free food supplement during the morning/afternoon break.
8. There were four cases in Portugal in which children were not entitled to a free or subsidised meal. Two were ineligible because the family income was too high (so they were SASE bracket C); one child's parent had not submitted an income tax return on time; a fourth child was from a migrant family who had not yet applied for FSMs.
9. In the families with no employed parents, most children received FSMs. However, in three families where the parent was not in employment, the children did not get FSMs. In one, the mother had lost her job but was still 'waiting for Income Support to be sorted'; this included waiting for the 'passported' FSM benefit. In two families, it was because the parents had NRPF. Although the eligibility for claiming FSMs is set by government, schools' practices – and the experiences of children and families – vary, depending on local circumstances.
10. In a few families, children did receive FSMs despite having at least one employed parent. In three instances, lunch was provided free by the school (one, because the child had a scholarship, and the other two because the school funded lunches for all children through its own budget). In another case, a mother had recently started working but this had not been fully processed and, in another, a mother received a benefit that qualified her children for FSMs despite her being in paid work.

Conclusions and reflections

> *It is not, as poverty was before, the result of natural scarcity but of a set of priorities imposed upon the rest of the world by the rich. Consequently, the modern poor are not pitied – except as individuals – but written off as trash. The twentieth-century consumer economy has produced the first culture for which a beggar is a reminder of nothing.* (John Berger in Sperling 2018, 222–3)

This book has aimed to explore the consequences of a major economic event in the twenty-first century – the 2008 global financial crisis and its aftermath – for the modern poor. The crisis has shaken most of those countries with the greatest gap between the rich and the poor (Hopkin 2020). As suggested by Narotzky and Besnier's (2014) conceptualisation of the lived realities of economic crisis, our concern has been with what 'ordinary people understand by "a life worth living" and what they do to strive toward that goal, particularly under conditions of radical uncertainty'. In particular, we set out to understand how, in well-off societies, parents care for their children and manage to feed them on a low income. We have also sought to examine children's experiences of food and eating and how lack of money has affected their lives at home and outside. To fulfil these aims, we adopted a comparative approach by studying low-income families in three contrasting countries. The purpose of this research design was to identify the particularity of social conditions, both objective and subjective, and how they played out in families' and children's lives; to detect the similarities and the differences, and which aspects of context made a difference.

As we write this concluding chapter the world is going through another seismic crisis, the Covid-19 pandemic, a time of unimaginable uncertainty and risk to the world, which has both massive health and economic consequences and is transforming the way of life of every one of us. As became clear in the 2008 financial crisis, and this book gives testimony to, those worst affected in such crises are the families and children who have the least resources (O'Connell and Brannen 2020). Between February and April 2020, the early months of the pandemic in the UK, analysis of the UK's Understanding Society Panel data found that household incomes fell and that those on the lowest incomes, notably lone-parent households and workers from black, Asian and minority ethnic households, were by far the worst affected (Crossley et al. 2020). Emerging research on the effects of the pandemic on unemployment suggests these are also gendered, self-employed men and part-time women workers being most affected (ONS 2020b). The impacts of the pandemic on the health and mortality of different groups are also highly unequal, with evidence that these are exacerbated by racial and socioeconomic inequalities, including stark differences in housing conditions (Abbs and Marshall 2020; Haque et al. 2020). Analysis of poll data suggests that the effects include rising food insecurity, particularly among families in black, Asian and minority ethnic groups (Food Foundation 2020a). Moreover, a growing number of families are moving into low income as redundancies, income loss and furlough impact upon those who were previously better off; hence, there has been a large increase in the number of new families claiming FSMs (Food Foundation 2020b).

In this context, long-standing questions about what children need in order to survive and thrive have renewed relevance and urgency. Debates have hinged on definitions of poverty: rights versus needs; absolute versus relative poverty; material and bodily experiences versus broader definitions of human flourishing. At another level are arguments about whether the resources, goods and services to prevent poverty and promote social inclusion should be provided collectively by the welfare state or accessed privately through the market. In focusing on food poverty in this book we have engaged with these debates in two ways. First, we have understood partaking of food as comprising customary practices that are both material and inextricably linked to symbolic and emotional meanings. Second, we have sought to understand the food practices of parents and children at risk of food poverty in a broad structural analysis of their positions in terms of the resources available and those they can access, as well as the opportunities they lack.

We have taken a long-distance, a medium-distance and a close-up view of low-income families (Hantrais 2009). This has meant working analytically at three levels: the national level of welfare states, the meso level of local institutions and informal social networks and the household level in which parents and children act on and convert the resources they access in order to sustain their families. We have shown how disruption and change leave their traces in different ways on individuals and families through a range of mediating institutions that affect their lives and the kinds of communities in which they live. This research design takes a critical realist approach (see, for example, Fletcher 2017). At one level, we have focused on families' own understandings of poverty and food poverty within the contexts of their own social networks and localities and the services to which they have access. At the same time, events, policies and other structural dimensions of political-economic contexts are ontologically presumed to exist irrespective of human interpretation. In this way we have pointed to some of the causal mechanisms that underpin the realities of poverty.

This multi-level methodology has the benefit of alerting the researcher to the significance of different levels of structure in each societal context. The significance of national policies for family food budgets is illustrated in the combined effects of housing and policies and benefit levels. Given that the size of the family food budget depends to a great extent on what is left after major expenditure such as rent, the fact of whether the state provides and subsidises housing can be a significant factor that interacts with other national policies such as levels of social security benefits. In the UK, many families are in the expensive private rental sector; these rents are subject to market forces and are not subsidised by the state above a certain level. In contrast, in Portugal, rents are low but benefit levels are also very low. In Norway, public housing that is generally of a high standard is available, but benefit levels are low for those, like migrant parents, who have no or limited employment records.

The level of analysis selected may be secondary to unravelling the interaction between different layers of reality (Lallement 2003 in Hantrais 2009, 55). In the UK, for example, policies concerning the delivery of school meals vary at the local level (between schools), whereas in Portugal national policy created uniformity in entitlement and provision. Which level – ontological or analytic – is most important in explaining social phenomena – in this case children's experience of school meals – therefore depends on the phenomenon under consideration. Although national school meals policy in both the UK and Portugal clearly determines the parameters for their local delivery, the causes of children's mixed experiences of school meals in the UK are not reducible to the (lack of) policy at the national level.

Food poverty in national context

National and international crises highlight the enduring importance of the nation state. The countries we have focused on in this book – the UK, Portugal and Norway – represent very different welfare regimes with different consequences for families struggling on low incomes. From 1979 the UK's welfare state, originally based on universal principles, has been steadily reduced as market forces have been introduced into all sectors of the economy and society. The UK's response to the 2008 crisis was to make substantial cuts to benefits and local authority funding for expenditure on public services. In contrast, Portugal's welfare state was only developed after the end of the Salazar dictatorship in 1974. Portugal was hit particularly hard by the 2008 crisis, when it was obliged to seek a bailout loan from the Troika (Chapter 1) which led a new right-wing government to impose draconian policies including severe retrenchment of social welfare, reductions in benefit levels and reduced eligibility. Norway, by contrast, was largely protected from the financial crisis because of its strategy of reinvesting the profits of its large oil industry for the benefit of its citizens (Chapter 1). Although its welfare state is relatively generous, this is premised on strong labour market policies that limit entitlement to full welfare benefits to those who have contributed through payment of taxes based on employment.

The effects of cuts to welfare benefits that took place in the UK following the 2008 crisis were savage, causing many families to become reliant on charities, including food banks, which have grown massively in number. Portugal is quite a different case, given its low rates of benefits and well-established charitable institutions that have long provided help to low-income families; this latter support was augmented by the government to meet the numbers of people hit very hard by the crisis. Norway, meanwhile, was only marginally affected by the global recession. Changes to its benefits system were much more to do with wider public-sector changes across Europe, relating to neoliberal ideas and New Public Management, which pre-dated the crisis (Christensen and Lægreid 2007). However, those with no, or weak, employment records, a disproportionate number of whom are migrants, have access to only a basic level of social assistance.

Labour market deregulation long pre-dated the crisis, especially in the UK, and became even more evident afterwards. Unlike many European countries, the UK has enlarged its labour force over the last decade or so, most of the growth being in low-paid employment, including self-employment and part-time and insecure work, often on zero-hours contracts. Portugal, meanwhile, has experienced high unemployment that has exacerbated its existing reliance on a large informal economy that depends on a low-paid workforce. Again, the Norwegian situation is very different, with a tightly regulated labour market that depends on a highly educated workforce and marginalises those without higher-level educational qualifications.

Changes at the national level intersect with events in individual lives. The circumstances and events that plunge people into poverty or contribute to low income include not only changes in the labour market but also benefits and immigration law. Many of the families in this book were contending with a combination of difficulties, some set in motion by an initial shock, such as loss of a job or legal status, or a reduction in their benefits. These in turn were sometimes linked to a series of connected experiences: domestic abuse, relationship dissolution, precarious housing, spiralling debt and mental health problems.

Employment did not necessarily protect families from food poverty, particularly in the UK and Portugal. Although some families with one parent or two parents in low-paid or unpredictable hours of employment managed to keep the wolf from the door, the situation was precarious; when an unexpected expense or a fluctuation in wages occurred, some were left with little support and lacked the resources to feed their families adequately. In Norway, where tripartite negotiations between government, employers and unions mean conditions are better and wages higher, parents who lacked the skills needed in the labour market were left no alternative but to rely on benefits. These low-income families were better off than their counterparts in the UK and Portugal, but were excluded from the norms of a wealthy society enjoyed by most families in Norway. At times they struggled to obtain sufficient nutritious food, the costs of which are kept high by market protectionism. As this book shows, this was disproportionately the experience of parents in the study who had migrated to Norway under its refugee programme.

Food poverty at the local level

Local institutions can mitigate some of the disruption caused by international crises and the policies of nation states which make the daily lives of the poor such a struggle. Since the global financial crisis, food 'aid', 'assistance' and 'charity' have risen across Europe and became commonplace as a means of providing food to people who struggle to obtain enough through the usual routes. In some countries, food aid is supplanting welfare state provision. Although, in the UK, households' access to sufficient healthy or 'good' food has not been considered a matter for government policy, in the Second World War and the early 1950s, faced with a large reduction in food availability, Britain arranged more equal access through rationing and social support. In contrast, over recent decades, successive UK governments have pursued 'cheap food' policies and, after the 2008 crisis, made changes and cuts to benefits which led to a huge rise in the number of food banks. Indeed, in Britain, food banks have become synonymous with the term 'poverty'. A popular narrative, underpinned by corporate social responsibility strategies of global food companies, posits the reduction of food waste as a solution to food poverty. Another is to suggest that the poor need to learn how to cook, ignoring the fact that cooking from scratch can cost more in money (and time) than many cheap pre-prepared meals. Both narratives deflect attention from governments' responsibilities to promote and protect household food security.

Because Portugal's welfare state was established later than in other countries, the church and civil society have long played an important part in providing welfare at a local level. Following the 2008 financial crisis, they continued to do so, alongside NGOs and local authorities, a wide variety of organisations being involved in the distribution of both cooked and uncooked food. Compared with Portugal and the UK, in Norway wages and food prices are high, and charity plays only a marginal role in addressing either poverty or food poverty. Indeed, perhaps because of its generous welfare state, the official discourse in Norway does not recognise food poverty. Nonetheless, as we show in the book, some low-income families in Norway have sought food from food banks and other voluntary organisations as well as seeking help from the local municipality and the social security office.

Local communities are also 'places' (Massey 1994) in which people struggling with food poverty experience their daily lives. The types of areas in which they live offer different services and opportunities for accessing food. In the study we recruited families from two types of communities in each country – inner city areas or suburbs of capital cities and small towns or semi-rural areas outside the same cities. The local area made a difference to the availability and cost of food that families could access, as we witnessed in the course of the fieldwork. The rural area where the study was carried out in Portugal afforded opportunities for some families to grow some of their own produce, and a few families with access to gardens in the UK areas grew vegetables. The close geographical proximity of some families to their kin was also a further potential resource offering the opportunity to pool and share food and other kinds of support, for example, enabling young people to eat at their grandparents' homes in the school holidays, as some children did in the Portuguese sample. Those who had no kin nearby were more reliant on welfare and local institutions, but overall the families in Portugal drew more on both types of support. In Norway, many of the recent migrants lacked family locally, as did some migrant families in the UK, though some had established and depended on social support, in some cases understood through the lens of fictive kinship (Ebaugh and Curry 2000).[1]

Education is among the collective resources to which children and families have access. Schools have historically provided support to children and families, including through meals, so that children may engage in learning and benefit from educational provision. However, there are variations between and within countries in the ways that school meals are funded and delivered, and in which children and families are eligible for free or subsidised meals. There have also been changes in the role that schools play and are expected to play in ameliorating the effects of poverty on children's and families' lives. In the UK, restricted eligibility for school meals means only around half of children growing up in poverty are entitled to a free school meal, and the allowance and food available to children may be inadequate and the systems of delivery stigmatising. Schools are increasingly using their own discretionary funds and accessing charitable support to feed hungry children, not only at lunchtime but also at breakfast, after school and in school holidays. In Portugal, a three-tier funding system and standardised menu means that most children in low-income families are entitled to a free or subsidised three-course meal and supplementary snacks are provided to some. In Norway, school meals are not provided, and so families must supply packed lunches. Given the relatively high cost of food, including bread, families can find it hard to make ends meet during term time, in contrast to the UK and Portugal, where school holidays without free school meals increase pressure on tight family food budgets. It is notable that in both Portugal and Norway, but no longer the UK, young people in some low-income families are entitled to, and receive, scholarships that cover some maintenance costs while they are at school.

Food poverty at the household level

In order to understand food poverty at the household level, we examined which types of families were most at risk across the three countries by analysing the international SILC dataset and looking at change over time – between 2005 and 2016. We found that, though poverty rates were generally highest among families in Portugal, rates of food insecurity were highest among families in the UK. We also found that family type was important in the UK, lone-parent families being consistently at much greater risk of food insecurity than couple households, even after adjusting for low income. The results for Norway also showed a widening gap over time (from 2013) between low-income lone parents and low-income couples in terms of the proportion at risk of food insecurity. In Portugal, by contrast, family type made less difference to whether low-income families experienced food insecurity, reflecting the pattern for poverty in general.

Our main task in the book has been to investigate the human stories behind statistical comparisons, to look for patterns not apparent in the survey evidence and suggest the complexity and specificity of people's lives. The low-income families that we succeeded in including in the study show how, in each country, a variety of multifaceted disadvantages intersect to place families at risk of poverty and food poverty: gender, family form, parental (non-)employment status, migration status and ethnicity. We have demonstrated intersectionality and diversity in our analysis of the distribution of food poverty across the sample households and in our selection of case studies. We have described the households of lone mothers who were not in paid work, couple households where one or both parents were in paid work and households in which one parent was an undocumented migrant and not allowed to work officially or to claim state benefits. Multi-generational households also occur, in which parents and grandparents shared food and other resources.

Our qualitative research with low-income families confirmed the pattern of food poverty among lone-parent families found in the quantitative research, suggested some reasons for this and explored how lone parents manage. In Portugal, reliance on extended family is a norm, although, as the case analysis showed, those on the lowest incomes may have less of such support to draw on. In the UK, lone mothers are among the hardest hit by cuts to welfare benefits and local social spending, while in Norway, lone mothers who are unable to access the labour market are reliant on basic social support. Reflecting extensive evidence about the gendered distribution of poverty and its management, most lone parents are mothers and it is mothers in most dual-parent families who manage limited budgets and do the work of food provisioning.

Looking across the sample and focusing on specific cases, we also examined how low income and family form intersect with other axes of inequality, including race and ethnicity. In both the UK and Norway, families in which mothers are migrants are over-represented among those experiencing a shortage of food at the household level, reflecting racialised hierarchies that restrict citizenship, limit employment opportunities and generate racism. In the UK, some ethnic minority groups have much higher risks of poverty than others. In Norway, poverty is highly concentrated among those who have migrated under the UN refugee quota system. Reduced entitlements to family benefits in the UK (notably the two-child limit) and Norway (reduced maternity allowance) disproportionately affect women in ethnic minority groups, as do cuts to local government spending in areas of the UK where ethnic minorities are most concentrated, especially since those on the lowest incomes rely most heavily on such publicly provided resources (Pearson 2019). In Portugal, fewer mothers who were migrants reported a compromised quantity of food at the household level, but, as the case of Lala's family showed, racially minoritised Roma were subject to discrimination and severe levels of poverty. These intersections reflect deep-seated inequalities in these societies of the Global North and institutional racism, based on skin colour, against those whose antecedents originate from the Global South.

In order to understand what makes a difference to how *particular* low-income families in *particular* contexts manage to feed themselves, we compared parents living in the same family form in each country and, where possible, in the same type of locality (city, suburban or semi-rural area). In this way we have sought both to describe the families and their resources and to identify the social conditions that have made a difference to their ability to feed themselves adequately.

In this endeavour we conceptualised families as household resource units in which food provisioning takes place. In each of the cases, we identified the income and other resources available to the parents; which types of food they were able to afford and how they accessed them; and the ways in which they transformed food into meals. Because our focus was on families with children, we prioritised both the feeding of children in the home and their access to food outside the home. We looked at food in school and the ways in which the type of school meals system affected what children were able to access and the social and emotional consequences for them. We also examined how low family income constrained children's social participation in buying snacks and eating out with peers.

As the cases demonstrate, food was a major outgoing for the families. For each family, we compared household food expenditure to the amount calculated in national food budget standards (FBS) for a particular family according to its size and the ages of the children. Almost all the families in the study were spending less than the FBS for families of a similar type and size. Because food is generally an 'elastic' part of the household budget, we also examined how the timing of income affected food provisioning: the methods the mothers adopted to make food 'stretch' among family members, over the course of a day and from one pay day to the next.

Our use of the concept of food provisioning also took into account the allocation of responsibility. The case studies show how food poverty is gendered: mothers in the large majority of families took charge of the management of food budgets and carried out the bulk of the food work: the preparation of meals and searching out cheap food in a diverse range of shops and markets. Cutting back on their own food intake to protect children was a common strategy adopted by mothers across the countries in their efforts to ensure the children ate a healthy diet, although the mothers were generally reluctant to admit to their children that they were going without enough to eat.

When we talked to the children, we found many reluctant to admit that their parents were unable to provide enough food, although in a questionnaire, around a quarter in each country sample ticked that they had on occasion gone to bed or to school hungry. In response to a vignette showing an empty food cupboard some said that such a thing had happened at home. Some mentioned a lack of fruit at home. Those children whose parents had irregular immigration status were most at risk of going without enough to eat, lacking both quantity and quality of food.

As the cases show, food work in low-income families is hard work. Mothers' routine ways of shopping and cooking involved the expenditure of a great deal of effort and time. In all three countries mothers shopped around for the best-value products. In the coastal town in the UK, this sometimes involved walking long distances; in Norway, it often entailed a free or subsidised bus ride to Sweden, where food is cheaper, or relying on family or friends for a lift. 'Stocking up' and 'running down' the freezer was a strategy common to some families in the three countries, not only as a method of food storage but also as a way of shifting time for food preparation. However, not all families had access to a freezer or other storage facilities, and many could not afford to buy in bulk. Instead, most shopped little and often, a method that also prevented children from eating more than their mothers had budgeted for at any one meal. Fluctuations in wages and benefits made the management of income and food harder, leading to anxiety about money and where the next meal would come from. Credit was used to fill the gaps in some cases and some mothers turned to formal and informal sources for support in times of shortage.

Some families relied on food charity, especially in Portugal. Reliance on food aid and special offers in supermarkets had implications for the timing of meals; domestic routines were dictated by when free and cheap foods were available. In Portugal, one food aid organisation did not open its doors until the evening; supermarkets in the UK reduced the prices of some products only at the end of the day. The quality of what families ate varied considerably across the cases, as children and mothers reported in interviews and we documented in composite daily menus. Whereas some mothers told us they found satisfaction in the careful planning of meals and in cooking creatively with the limited ingredients available to them, others were frustrated and depressed by being unable to cook what they wanted because of lack of money and, in some cases, lack of access to facilities, including fuel for cooking. Thus, to put meals on the table was often daily drudgery. As some mothers in the UK sample experienced, cooking from scratch was not often an option on account of the high cost of ingredients, the amount of time required or the unavailability of cooking facilities.

As we have shown, poverty and inequality are not simply about material deprivation but entail the symbolic violence of discredited identity and damage to social relations. Low income had major effects on mothers' and children's social participation involving food. Parents not only sacrificed their material needs to protect their children's food intake, but also sought to ensure that children did not miss out on a social life with friends. Even in families where there was little or no 'spare' money, most mothers managed to give children some cash to be 'like their friends' and buy snacks and sweets at school or outside school, activities that are part of young people's increasing autonomy as they get older. In the UK and Portugal, although many of the families had always been on low incomes, some had once enjoyed a comfortable middle-class lifestyle before jobs were lost or work hours were reduced, either directly or indirectly as a result of the 2008 recession. For the latter group of parents, sustaining a social life and customary food practices seemed to be a way of maintaining a semblance of 'normality', especially for their children.

Around a third of parents said they could not afford to allow their children to have their friends home for something to eat, and about the same proportion of young people said they did not socialise with friends in activities involving food and eating. Some children described feelings of exclusion and 'difference'. More commonly, children made 'excuses', both to friends and to the interviewers, for not being able to join in. Clearly aware of constraints on their families' incomes, they also described moderating their own needs, saying they tried not to ask their parents for money for food, clothes or luxury items. In the UK, where children look to consumer culture to establish a sense of belonging, some young people described lives that were limited and lacking in spontaneity compared with their peers. In order not to be left out they set aside money meant for transport and school lunch so that they had money to spend with friends outside school. Families who had once enjoyed higher incomes were better resourced to protect their children from shame, whereas parents who had been in poverty a long time could not offer their children what other parents provided and so their children were more exposed to shame.

The extent to which families depended on others – for both formal and informal support – depended upon several factors: the availability of support, the nature of the need, whether they considered seeking help socially acceptable and their capacities to return support. In Portugal, family support was more commonly sought than in the UK or Norway, where reliance on family and friends was equal. For some Portuguese families, support from kin was embedded in the everyday practices of family life – for example, pooling resources and eating together routinely and on special occasions. Grandparents played a critical role, providing grandchildren with meals after school and in the school holidays in some families in Portugal as well as a few cases in the UK.

In times of acute need, mothers were reluctant to strain the norms of family relations and fearful of being unable to repay support. The lack of capacity to provide the basic necessities for their children and the need to resort to charity were described by mothers as a shaming experience. To avoid this, some mothers in the UK and Norway used other avenues, including turning to loan companies, which led to mounting personal debt that they were unable, or unlikely to be able, to repay. It was common in Norway for parents to make requests for assistance with specific items of expenditure, such as children's sports equipment, from the social security office or the municipality. However, they described intrusive questioning by officials into their personal circumstances by officials, which they found embarrassing. Likewise, they found the bureaucratic process intended to determine who was 'deserving' of help humiliating, especially when, as often happened, requests were turned down. The material imperative to seek support was, however, typically accompanied by a moral imperative *not* to be seen to exploit the state or charity. Even those families on the lowest incomes sought to distance themselves from 'others' on benefits – those deemed to be 'undeserving' or 'feckless'. For their own part, they claimed entitlement to support based on their current or past employment records and presented themselves as morally upright people who lived 'within their means'.

A key resource that had the potential to mitigate child food poverty in Portugal and the UK was the school meal (school meals are not generally provided in Norway). In practice, we found that the availability, cost and quality of school food varied strikingly across the countries. In Portugal, children are provided with a three-course school meal that for almost all the low-income families was free or subsidised. The meal included meat or fish each day; this was especially important, since mothers mentioned being unable to give their children as much good-quality meat or fish as they would expect and wish to do. Children were routinely expected to eat the typical Portuguese soup, which is a central part of a Portuguese meal as well as a staple source of vegetables. Consequently, school meals made a substantial contribution to children's daily diets and nutrition and mitigated food poverty in the families in Portugal, supplementing or, in some cases, substituting for lack of food at home. However, some children complained about the quality of some of the school food and refused to eat it, despite their mothers' protestations.

In the UK, eligibility for FSMs is limited to recipients of certain benefits. Children whose (migrant) families had no access to 'public funds', and most children whose parents were in low-paid work, were not eligible for free school meals. Furthermore, we found great variation in the UK secondary schools we studied in the types of food available and the ways meals were delivered. For children in some schools, shared meals delivered free at the point of purchase were a vital source of nutrients and means of inclusion. In other schools, children said the FSM allowance was insufficient to purchase an adequate meal and they felt excluded and ashamed. In schools where school meals were mandatory, this was a drain on mothers' limited resources if children were not entitled to FSMs. In Norway, unlike other Nordic countries, children were expected to bring a traditional Norwegian packed lunch to school. The cost of packed lunches was therefore a major expense for low-income parents, given the high cost of food, including bread. Feeding children in the school holidays was described as difficult by the mothers in the UK and Portugal, whereas in Norway holidays provided relief from the need to supply packed lunches and the families could save money by eating customary foods at home.

Food poverty: whose responsibility?

This book raises urgent questions for our societies concerning the future and the need to transform society in ways that lead both to a more equitable redistribution of income, assets and collective resources. It also requires a resetting of values about *human* worth so that the growing numbers of low-income people are no longer shamed and stigmatised. In so far as crisis means a time of danger and opportunity, it is evident that the 2008 economic crisis exacerbated poverty and social inequality. It made the lives of many families even more precarious and destroyed possibilities and dreams of a better future. How damaging and irreversible the long-term effects of the current global crisis will be, we have no idea.

This book brings to the fore questions about government's responsibility to ensure that all citizens have an equal entitlement to a level of income that enables them to obtain appropriate and adequate food as a basic human right. As the families' stories document, the policies of government have denied many families this right. On his visit to the UK in 2018, Philip Alston, the UN Special Rapporteur on extreme poverty and human rights, noted in his report, 'Austerity could easily have spared the poor, if the political will had existed to do so' (Alston 2018, 22).

This conclusion is echoed by children, as well as their parents, who were asked to give their views about the locus of responsibility for ensuring that families have access to adequate food. In all three countries, although children took it as given that, under normal conditions, it was parents' duty to ensure their children were well fed, they also thought it was government's responsibility, often in concert with other institutions, to guarantee that parents could fulfil this obligation (O'Connell et al. 2019a). Children took seriously the moral questions of the obligation to act responsibly. They spoke about the need for parents to prioritise essential expenditure and not waste money on less important things. They also made the case for government and society to act humanely and responsibly, as these four children poignantly articulate in response to the question of where responsibility and blame lie:

> The parents, because it is their job to take care of their children and make sure they have food. It isn't always their fault, but still their responsibility. (Andressa, girl, age 12, with South American migrant lone mother employed full-time in an after-school club, own flat, east central Oslo)

Because they [members of government], since they are very rich, could increase the income or the family allowance ... or then poor people ... me, for instance, if I won the EuroMillions [lottery], I'd ... you know that thing we passed by? It has a tunnel and there are only homeless there ... and I could go there ... and give them money. (Jessica, girl, age 12, two-parent white Portuguese household, both parents unemployed, inadequate rented housing, Lisbon)

Family is the power of love and family is the power of team. And secondly, the government is – I said the government because government is the one that takes care of like the hospitals and the charities and well, not really charity, but would control yeah. So, I think the government should probably be monitoring what is going on. (Dayo, one of two brothers, aged 15 and 12, two-parent household, West African migrant parents with NRPF, rented housing, inner London)

I think the parents because of what he said, and government because if a child dies the government is always serious about it. So, if the child doesn't die, they should still be serious about the child anyway. (Ayo, Dayo's brother)

It is no wonder that many of the families we spoke to talked about life as a matter of 'survival' and beyond their control. In the short term, few were able to imagine radical changes to their circumstances, especially those experiencing racialised discrimination, as well as penury, who had little realistic expectation of improvement to their lives. Yet they still hoped the future would be better. While parents nurtured aspirations for their children, the children harboured ambitions. Especially those from migrant backgrounds, who placed their faith in education and hard work as 'the' routes out of poverty.

Thoughts for the future

The Covid-19 pandemic has exposed and exacerbated pre-existing stark inequalities in families' lives, health and diets. Although we are yet to see the full extent of its devastating consequences on the food security of low-income countries and their citizens, tens of millions of lives and livelihoods are at risk (WFP 2020). In the UK and other countries in the Global North, food 'shortages' are the result of panic buying and food policies that have left food supply and security to global food markets and retailers, with little or no regard for environmental or social justice. In these circumstances, banquet and hunger coexist, as those who *can* put themselves and their families first, while those who *cannot* are left to feed themselves through diminishing supplies of emergency charitable provision.

If the world is to survive this new global crisis, international collaboration will be essential and national governments and local infrastructure and communities will need to work together. All four levels – international, national, local and household/individual – are fundamental to creating a democratic basis for social solidarity (Klinenberg 2018, 2020). The challenges are vast. As the Portuguese writer and recipient of the 1998 Nobel Prize in Literature José Saramago said in an interview in *The Guardian* (Merritt 2006), 'We live in a world that is governed by institutions that are not democratic – The World Bank, the IMF [International Monetary Fund] and WTO [World Trade Organization].' As nationalism sweeps the US and many European countries, we are living in a time when ideas of the common good are under threat. In T. H. Marshall's terms, a shared society rests on 'a direct sense of community membership based on loyalty to a civilisation that is a common possession' (1963, 96).

In this era of late consumer capitalism, under policies of neoliberalism and austerity, those on low incomes and especially women, 'are increasingly treated as an expandable and costless resource that can absorb all the extra work that results from cuts to the resources that sustain life' (Pearson 2019, 28). An alternative economic logic that recognises the centrality of reproductive work to livelihoods and invests in social as well as physical infrastructure must be a central priority. As sociologist and lifelong anti-poverty campaigner John Veit-Wilson wrote in a blog post about the future of poverty and social security in the UK, this requires not only redistribution but also a reconceptualisation and reprioritisation of the 'common wealth':

> In our marketised and consumerist society in which everyone's freedom of choice is expressed by spending one's own money, it is essential to have enough income to be recognised as included in society and to achieve a respectable minimum level of living. But our capacities for interaction, mobility and cultural and economic participation at levels indispensable for social inclusion can't all be bought individually ... Strategies for abolishing poverty must therefore ensure not only adequate individual incomes

but also publicly available collective resources to prevent poverty. (Veit-Wilson 2019)

In the UK, media discourse pits the economy against public health, Westminster against the devolved nations, the North against the South, the young against the old, the haves against the have-nots. On the ground, however, at the level of the school and neighbourhood, everyday acts of social solidarity mitigate some of the worst effects of the pandemic on children's and families' health and lives. At a societal level, as the economy shrinks, more families are falling into low income. Many are claiming social benefits for the first time, and the numbers applying for free school meals have increased despite the desperately low threshold and stingy qualifying criteria (Food Foundation 2020b). In this context, the ideology of 'choice' and the 'welfare myth' of 'them' and 'us' (Hills 2014) will become increasingly difficult to sustain.

The pandemic offers the chance to challenge the politics of division and the discourse of 'choice' that pervade the dominant populist rhetoric, however difficult that will be. This requires forging a new political narrative that foregrounds families like those in this book and includes not only those at the bottom of the income pyramid but the growing numbers who are just about 'getting by'. If we are to create the possibilities, both subjective and objective, to develop better lives in the future, a strong citizenship narrative needs to be created that is rooted in communities and institutions such as political parties, unions and civic associations which give meaning to collective identity (Hallgrimsdottir et al. 2020).

A long-term strategy has never been more urgent nor indeed more difficult, given that public institutions are under enormous strain in dealing with the current situation. Given the abject failure of the years of neoliberal capitalism to engender prosperity and stability, at the national level governments need to set an agenda for the ways in which they can carry out their democratic duty to take responsibility for the health and well-being of their citizens. This begins, but does not end, with the recognition that the goals of public health and capitalism are inconsistent (Warde 2014). At the local level, long-term strategies are needed so that local authorities, trades unions, schools and civil society organisations – environmentalists, housing activists, food aid providers, anti-racists, feminists and other groups – will play a full part in transforming society and the economy in democratic ways.

Children living in poverty should be at the forefront of long-term strategies and the political agenda. Compared with older generations, especially in the UK, the needs of children and young people have not been prioritised; funding for youth services, adequate training, employment and housing has been woeful, a situation compounded by the Covid-19 pandemic (Gardiner et al. 2020). Young people's mental health has suffered considerably; their education and access to friends and to school food have been severely disrupted. Young people are the future and they must be able to participate in the decisions that affect their lives.

Social scientists also need to think about an agenda for future research that will inform the building of a just society in which children, families and future generations have the right to decent food, adequate housing, equal access to good health and opportunities for full social participation. The pandemic has highlighted the need for social science to review its potential contribution, given that other disciplines – public health, behavioural science, psychology – are currently pre-eminent. We also need to consider the contribution of our methodology and to examine the methods we employ given the constraints of physical distancing. Which of our typical repertoire of methods are feasible and which new ones do we need to develop?

Expertise in the field of families and food is of particular relevance to the pressing problems that face society. Questions arise about the effects of the coming recession on the already large numbers of families and children living in poverty and food poverty as well as those who will undoubtedly move into poverty as the economy shrinks. In the short term, we need to monitor which groups of children and young people are most, and which are least, affected by the pandemic and in what ways, including access to (a good) education, (decent) school food and opportunities for social participation. An imminent concern is the effect of new immigration policies and rising nationalist sentiment on the lives of children in migrant families.

Other areas fertile for research, now and in the future, concern the role of charities and corporate philanthropy; how far will they, and should they, supplant welfare states as their coffers empty? The role of civil society organisations is also ripe for study, particularly their contribution to rebalancing a society riven by inequality and the weakening of democratic institutions and processes. In the longer term, we need to investigate the extent to which changes in material and environmental circumstances lead to changes in social expectations and practices among different socioeconomic groups. In this period of huge uncertainty, how and in what forms social infrastructure and social solidarity will be rebuilt are pressing matters.

Whichever questions we prioritise, we will have to take careful account of what is already known and not known and reconsider the contribution that social science can make to scientific knowledge and social policy and practice. This means being strategic, eschewing poorly designed, underfunded and disconnected pieces of research. Instead, researchers should consider how we can ethically navigate and coordinate our efforts in a sector (higher education) that is, all too often, beset by competition and opportunism and driven by a business culture.

In the work undertaken for this book, we have experienced the benefits of taking a comparative viewpoint and working in an international team. The importance of international and interdisciplinary collaboration cannot be understated, especially in a climate in which the UK seeks to exercise its so-called new sovereignty in a post-Brexit world. Researchers in the field of families and food need to work with others across the Global North and Global South who have experience of the fields of social inequality, food security and child poverty and have accumulated the methodological expertise and capacity to carry out research that can address in a rigorous way the most important questions that we all face, both now and in the future. Carrying out comparative research in an international team and working with data from different societies underline the value and importance of working collectively. Politically, comparative research means building the international solidarities necessary to bring about radical social change.

Note

1. The concept of 'fictive kin', which has a long history in anthropology, has been used to refer to providers of material and social support who are not kin but are treated like kin and enable one to become incorporated into a new and often hostile society (Ebaugh and Curry 2000).

References

Abbs, I. and L. Marshall. 2020. 'Emerging evidence on COVID-19's impact on health and health inequalities linked to housing', Health Foundation. https://www.health.org.uk/news-and-comment/blogs/emerging-evidence-on-covid-19s-impact-on-health-and-health-inequalities.

Abel-Smith, B. P. and P. Townsend. 1965. *The Poor and the Poorest: A new analysis of the Ministry of Labour's Family Expenditure Surveys of 1953–54 and 1960*. London: G. Bell.

Agresti, A. 2018. *An Introduction to Categorical Data Analysis*, 3rd edn. Hoboken, NJ: John Wiley.

Alanen, L. 2003. 'Childhoods: The generational ordering of social relations', in *Childhood in Generational Perspective*, edited by B. Mayall and H. Zeiher, 27–46. London: Institute of Education.

Albertini, M., M. Kohli and C. Vogel. 2007. 'Intergenerational transfers of time and money in European families: Common patterns – different regimes?', *Journal of European Social Policy* 17(4): 319–34.

Almeida, J. F. de, L. Capucha, A. F. da Costa, F. L. Machado, I. Nicolau and E. Reis. 1992. *Exclusão social: factores e tipos de pobreza em Portugal*. Oeiras: Celta.

Alston, P. 2018. 'Statement on visit to the United Kingdom, by Professor Philip Alston, United Nations Special Rapporteur on extreme poverty and human rights', London, 16 November. https://www.ohchr.org/Documents/Issues/Poverty/EOM_GB_16Nov2018.pdf.

Alston, P. 2019. 'Climate change and poverty: Report of the Special Rapporteur on extreme poverty and human rights', UN Human Rights Council. https://digitallibrary.un.org/record/3810720?ln=en.

Alves, S. 2014. 'Welfare state changes and outcomes: The cases of Portugal and Denmark from a comparative perspective', *Social Policy and Administration* 49(1): 1–23.

Amilien, V. 2012. 'Nordic food culture: A historical perspective', *Anthropology of Food* S7. https://doi.org/10.4000/aof.6950.

Anderson, B. 1983. *Imagined Communities: Reflections on the origin and spread of nationalism*. London: Verso.

Anitha, S. and R. Pearson. 2018. *Striking Women: Struggles & strategies of South Asian women workers from Grunwick to Gate Gourmet*. London: Lawrence & Wishart.

Araújo, J., M. Severo, C. Lopes and E. Ramos. 2011. 'Food sources of nutrients among 13-year-old Portuguese adolescents', *Public Health Nutrition* 14(11): 1970–8.

Archer, M. 1995. *Realist Social Theory: The morphogenetic approach*. Cambridge: Cambridge University Press.

Arnold, J. and C. Farinha Rodrigues. 2015. Reducing Inequality and Poverty in Portugal. Paris: OECD. http://dx.doi.org/10.1787/5jrw21ng3ts3-en.

Atkinson, A. B. 1998a. 'Social exclusion, poverty and unemployment', in *Exclusion, Employment and Opportunity*, edited by A. B. Atkinson and J. Hills, 1–21. London: CASE.

Atkinson, A. B. 1998b. *Poverty in Europe*. Oxford: Blackwell

Atkinson, A. B. and E. Marlier, eds. 2010. *Income and Living Conditions in Europe*. Brussels: Eurostat European Commission. https://ec.europa.eu/eurostat/documents/3217494/5722557/KS-31-10-555-EN.PDF.

Attree, P. 2005. 'Low-income mothers, nutrition and health: A systematic review of qualitative evidence', *Maternal and Child Nutrition* 1: 227–40.

Augusto, F. Forthcoming. 'Food aid initiatives: The vision of volunteers and beneficiaries', PhD thesis, University of Lisbon.

Bacchi, C. and S. Goodwin. 2016. *Poststructural Policy Analysis: A guide to practice* Basingstoke: Palgrave Macmillan.

Backett-Milburn, K., W. Wills, M. Roberts and J. Lawton. 2011. 'Food, eating and taste: Parents' perspectives on the making of the middle-class teenager', *Social Science and Medicine*, 71: 1316–23.

Baillie, R. 2011. 'An examination of the public discourse on benefit claimants in the media', *Journal of Poverty and Social Justice* 19(1): 67–70.

Bajić-Hajduković, I. 2013. 'Food, family, and memory: Belgrade mothers and their migrant children', *Food and Foodways* 21(1): 46–65.

Ballard, T., A. Kepple and C. Cafiero. 2013. *The Food Insecurity Experience Scale: Development of a global standard for monitoring hunger worldwide*. Rome: FAO. http://www.fao.org/economic/ess/ess-fs/voices/en/.

Bambra, C. 2019. 'Introduction', in *Health in Hard Times: Austerity and health inequalities*, edited by C. Bambra, 1–34. Bristol: Policy Press.

Baptista, I. 2011. *Promoting Social Inclusion of Roma: A study of national policies*. Brussels: European Commission DG Employment, Social Affairs and Inclusion.

Barbosa, M. de Araújo. 2012. 'Isabel Jonet: We live in an idiotic way', *Dinheirovivo*. https://www.dinheirovivo.pt/economia/nos-vivemos-de-uma-maneira-idiota/.

Barreto, A. 2004. 'Mudança Social em Portugal 1960–2000', in *Portugal Contemporâneo*, edited by A. Pinto, 137–62. Lisbon: D. Quixote.

Bauman, Z. 1998. *Globalization: The human consequences*. New York: Columbia University Press.

Benjamin, O. 2020. 'Shame and ("managed") resentment: Emotion and entitlement among Israeli mothers living in poverty', *British Journal of Sociology* 71(4): 785–99.

Bennett, F. and M. Daly. 2014. *Poverty through a Gender Lens: Evidence and policy review on gender and poverty*. York: JRF.

Bere, E., M. Hilsen and K. Klepp. 2010. 'Effect of the nationwide free school fruit scheme in Norway', *British Journal of Nutrition* 104: 589–94.

Beveridge, W. 1942. *Social Insurance and Allied Services (Beveridge Report)*. London: Her Majesty's Stationary Office.

Bjelland, I. 2007. 'Ren i skinn er ren i sinn – skolefolk og medisineres ordskifte om norske skolebarns helse 1920–1957', master's thesis, University of Bergen. https://bora.uib.no/bitstream/1956/2364/1/Masterthesis_Bjelland.pdf.

Blom, S. 2002. *Innvandrernes bosettingsmønster i Oslo*. Oslo: Statistics Norway. https://www.ssb.no/a/publikasjoner/pdf/sos107/sos107.pdf.

Blom, S. 2010. 'Sysselsetting blant innvandrere: Hvilken betydning har individuelle egenskaper og tilpasningsstrategier?', *Søkelys på arbeidslivet* 27(1–2): 59–75.

Borch, A. and U. Kjaerness. 2016. 'Food security and food insecurity in Europe: An analysis of the academic discourse (1975–2013)', *Appetite* 103: 137–47.

Bourdieu, P. 1990. *In Other Words*. Stanford, CA: Stanford University Press.

Bourdieu, P. 2010. *Distinction: A social critique of the judgement of taste*, translated by R. Nice. Oxford: Taylor & Francis.

Boyden, J. and G. Mann. 2005. 'Children's risk, resilience, and coping in extreme situations', in *Handbook for Working with Children and Youth: Pathways to resilience across cultures and contexts*, edited by M. Ungar, 3–26. Thousand Oaks, CA: SAGE.

Bradley, K. 2009. *Poverty, Philanthropy and the State: Charities and the working classes in London*. Manchester: Manchester University Press.

Bradshaw, J. and Y. Chzhen. 2011. 'Lone-parent families: Poverty and policy in comparative perspective', in *Bienestar, protección social y monoparentalidad*, edited by A. Samaranch and D. Nella, 25–46. Barcelona: Copalqui Editorial.

Bradshaw, J., Y. Chzhen, G. Main, B. Martorano, L. Menchini, L. and C. Neubourg, 2012. *Relative Income Poverty among Children in Rich Countries*. Florence: UNICEF Innocenti Research Centre.

Bradshaw, J., N. Finch, E. Mayhew, V.-M. Ritakallio and C. Skinner. 2006. *Child Poverty in Large Families*. Bristol: Policy Press.

Bradshaw, J. and E. Mayhew. 2011. *The Measurement of Extreme Poverty in the European Union*. Brussels: European Commission DG Employment, Social Affairs and Inclusion.

Bradshaw, J. and O. Movshuk. 2019. 'Measures of extreme poverty applied in the European Union', in *Absolute Poverty in Europe: Interdisciplinary perspectives on a hidden phenomenon*, edited by H. P. Gaisbauer, G. Schweiger and C. Sedmark, 39–72. Bristol: Policy Press.

Bradshaw, J. and R. Sainsbury, eds. 2000. *Researching Poverty: A study of town life*. Bristol: Policy Press.

Brannen, J. 1988. 'The study of sensitive subjects: Notes on interviewing', *Sociological Review* 36(3): 552–63.

Brannen, J. 2005. 'Introduction: Cross-national seminar on biographical methods', introduction to workshop, Thomas Coram Research Unit, Institute of Education, UCL, 24–25 November. http://eprints.ncrm.ac.uk/10/1/JuliaBrannen-Introduction.pdf.

Brannen, J. 2015. *Fathers and Sons: Generations, families and migration*. London: Palgrave Macmillan.

Brannen, J. 2019. *Social Research Matters: A life in family sociology*. Bristol: Bristol University Press.

Brannen, J. 2020. 'The study of childhood: Thoughts from a family life researcher', *Families, Relationships and Societies* 9(1): 161–7.

Brannen, J., E. Heptinstall and K. Bhopal. 2000. *Connecting Children: Care and Family Life in Later Childhood*. London: Falmer.

Brannen, J. and A. Nilsen. 2002. 'Young people's time perspectives: From youth to adulthood', *Sociology* 36(3): 513–37.

Brannen, J. and A. Nilsen. 2011. 'Comparative biographies in case-based cross-national research: Methodological considerations', *Sociology* 45(4): 603–19.

Brannen, J. and M. O'Brien, eds. 1996. *Children in Families: Research and policy*. London: Falmer Press.

Brannen, J. and G. Wilson, eds. 1987. *Give and Take in Families: Studies in resource distribution*. London: Unwin Hyman.

Brembeck, H. 2009. 'Children's "becoming" in frontiering foodscapes', in *Children, Food and Identity in Everyday Life*, edited by A. James, A. T. Kjorholt and V. Tingstad, 130–48. London: Palgrave Macmillan.

Briggs, A. 2000. 'Seebohm Rowntree's poverty: A study of town life in historical perspective', in *Getting the Measure of Poverty: The early legacy of Seebohm Rowntree*, edited by J. Bradshaw and R. Sainsbury, 5–22. Aldershot: Ashgate.

Brooks, F. 2014. *The Link between Pupil Health and Wellbeing and Attainment: A briefing for head teachers, governors and staff in education settings*. London: Public Health England.

Brown, H. and C. Bambra. 2019. 'Do your parents mess you up? Exploring the intergenerational correlation in physical health, mental health, and wages over time', executive summary for London policy event, June 2019, using findings from 'The Intergenerational Persistence of Inequalities in Health and Income: Where Can We Target Policy to Best Reduce Inequalities?', Understanding Society Policy Fellowship. https://www.ncl.ac.uk/ihs/staff/profile/heather-brown.html#research.

Browne, J., R. Hyee, H. Immervoll, D. Neumann, D. Pacifico and O. Rastrigina. 2020. 'The OECD tax-benefit model for Portugal: Description of policy rules for 2019', OECD, Directorate for Employment, Labour and Social Affairs. http://www.oecd.org/els/benefits-and-wages.htm.

Bugge, A. 2011. 'Lovin' it? A study of youth and the culture of fast food', *Food, Culture and Society* 14(1): 71–89.

Burridge, J. 2012. 'Introduction: Frugality and food in contemporary and historical perspective', *Food and Foodways* 20(1): 1–7.

Callan, T., B. Nolan, B. J. Whelan, D. F. Hannan and S. Creighton. 1989. *Poverty, Income and Welfare in Ireland*. Dublin: Economic and Social Research Institute.

Caplan, P. 1996. 'Why do people eat what they do? Approaches to food and diet from a social science perspective', *Clinical Child Psychology and Psychiatry* 1(2): 213–27.

Caplan, P. 2017. 'Win–win?: Food poverty, food aid and food surplus in the UK today', *Anthropology Today* 33(3): 317–22.

Cappelen, A., J. Jørgen Ouren and T. Skjerpen. 2011. *Effects of Immigration Policies on Immigration to Norway, 1969–2010*. Oslo: Statistics Norway. https://www.ssb.no/a/english/publikas-joner/pdf/rapp_201140_en/rapp_201140_en.pdf.

Cardoso, S., F. Augusto and M. Truninger. 2017. 'Children, families, food poverty and the media: Analysis of Portugal newspapers 2007–2016', unpublished report, Families and Food in Hard Times Project, July.

Cardoso, S., M. Truninger, V. Ramos and F. Augusto. 2019. 'School meals and food poverty: Children's views, parents' perspectives and the role of school', *Children & Society* 33(6): 572–86.

Carney, C. and B. Maitre. 2012. *Constructing a Food Poverty Indicator for Ireland Using the Survey of Income and Living Conditions*. Dublin: Department of Social Protection.

Chase, E. and R. Walker. 2013. 'The co-construction of shame in the context of poverty: Beyond a threat to the social bond', *Sociology* 47(4): 739–54.

Chase, E. and R. Walker. 2015. 'Constructing reality? The "discursive truth" of poverty in Britain and how it frames the experience of shame', in *Poverty and Shame: Global perspectives*, edited by E. Chase and G. Bantebya-Kyomuheno, 256–69. Oxford: Oxford University Press.

Christensen, T. and P. Lægreid, eds. 2007. *Transcending New Public Management: The transformation of public sector reforms*. Aldershot: Ashgate.

Christie, I., M. Harrison, C. Hitchman and T. Lang. 2002. *Inconvenience Food: The struggle to eat well on a low income*. London: Demos.

Chzhen, Y., Z. Bruckauf and UNICEF Office of Research Innocenti. 2018. 'Monitoring progress towards sustainable development: Multidimensional child poverty in the European Union', *Journal of Poverty and Social Justice* 26(2): 129–50.

Coates, J., E. A. Frongillo, B. L. Rogers, P. Webb, P. E. Wilde and R. Houser. 2006. 'Commonalities in the experience of household food insecurity across cultures: What are measures missing?', *Journal of Nutrition* 136(5): 1438S–48S.

Colas, A., J. Edwards, J. Levi and S. Zubaida. 2018. *Food, Politics and Society: Social theory and the modern food system*. Oakland: University of California Press.

Collett, E. 2011. *The Future of Immigrant Integration in Europe in a Time of Austerity*. Washington, DC: Migration Policy Institute.

Cook, D. 2009. 'Semantic provisioning of children's food: Commerce, care and maternal practice', *Childhood* 16(3): 317–34.

Corden, A. and J. Millar. 2007. 'Qualitative longitudinal research for social policy: Introduction to themed section', *Social Policy & Society* 6(4): 529–32.

Corkill, D. and M. Eaton. 1998. 'Multicultural insertions in a small economy: Portugal's immigrant communities', *South European Society and Politics* 3(3): 149–68.

Costa, A. B., I. Baptista, P. Perista and P. Carrilho. 2008. *Um olhar sobre a pobreza. Vulnerabilidade e exclusão social no Portugal Contemporâneo*. Lisbon: Gradiva.

Coulter, S. 2016. 'The UK labour market and the "Great Recession"', in *Unemployment, Internal Devaluation and Labour Market Deregulation in Europe*, edited by M. Myant, T. Sotiria and A. Piasna, 197–227. Brussels: European Trade Union Institute.

Coveney, J. 2006. *Food, Morals and Meaning: The pleasure and anxiety of eating*, 2nd edn. Abingdon: Routledge.

Crafter, S. and H. Iqbal. 2018. 'Child language brokering: Spaces of belonging and mediators of cultural knowledge', Final Report, Open University and Institute of Education, UCL.

Crettaz, E. 2011. *Fighting Working Poverty in Post-industrial Economies: Causes, trade-offs and policy solutions*. Cheltenham: Edward Elgar.

Crompton, R. 2006. *Employment and the Family*. Cambridge: Cambridge University Press.

Crossley, T., P. Fisher, H. Low, M. Benzeval, J. Burton, A. Jäckle and B. Read. 2020. 'Understanding society COVID-19 survey, April briefing note: The economic effects', Working Paper No. 10/2020, ISER, University of Essex, Colchester.

Croucher, K., D. Quilgars and A. Dyke. 2019. *Housing and Life Experiences: Making a home on a low income*. York: JRF. https://www.jrf.org.uk/report/housing-and-life-experiences-making-home-low-income.

Cuadra, C. B. 2012. 'Right of access to health care for undocumented migrants in the EU: A comparative study of national policies', *European Journal of Public Health* 22(2): 267–71.

Currie, C., C. Zanotti, A. Morgan, D. Currie, M. de Looze, C. Roberts, O. Samdal, O. R. F. Smith and V. Barnekow. 2012. *Social Determinants of Health and Well-Being among Young People. Health Behaviour in School-Aged Children (HBSC) Study: International report from the 2009/2010 Survey*. Copenhagen: WHO Regional Office for Europe. http://www.euro.who.int/__data/assets/pdf_file/0003/163857/Social-determinants-of-health-and-well-being-among-young-people.pdf?ua=1.

Dagdeviren, H., M. Donoghue and L. Meier. 2017. 'The narratives of hardship: The new and the old poor in the aftermath of the 2008 crisis in Europe', *Sociological Review* 65(2): 369–85.

Daly, M. 2017. 'Money-related meanings and practices in low-income and poor families', *Sociology* 51(2): 450–65.

Daly, M. and G. Kelly. 2015. *Families and Poverty: Everyday life on a low income*. Bristol: Policy Press.

Danesi, G. 2018. 'A cross-cultural approach to eating together: Practices of commensality among French, German and Spanish young adults', *Social Science Information* 57(1): 99–120.

Daniels, A. K. 1987. 'Invisible work', *Social Problems* 34(5): 403–15.

Darmon, I. and A. Warde. 2014. 'Introduction: Towards dynamic comparative analysis', *Anthropology of Food* S10. https://journals.openedition.org/aof/7700.

Davis, A., D. Hirsch and M. Padley. 2014. *A Minimum Income Standard for the UK in 2014*. York: JRF.

Davis, A., D. Hirsch, N. Smith, J. Beckhelling and M. Padley. 2012. *A Minimum Income Standard for the UK in 2012: Keeping up in hard times*. York: JRF.

Davis, O. and B. Geiger. 2017. 'Did food insecurity rise across Europe after the 2008 crisis? An analysis across welfare regimes', *Social Policy and Society* 16(3): 343–60

Dean, H. 1998. 'Benefit fraud and citizenship', in *Choice and Public Policy*, edited by P. Taylor-Gooby, 183–200. Basingstoke: Palgrave Macmillan.

Defra (Department for Environment, Food & Rural Affairs). 2020. 'Family food 2017/18'. https://www.gov.uk/government/publications/family-food-201718/family-food-201718#household-spending-on-food.

De Sousa, A. 2019. 'Lisbon's bad week: Police brutality reveals Portugal's urban reality', The *Guardian*, 31 January. https://www.theguardian.com/cities/2019/jan/31/lisbons-bad-week-police-brutality-reveals-portugals-urban-reality.

Despacho no. 8452-A. 2015. 'The price of a school meal is 1.46€', *Diário da República*, n.°148/2015, 2° Suplemento, Série II de 2015-07-31, 31 July.

DeVault, M. 1991. *Feeding the Family: The social organization of caring as gendered work*. Chicago: University of Chicago Press.

Dexter, Z., L. Capron and L. Gregg. 2016. *Making Life Impossible: How the needs of destitute migrant children are going unmet*. London: Children's Society.

DG Employment and Social Affairs. 2014. *Study on Mobility, Migration and Destitution in the European Union Final Report. PROGRESS 2007–2013*. Brussels: European Community Programme for Employment and Social Solidarity.

Dickens, C. 1854. *Hard Times*. London: Bradbury & Evans.

Dimbleby, H. and J. Vincent. 2013. *The School Food Plan*. London: Department for Education.

Douglas, M. 1975. *Implicit Meanings: Essays in anthropology*. London: Routledge & Kegan Paul.

Døving, R. 1999. 'Matpakka – den store norske fortellingen om familien og nasjonen', *Tidsskrift for religion og kultur* 1. http://www.hf.ntnu.no/din/doving.html.

Dowler, E. 2008. 'Policy initiatives to address low-income households' nutritional needs in the UK', *Proceedings of the Nutrition Society* 67: 289–300.

Dowler, E. and C. Calvert. 1995. 'Diets of lone parent families'. *Social Policy Research* 71: 1–4.

Dowler, E., M. Kneafsey, H. Lambie, A. Inman and R. Collier. 2011. 'Thinking about "food security": Engaging with UK consumers', *Critical Public Health* 21(4): 403–16.

Dowler, E. and S. Leather. 2000. 'Spare some change for a bite to eat? From primary poverty to social exclusion: The role of nutrition and food', in *Experiencing Poverty*, edited by J. Bradshaw and R. Sainsbury, 200–18. Aldershot: Ashgate.

Dowler, E. and D. O'Connor. 2012. 'Rights based approaches to addressing food poverty and food insecurity in Ireland and UK', *Social Science and Medicine* 74(1): 44–51.

Dowler, E., S. Turner and B. Dobson. 2001. *Poverty Bites: Food, health and poor families*. London: Child Poverty Action Group.

Duffy, K. 2013. *Lifeboat or Life Sentence? The Troika and emergency assistance programmes and their impact on poverty and social exclusion*. Brussels: European Anti-Poverty Network. https://www.eapn.eu/wp-content/uploads/2016/01/2013-EAPN-troika-report-N-print.pdf.

Duncan, S. and R. Edwards. 1997. 'Lone mothers and paid work: Rational economic man or gendered moral rationalities?', *Feminist Economics* 3(2): 29–61.

Duncan, S. and R. Edwards. 1999. *Lone Mothers, Paid Work and Gendered Moral Rationalities*. Basingstoke: Palgrave Macmillan.

Dupuis, A. and D. Thorns. 2002. 'Home, home ownership and the search for ontological security', *Sociological Review* 46(1): 24–47.

Durkheim, E. 1981. *The Rules of Sociological Method*, translated by W. D. Halls. London: Free Press.

EAPN (European Anti-Poverty Network). 2015. *Report on Income and Social Protection for the EU Drivers Project: Synthesis of Case Study Evidence Compiled by European Anti-Poverty Network*. Brussels.

Eardley, T., J. Bradshaw, J. Ditch and I. Gough. 1996. *Social Assistance in OECD Countries: Synthesis report*. London: Her Majesty's Stationary Office.

Ebaugh, H. and M. Curry. 2000. 'Fictive kin as social capital in new immigrant communities', *Sociological Perspectives* 43(2): 189–209.

ECRI (European Commission against Racism and Intolerance). 2007. *Third Report on Portugal: European Commission against Racism and Intolerance*. Strasbourg: European Commission against Racism and Intolerance. http://hudoc.ecri.coe.int/XMLEcri/ENGLISH/Cycle_03/03_CbC_eng/PRT-CbC-III-2007-4-ENG.pdf.

Edin, K. and M. Kefalas. 2005. *Promises I Can Keep: Why poor women put motherhood before marriage*. Berkeley: University of California Press.

Erel, U. and L. Ryan. 2019. 'Migrant capitals: Proposing a multi-level analytical spatio-temporal framework', *Sociology* 53: 246–84.

Esping-Andersen, G. 1990. *The Three Worlds of Welfare Capitalism*. Cambridge: Polity Press.

EU-FRA (European Union: European Agency for Fundamental Rights). 2018. 'Fundamental rights report 2018', June. https://www.refworld.org/docid/5b18f1b44.html.

Eurofound. 2017. 'Working poor in Europe – Portugal'. https://www.eurofound.europa.eu/publications/report/2010/working-poor-in-europe-portugal.

Eurofound. 2020. 'Working poor', 8 December. https://www.eurofound.europa.eu/topic/working-poor.

European Commission. 2016. *Eurostat*. Luxembourg.

Eurostat. 2016. *Consumer price levels in the EU, 2016*. Luxembourg: European Commission.

Eurostat. 2017. 'EU statistics on income and living conditions (EU-SILC) methodology'. https://ec.europa.eu/eurostat/statistics-explained/index.php/EU_statistics_on_income_and_living_conditions_(EU-SILC)_methodology.

Eurostat. 2018. *Living Conditions in Europe: 2018 Edition*. Luxembourg: Publications Office of the European Union. https://ec.europa.eu/eurostat/documents/3217494/9079352/KS-DZ-18-001-EN-N.pdf/884f6fec-2450-430a-b68d-f12c3012f4d0.

Eurostat. 2019. 'Consumer price levels in 2018', news release. https://ec.europa.eu/eurostat/documents/2995521/9832355/2-20062019-AP-EN.pdf/6dbde954-2750-46fa-9cb5-84eff9eda121.

Evans, D. 2011. 'Thrifty, green or frugal: Reflections on sustainable consumption in a changing economic climate', *Geoforum* 42: 550–7.

Eydoux, A. and M.-T. Letablier. 2009. 'Familles monoparentales et pauvreté en Europe: Quelles réponses politiques?', *Politiques sociales et familiales* 98: 21–36.

Fafo. 2019. 'Survey indicates underlying racism', *News in English*, 20 May. https://www.newsinenglish.no/2019/05/20/survey-indicates-underlying-racism/.

FAO (Food and Agriculture Organisation), International Fund for Agricultural Development (IFAD), United Nations International Children's Emergency Fund (UNICEF), World Food Programme (WFP) and World Health Organization (WHO). 2018. *The State of Food Security and Nutrition in the World: Building climate resilience for food security and nutrition*. Rome: Food and Agriculture Organisation.

Farkas, L. 2017. *Analysis and Comparative Review of Equality Data Collection Practices in the European Union Data Collection in the Field of Ethnicity*. Brussels: European Commission.

Farthing, R. 2012. *Going Hungry? Young people's experiences of free school meals*. London: Child Poverty Action Group and British Youth Council.

FEBA (Federação Europeia de Bancos Alimentares). 2015. 'Pessoas Assistidas'. goo.gl/S92Zj9

Ferragina, F., M. Tomlinson and R. Walker. 2013. *Poverty, Participation and Choice: The legacy of Peter Townsend*. York: JRF.

Ferrara, M. 2009. 'From the welfare state to the social investment state', *Rivista Internazionale di Scienze Sociali* 117(3–4): 513–28.

Festinger, L. 1954. 'A theory of social comparison process', *Human Relations* 7(2): 117–40.

Filandri, M. and E. Struffolino. 2019. 'Individual and household in-work poverty in Europe: Understanding the role of labor market characteristics', *European Societies* 21(1): 130–57.

Finch, J. 1989. *Family Obligations and Social Change*. Cambridge: Polity Press.

Finch, J. and J. Mason. 1993. *Negotiating Family Responsibilities*. London: Routledge.

Fischler, C. 1988. 'Food, self and identity', *Social Science Information* 27: 275–93.

Fischler, C. 2011. 'Commensality, society and culture', *Social Science Information* 50(3–4): 528–48.

Fischler, C. 2015. 'Introduction', in *Selective Eating: The rise, meaning and sense of personal dietary requirements*, edited by C. Fischler, 1–15. Paris: Odile Jacob.

Fletcher, A. 2017. 'Applying critical realism in qualitative research', *International Journal of Social Research Methodology* 20(2): 181–94.

Fligstein, N. and A. Goldstein. 2011. 'The roots of the Great Recession', in *The Great Recession*, edited by D. Grusky, B. Western and C. Wimer, 21–57. New York: Russell Sage Foundation.

Flyvbjerg, B. 2004. 'Five misunderstandings about case-study research', in *Qualitative Research Practice*, edited by C. Seale, G. Gobo, J. Gubrium and D. Silverman, 420–35. London: SAGE.

Fog Olwig, K. 1998. 'Narratives of the children left behind: Home and identity in globalised Caribbean families', *Journal of Ethnic and Migration Studies*, 25(2): 267–84.

Fonseca, M. and J. McGarrigle. 2014. 'Immigration and policy: New challenges after the economic crisis in Portugal', in *Impacts of the Recent Economic Crisis (2008–2009) on International Migration*, edited by E. Levine and M. Verea, 51–75. Coyoacán: Universidad Nacional Autónoma de México.

Food Foundation. 2020a. 'Covid-19 tracker: The impact of coronavirus on food'. https://foodfoundation.org.uk/vulnerable-groups/.

Food Foundation. 2020b. 'Demand for free school meals rises sharply as the economic impact of Covid 19 on families bites'. https://foodfoundation.org.uk/demand-for-free-school-meals-rises-sharply-as-the-economic-impact-of-covid-19-on-families-bites/.

Fram, M. S., J. Bernal and E. A. Frongillo. 2015. *The Measurement of Food Insecurity among Children: Review of literature and concept note*. Florence: UNICEF Office of Research.

Fram, M. S., E. A. Frongillo, S. J. Jones, R. C. Williams, M. P. Burke, K. P. DeLoach and C. E. Blake. 2011. 'Children are aware of food insecurity and take responsibility for managing food resources', *Journal of Nutrition* 141(6): 1114–19.

Frazer, H. and E. Marlier. 2016. *Minimum Income Schemes in Europe: A study of national policies 2015*. Brussels: European Commission.

Gaisbauer, H. P., G. Schweiger and C. Sedmark., eds. 2019. *Absolute Poverty in Europe: Interdisciplinary perspectives on a hidden phenomenon*. Bristol: Policy Press.

Gardiner, L., M. Gustafsson, M. Brewer, K. Handscomb, K. Henehan, L. Judge and F. Rahma. 2020. *An Intergenerational Audit for the UK*. London: Resolution Foundation. https://www.resolutionfoundation.org/publications/intergenerational-audit-uk-2020/.

Gardiner, K. and J. Millar. 2006. 'How low-paid employees avoid poverty: An analysis by family type and household structure', *Journal of Social Policy*, 35(3): 351–69.

Garrett, P. 2015. 'Words matter: Deconstructing "welfare dependency" in the UK', *Critical and Radical Social Work* 3(3): 389–406.

Geertz, C. 1973. *The Interpretation of Cultures: Selected essays*. New York: Basic Books.

Gentilini, U. 2013. 'Banking on food: The state of food banks in high-income countries', *IDS Working Papers* 415: 1–18.

GESIS (Gesellschaft Sozialwissenschaftlicher Infrastruktureinrichtungen). 2016. *Codebook EU-SILC 2013 Cross-Sectional File*. Mannheim: Leibniz Institute for the Social Sciences.

Giddens, A. 1984. *The Constitution of Society*. Oxford: Polity Press.

Gillard, D. 2003. 'Food for thought: Child nutrition, the school dinner and the food industry'. http://www.educationengland.org.uk/articles/22food.html.

Glennerster, H., J. Hills, D. Piachaud and J. Webb. 2004. *One Hundred Years of Poverty and Policy*. York: JRF.

Goerne, A., 2011. 'A comparative analysis of in-work poverty in the European Union', in *Working Poverty in Europe: A comparative approach*, edited by N. Fraser, R. Gutiérrez and R. Peña-Casas, 15–45. Basingstoke: Palgrave Macmillan.

Goffman, E. 1967. *Interaction Ritual: Essays in Face to Face Behaviour*. New Brunswick, NJ: Transaction.

Goffman, E. 1974. *Stigma: Notes on the Management of Spoiled Identity*. London: Penguin Books.

Goode, J. 2012. 'Feeding the family when the wolf's at the door: The impact of over-indebtedness on contemporary foodways in low-income families in the UK', *Food and Foodways* 20(1): 8–30.

Goode, J., C. Callendar and R. Lister. 1998. *Purse or Wallet? Gender inequalities within families on benefits*. London: Policy Studies Institute.

Gordon, D. 2006. 'The concept and measurement of poverty', in *Poverty and Social Exclusion in Britain*, edited by C. Pantazis, D. Gordon. and R. Levitas, 29–63. Bristol: Policy Press.

Gordon, I., K. Scanlon, T. Travers and C. Whitehead. 2009. *Economic Impact on the London and UK Economy of an Earned Regularisation of Irregular Migrants to the UK*. London: London School of Economics.

Gordon, K., J. Wilson and A. Tonner. 2018. 'Tackling the determinants of food insecurity: The potential of local food projects', presentation at the Multi-disciplinary Research Conference on Food and Poverty in the UK: Taking Stock, Moving Forward, London School of Economics, London, 16–17 April.

Gosling, V. 2008. '"I've always managed, that's what we do": Social capital and women's experiences of social exclusion', *Sociological Research Online* 13(1): 1–18.

Gough, I. 1996. 'Social assistance in Southern Europe', *South European Society and Politics* 1(1): 1–23.

Gregório, M., P. Graça, A. Costa and P. Nogueira. 2014a. 'Time and regional perspectives of food insecurity during the economic crisis in Portugal, 2011–2013', *Saúde e Sociedade* 23(4): 1127–41.

Gregório, M., P. Graça and P. Nogueira. 2014b. 'Promoting a food and nutrition policy in the age of austerity – the Portuguese case'. Paper presented to the conference 'The Welfare State in Portugal in the Age of Austerity', Lisbon School of Economics & Management, Universidade de Lisboa, 9–10 May. https://www.iseg.ulisboa.pt/aquila/mkt/content/the-welfare-state-in-portugal-in-the-age-of-auterity/Papers/index.jsp.

Grieshaber, S. 1997. 'Mealtime rules: Power and resistance in the construction of mealtime rules', *British Journal of Sociology* 48(4): 649–66.

Grignon, C. 2001. 'Commensality and social morphology: An essay of typology', in *Food, Drink and Identity: Cooking, eating and drinking in Europe since the Middle Ages*, edited by P. Scholliers, 23–33. Oxford: Berg.

Grødem, A. 2017. 'Family-oriented policies in Scandinavia and the challenge of immigration', *Journal of European Social Policy* 27(1): 77–8.

Guerreiro, das dores, M. 2014. 'Family policies in Portugal', in *Handbook of Family Policies across the Globe*, edited by M. Robila, 195–210. New York: Springer.

Guio, A., Gordon, D., Najera, H. and Pomati, M. 2017. *Revising the EU Material Deprivation Variables, Working Papers*. Luxembourg: Eurostat.

Guptill, A., D. Copelton and B. Lucal. 2017. *Food & Society*, 2nd edn. Cambridge: Polity Press.

Hagen, K. and I. Lødemel. 2003. 'Fattigdomstiåret 2000–2010', in *Det Norske samfunn*, edited by I. Frønes and L. Kjølsrød, 284–307. Oslo: Gyldendal.

Halleröd, B. 1995. 'Perceptions of poverty in Sweden', *Scandinavian Journal of Social Welfare* 4(3): 174–89.

Halleröd, B., H. Ekbrand and M. Bengsstron. 2015. 'In-work poverty and labour market trajectories: Poverty risks among the working population in 22 European countries', *Journal of European Social Policy* 25(5): 473–88.

Halleröd, B. and D. Larsson. 2008. 'In-work poverty in a transitional labour market: Sweden', in *The Working Poor in Europe: Employment, poverty and globalization*, edited by H.-J. Andreß and H. Lohmann, 155–78. Cheltenham: Edward Elgar.

Hallgrimsdottir, H., A. Finnsson and E. Brunet-Jailly. 2020. 'Austerity talk and crisis narratives: Memory politics, xenophobia, and citizenship in the European Union', *Frontiers in Sociology*, 13 March. https://doi.org/10.3389/fsoc.2020.00014.

Hamelin, A., M. Beaudry and J. Habicht. 2002. 'Characterization of household food insecurity in Québec: Food and feelings', *Social Science and Medicine* 54(1): 119–32.

Hammersley, M. 2015. 'On ethical principles for social research', *International Journal of Social Research Methodology* 18(4): 433–49.

Hanmer, J. and J. Hearn. 1999. 'Gender and welfare research', in *Welfare Research: A Critical Review*, edited by F. Williams, J. Popay and A. Oakley, 106–30. London: UCL Press.

Hansen, R. 2003. 'Migration to Europe since 1945: Its history and its lessons', *Political Quarterly* 74(S1): 25–38.

Hantrais, L. 1999. 'Contextualization in cross-national comparative research', *International Journal of Social Research Methodology* 2(2): 93–108.

Hantrais, L. 2009. *International Comparative Research: Theory, methods, and practice*. Basingstoke: Palgrave Macmillan.

Haque, Z., Becares, L. and Treloar, N. 2020. *Over-Exposed and Under-Protected: The devastating impact of COVID-19 on Black and minority ethnic communities in Great Britain. A Runnymede Trust and ICM Survey*. London: Runnymede. https://www.runnymedetrust.org/uploads/Runnymede%20Covid19%20Survey%20report%20v3.pdf.

Harden, J., K. Backett-Milburn, M. Hill and A. MacLean. 2010. 'Oh, what a tangled web we weave: Experiences of doing "multiple perspectives" research in families', *International Journal of Social Research Methodology* 13(5): 441–52.

Harkness, S. 2013. 'Women, families and the "Great Recession" in the UK', in *Social Policy Review 25: Analysis and Debate in Social Policy 2013*, edited by G. Ramia, K. Farnsworth and Z. Irving, 293–314. Bristol: Policy Press.

Harvey, M. 2014. 'Comparing comparing: Exercises in stretching – concepts', *Anthropology of Food* S10. https://doi.org/10.4000/aof.7689.

Hawkes, C., Harris, J. and Gillespie, S. 2017. *Changing Diets: Urbanization and the nutrition transition. Global Food Policy Report*. Brighton: International Food Policy Research Institute.

HBS (Household Budget Surveys). 2017. 'Household Budget Surveys (HBS) – Overview', Eurostat. https://ec.europa.eu/eurostat/web/household-budget-surveys.

Head, E. 2009. 'The ethics and implications of paying participants in qualitative research', *International Journal of Social Research Methodology* 12(4): 335–44.

Healy, A. 2019. 'Measuring food poverty in Ireland: The importance of including exclusion', *Irish Journal of Sociology* 27(2): 105–27.

Heath, A. and L. Richards. 2020. 'How racist is Britain today? What the evidence tells us', *The Conversation*. Online: https://theconversation.com/how-racist-is-britain-today-what-the-evidence-tells-us-141657.

Hernes, V., J. Arendt, P. Joona and K. Tronstad. 2019. *Nordic Integration and Settlement Policies for Refugees: A comparative analysis of labour market integration outcomes*. Copenhagen: Nordic Council of Ministers.

Hick, R. 2014. 'Poverty as capability deprivation: Conceptualising and measuring poverty in contemporary Europe', *European Journal of Sociology* 55(3): 295–323.

Hick, R. and A. Lanau. 2017. *In-Work Poverty in the UK: Problem, policy analysis and platform for action*. Cardiff: Cardiff University. http://orca.cf.ac.uk/103013/1/Hick%20and%20Lanau%20_%20In-Work%20Poverty%20in%20the%20UK.pdf.

Hill, K., A. Davis, D. Hirsch, M. Padley and N. Smith. 2015. *Disability and Minimum Living Standards: The additional costs of living for people who are sight impaired and people who are deaf*. Loughborough: Centre for Research in Social Policy. https://www.lboro.ac.uk/media/wwwlboroacuk/content/crsp/downloads/reports/Disability%20and%20Minimum%20Living%20Standards%20Report.pdf.

Hill, K., D. Hirsch and A. Davis. 2020. 'The role of social support networks in helping low income families through uncertain times', *Social Policy & Society* 20(1): 1–16.

Hills, J. 2014. *Good Times, Bad Times: The welfare myth of them and us*. Bristol: Policy Press.

Hills, J., R. Smithies and A. McKnight. 2006. *Tracking Income: How working families' incomes vary through the year*. London: ESRC Research Centre for Analysis of Social Exclusion.

Hippe, J. M., Ø. Berge, et al. 2013. *Ombyggingens periode: Landrapport om Norge 1990–2012*. Oslo: Fafo. https://www.fafo.no/images/pub/2013/20305.pdf.

Hjelde, K. H. 2009. *Jeg er alltid bekymret: Om udokumenterte migranter og deres forhold til helsetjenestene i Oslo*. Oslo: Norwegian Centre for Minority Health Research.

Hobsbawm, E. and T. Ranger. 1983. *The Invention of Tradition*. Cambridge: Cambridge University Press.

Holm, L., M. Ekström, J. Gronow, U. Kjærnes, T. Bøker Lund, J. Mäkelä and M. Niva. 2012. 'The modernisation of Nordic eating: Studying changes and stabilities in eating patterns', *Anthropology of Food* S7: 2–14.

Hood, A. and T. Waters. 2017. *Living Standards, Poverty and Inequality in the UK: 2016–17 to 2021–22*. London: Institute for Fiscal Studies.

Hopkin, J. 2020. *Anti-system Politics: The crisis of market liberalism in rich democracies*. Oxford: Oxford University Press.

Horemans, J., I. Marx and B. Nolan. 2016. 'Hanging in, but only just: Part-time employment and in-work poverty throughout the crisis', *IZA Journal of European Labor Studies* 5(5). https://doi.org/10.1186/s40174-016-0053-6.

Horta, A., M. Truninger, S. Alexandre, J. Teixeira and V. Aparecida da Silva. 2013. 'Children's food meanings and eating contexts: Schools and their surroundings', *Young Consumers* 14(4): 312–20.

Horta, A. and P. White. 2008. 'Post-colonial migration and citizenship regimes: A comparison of Portugal and the United Kingdom', *Revista Migrações* 4: 33–57. https://ec.europa.eu/migrant-integration/librarydoc/post-colonial-migration-and-citizenship-regimes-a-comparison-of-portugal-and-the-united-kingdom.

Horvath, K. and R. Latcheva. 2019. 'Mixing methods in the age of migration politics: A commentary on validity and reflexivity in current migration research', *Journal of Mixed Methods* 13(2): 127–31.

Husebø-Evensen, M. 2016. 'Matvarekrigen skaper krise på Fattighuset: Vi er snart tomme for mat', TV2, 4 February. https://www.tv2.no/a/8010464/.

Independent Working Group on Food Poverty. 2016. 'Dignity: Ending hunger together in Scotland'. https://www.gov.scot/publications/dignity-ending-hunger-together-scotland-report-independendent-working-group-food/.

INE (Instituto Nacional de Estatística). 2014. 'EU Statistics on Income and Living Conditions (EU-SILC) 2013'.

Jackson, P., S. Olive and G. Smith. 2009. 'Myths of the family meal: Re-reading Edwardian life histories', in *Changing Families, Changing Food*, edited by P. Jackson, 131–45. Basingstoke: Palgrave Macmillan.

Jaehrling, K., T. Kalina and L. Mesaros. 2015. 'A paradox of activation strategies: Why increasing labour market participation among single mothers failed to bring down poverty rates', *Social Politics* 22(1): 86–110.

James, A. 1979. 'Confections, concoctions and conceptions', *Journal of the Anthropological Society of Oxford*, 10: 83–95.

James, A., P. Curtis and K. Davis. 2009. 'Negotiating family, negotiating food: Children as family participants?', in *Children, Food and Identity in Everyday Life*, edited by A. James, A. Kjørholt and V. Tingstad, 35–51. London: Palgrave Macmillan.

Jamie Oliver Foundation. 2017. *A Report of the Food Education Learning Landscape*. London: AKO Foundation.

Jolly, A. 2018. 'No recourse to social work? Statutory neglect, social exclusion and undocumented migrant families in the UK', *Social Inclusion* 6(3): 190–200.

Jones, N. R. V., A. I. Conklin, M. Suhrcke and P. Monsivais. 2014. 'The growing price gap between more and less healthy foods: Analysis of a novel longitudinal UK dataset', *PLoS ONE* 9(10): e109343.

Jonsson, S. 2020. 'A society which is not: Political emergence and migrant agency', *Current Sociology* 68(2): 204–22.

JRF (Joseph Rowntree Foundation). 2020. 'Poverty levels and trends in England, Wales, Scotland and Northern Ireland'. https://www.jrf.org.uk/data/poverty-levels-and-trends-england-wales-scotland-and-northern-ireland#:~:text=In%20Wales%2C%20the%20pensioner%20poverty,12%25%20in%202016%2F19.

Julier, A. 2013. *Eating Together: Food, friendship and inequality*. Urbana: University of Illinois Press.

Kenway, P. and G. Palmer. 2007. *Poverty among Ethnic Groups: How and why does it differ?* York: JRF. https://www.npi.org.uk/files/5813/7536/3916/2042-ethnicity-relative-poverty.pdf.

King, C. 1995. 'Viewpoint: What is hospitality?', *International Journal of Hospitality Management* 14: 219–23.

Kirkpatrick, S., L. McIntyre and M. Potestio. 2010. 'Child hunger and long-term adverse consequences for health', *Archives of Pediatrics and Adolescent Medicine* 164(8): 754–62.

Klinenberg, E. 2018. *Palaces for the People: How social infrastructure can help fight inequality, polarization, and the decline of civic life*. New York: Penguin Random House.

Klinenberg, E. 2020. 'We need social solidarity, not just social distancing: To combat the coronavirus, Americans need to do more than secure their own safety', *New York Times*, 14 March. https://www.nytimes.com/2020/03/14/opinion/coronavirus-social-distancing.html.

Kmietowicz, Z. and G. Iacobucci. 2017. 'Government fails to assuage doctors' concerns over NHS crisis', *British Medical Journal* 356: j153.

Kneafsey, M., E. Dowler, H. Lambie, A. Inman and R. Collier. 2012. 'Consumers and food security: Uncertain or empowered?', *Journal of Rural Studies* 28: 1–12.

Knight, A., J. Brannen, R. O'Connell and L. Hamilton. 2018. 'How do children and their families experience food poverty according to UK newspaper media 2006–2015?' *Journal of Poverty and Social Justice* 26(2): 207–33.

Knijn, T., C. Martin and J. Millar. 2007. 'Activation as a common framework for social policies towards lone parents', *Social Policy & Administration* 41(6): 638–52.

Kohn, M. 1987. 'Cross-national research as an analytic strategy: American Sociological Association, 1987 presidential address', *American Journal of Sociology* 52(6): 713–31.

Krumer-Nevo, M. and O. Benjamin. 2010. 'Critical poverty knowledge: Contesting othering and social distancing', *Current Sociology* 58(5): 693–714.

Kvamme, E. and S. Ytrehus. 2015. 'Barriers to health care access among undocumented migrant women in Norway', *Society, Health and Vulnerability* 6(1): article 28668. https://doi.org/10.3402/shv.v6.28668.

Lallement, L. 2003. 'Pragamatique de la comparaison', in *Stratégies de la comparaison internationale*, edited by M. Lallement and J. Spurk, 295–306. Paris: CNRS.

Lambie-Mumford, H. 2013. '"Every town should have one": Emergency food banking in the UK', *Journal of Social Policy* 42(1): 73–89.

Lambie-Mumford, H. 2017. *Hungry Britain: The rise of food charity*. Bristol: Policy Press.

Lambie-Mumford, H. and E. Dowler. 2014. 'Rising use of "food aid" in the United Kingdom', *British Food Journal* 116(9): 1418–25.

Lambie-Mumford, H. and E. Dowler. 2015. 'Hunger, food charity and social policy: Challenges faced by the emerging evidence base', *Social Policy and Society* 14(3): 497–506.

Lambie-Mumford, H. and T. Silvasti, eds. 2020. *The Rise of Food Charity in Europe*. Bristol: Policy Press.

Lang, T. 1997. 'Dividing up the cake: Food as social exclusion', in *Britain Divided: The growth of social exclusion in the 1980s and 1990s*, edited by A. Walker and C. Walker, 213–28. London: Child Poverty Action Group.

Lang, T. 2020. *Feeding Britain: Our food problems and how to fix them*. London: Pelican.

Lang, T., D. Barling and M. Caraher. 2009. *Food Policy: Integrating health, environment and society*. Oxford: Oxford University Press.

Lang, T., E. Millstone and T. Marsden. 2017. *A Food Brexit: Time to get real. A Brexit Briefing*. Brighton: University of Sussex Science Policy Research Unit.

Langsted, O. 1994. 'Does anyone regard children as experts when it comes to their own lives?', in *Valuing Quality in Early Childhood Services: New approaches to defining quality*, edited by P. Moss and A. Pence, 28–42. London: Paula Chapman.

Lansley, S. and Mack, J. (2015). Breadline Britain: the rise of mass poverty. London: Oneworld Publications.

Leather, S. 1996. *The Making of Modern Malnutrition*. London: Caroline Walker Trust.

Lems, E., F. Hilverda, A. Sarti, L. van der Voort, A. Kegel, C. Pittens, P. Broerse and C. Dedding. 2020. '"McDonald's is good for my social life": Developing health promotion together with adolescent girls from disadvantaged neighbourhoods in Amsterdam', *Children and Society* 34(3): 204–19.

Letablier, M. and K. Wall. 2018. 'Changing lone parenthood patterns: New challenges for policy and research', in *Lone Parenthood in the Life Course*, edited by L. Bernardi and D. Mortelmans, 29–54. Basel: Springer Open.

Levitas, R., E. Head and N. Finsh. 2006. 'Lone mothers, poverty and social exclusion', in *Poverty and Social Exclusion in Britain: The millennium survey*, edited by C. Pantazis, D. Gordon and R. Levitas, 405–30. Bristol: Policy Press.

LeVoy, M., N. Verbruggen and J. Wets, eds. 2003. *Undocumented Migrant Workers in Europe*. Brussels: Katholieke Universiteit.

Lewis, J. and B. Hobson. 1997. 'Introduction', in *Lone Mothers in European Welfare Regimes: Shifting policy logics*, edited by J. Lewis, 1–20. London: Jessica Kingsley Publishers.

Lightman, E., A. Mitchell and D. Herd. 2008. 'Globalization, precarious work, and the food bank', *Journal of Sociology and Social Welfare* 35(2): 9–28.

Lima, R. 2018. *Orientações sobre ementas e refeitorios escolares*. Lisbon: Ministerio da Educacao, Direccao-Geralda Educacao.

Lipsky, M. 2010. *Street-Level Bureaucracy: Dilemmas of the individual in public services*. Rev. edn. New York: Russell Sage Foundation.

Lister, R. 2004. *Poverty*. Cambridge: Polity Press.

Lister, R. 2007. 'Inclusive citizenship: Realizing the potential', *Citizenship Studies* 11(1): 49–61.

Lister, R. 2013. '"Power not pity": Poverty and human rights', *Ethics and Social Welfare* 7: 109–23.

Lister, R. 2015. '"To count for nothing": Poverty beyond the statistics', *Journal of the British Academy* 3: 139–65.

Livanos, I. and L. Papadopoulos. 2019. *The Rise of Precarious Employment in Europe: Theoretical perspectives, reforms and employment trends in the era of economic crisis*. Bingley: Emerald Publishing.

Lødemel, I. 1992. 'European poverty regimes', paper presented at the International Research Conference on Poverty and Distribution, Oslo, 16 November.

Lødemel, I. and B. Schulte. 1992. 'Social assistance: A part of social security or the Poor Law in new disguise?', paper presented at the Beveridge Conference, York, September.

Løes, A. 2010. 'Organic and conventional public food procurement for youth', *NorwayBioforsk Report* 5(110): iPOPY discussion paper 7.

Long, S. 1991. 'Do the school nutrition programs supplement household food expenditures?', *Journal of Human Resources*, 26(4): 654–78.

Loopstra, R., A. Reeves, D. Taylor-Robinson, B. Barr, M. McKee and D. Stuckler. 2015. 'Austerity, sanctions, and the rise of food banks in the UK', *British Medical Journal* 350: h1775.

Loopstra, R., A. Reeves, M. McKee and D. Stuckler. 2016. 'Food insecurity and social protection in Europe: Quasi-natural experiment of Europe's great recessions 2004–2012', *Preventive Medicine*, 89: 44–50.

Loopstra, R. and V. Tarasuk. 2013. 'What does increasing severity of food insecurity indicate for food insecure families? Relationship between severity of food insecurity and indicators of material hardship and constrained food purchasing', *Journal of Hunger and Environmental Nutrition* 8: 337–49.

Lund, T., U. Kjaernes and L. Holm. 2017. 'Eating out in four Nordic countries: National patterns and social stratification', *Appetite* 119: 23–33.

Lupton, D. 1996. *Food, the Body and the Self*. London: SAGE.

Lyngø, I. 2001. 'The National Nutrition Exhibition: A new nutritional narrative', in *Norway in the 1930s in Food, Drink and Identity: Cooking, eating and drinking in Europe since the Middle Ages*, edited by P. Scholliers, 141–63. Oxford: Berg.

Lyngø, I. 2003. 'Vitaminer! Kultur og vitenskap i mellomkrigstidens kos-tholdspropaganda', PhD dissertation, University of Oslo.

MacKay, K. and M. Quigley. 2018. 'Exacerbating inequalities? Health policy and the behavioural sciences', *Health Care Analysis* 26(4): 380–97.

Maeso, S. 2014. '"Civilising" the Roma? The depoliticisation of (anti)racism within the politics of integration', *Identities Global Studies in Culture and Power* 22(1): 53–70

Maguire, E. and P. Monsivais. 2015. 'Socio-economic dietary inequalities in UK adults: An updated picture of key food groups and nutrients from national surveillance data', *British Journal of Nutrition* 113: 181–9.

Mahony, S. and L. Pople. 2018. *Life in the Debt Trap: Stories of children in families struggling with debt*. Bristol: Policy Press.

Main, G. 2013. 'A child-derived material deprivation index', PhD thesis. University of York.

Main, G. 2018. 'Fair shares and families: A child-focused model of intra-household sharing', *Childhood Vulnerability Journal* 1: 31–49.

Main, G. and J. Bradshaw. 2018. 'Improving lives? Child poverty and social exclusion', in *Poverty and Social Exclusion in the UK. Volume 1: The nature and extent of the problem*, edited by E. Dermott and G. Main, 135–54. Bristol: Policy Press.

Margerison-Zilko, C., S. Goldman-Mellor, A. Falconi and J. Downing. 2016. 'Health impacts of the Great Recession: A critical review', *Current Epidemiology Reports* 3(1): 81–91.

Marshall, T. H. 1963. *Sociology at the Crossroads*. London: Heinemann.

Martens, L. 2018. *Childhood and Markets: Infants, parents and the business of childcaring*. Basingstoke: Palgrave Macmillan.

Marx, I., J. Vanhille and G. Verbist. 2012. 'Combating in-work poverty in continental Europe: An investigation using the Belgian case', *Journal of Social Policy* 41(1): 19–41.

Massey, D. 1994. *Space, Place and Gender*. Minneapolis: Minnesota Press.

Matlin, S., A. Depoux, S. Schütte, A. Flahault and L. Saso. 2018. 'Migrants' and refugees' health: Towards an agenda of solutions', *Public Health Reviews* 39: 27.

Mauss, M. 1990. *The Gift: The Form and Reason for Exchange in Archaic Societies*. New York: W.W. Norton & Company.

Maxwell, G. 1996. 'Measuring food insecurity: The frequency and severity of "coping strategies"', *Food Policy* 21(3): 291–303.

May, C., G. Brown, N. Cooper and L. Brill. 2009. *The Sustainable Livelihoods Handbook: An asset approach to poverty*. Manchester: Church Action on Poverty and Oxfam.

McGiffen, S. 1999. Interview: Tony Benn. *Spectrezine*, 20 April. Online: http://www.spectrezine.org/europe/tonybenn.html.

McKee, L. 1987. 'Households during unemployment the resourcefulness of the unemployed', in *Give and Take in Families: Studies in resource distribution*, edited by J. Brannen and G. Wilson, 96–116. London: Allen & Unwin.

McKee, M., M. Karanikolos, P. Belcher and D. Stuckler. 2012. 'Austerity: A failed experiment on the people of Europe', *Clinical Medicine* 12(4): 346–50.

McKendrick, J. H., S. Cunningham-Burley and K. Backett Milburn. 2003. *Life in Low Income Families in Scotland: Research report*. Edinburgh: Scottish Executive Social Research.

Merritt, S. 2006. 'Still a street-fighting man. Interview with José Saramago', The *Guardian*, 30 April. https://www.theguardian.com/books/2006/apr/30/fiction.features.

Midtbøen, A. and J. Rogstad. 2012. *Diskriminerings Omfang og Årsaker. Etniske Minoriteters Tilgang til Norsk Arbeidsliv*. Oslo: Institut for samfunnsforskning.

Midthjell, L. 2011. 'Fiscal policy and financial crises – what are the actual effects of fiscal policy?', *Norges Bank Economic Bulletin* 82: 24–38. https://www.norges-bank.no/contentassets/bdc-cffbe63374cca96a00cdf312888ab/fiscal_policy_and_financial_crisis.pdf.

Millar, J. 2007. 'The dynamics of poverty and employment: The contribution of qualitative longitudinal research to understanding transitions, adaptations and trajectories', *Social Policy & Society* 6(4): 533–44.

Millar, J. and T. Ridge. 2013. 'Lone mothers and paid work: The "family–work project"', *International Review of Sociology* 23(3): 564–77.

Miller, D. 1988. 'Appropriating the state on the council estate', *Man, New Series* 23: 353–72.

Mills. C. W. 1983. *The Sociological Imagination*. Oxford: Oxford University Press.

Moisio, R., E. Arnould and L. Price. 2004. 'Between mothers and markets: Constructing family identity through homemade food', *Journal of Consumer Culture* 4(3): 361–84.

Monteiro, C., J. Moubarac, R. Levy, D. Canella, M. Louzada and G. Cannon. 2018. 'Household availability of ultra-processed foods and obesity in nineteen European countries', *Public Health Nutrition* 21(1): 18–26.

Moreira, P. and P. Padrão. 2004. 'Educational and economic determinants of food intake in Portuguese adults: A cross-sectional survey', *BMC Public Health* 4: 58.

Morgan, D. 1996. *Family Connections: An Introduction to Family Studies*. Cambridge: Polity Press.

Morgan, D. 2011. *Rethinking Family Practices*. London: Palgrave Macmillan.

Motel-Klingebiel, A., C. Tesch-Roemer and H. von Kondratowitz. 2005. 'Welfare states do not crowd out the family: Evidence for mixed responsibility from comparative analyses', *Ageing and Society* 25: 863–82.

Najman, J. and G. Davey Smith. 2000. 'The embodiment of class-related and health inequalities: Australian policies', *Australian and New Zealand Journal of Public Health* 24(1): 3–4.

Narotzky, S. and N. Besnier. 2014. 'Crisis, value, and hope: Rethinking the economy. An introduction to Supplement 9', *Current Anthropology* 55(S9): S4–16.

National Institute of Statistics. 2014. *Food Balance Sheet*. Lisbon: National Institute of Statistics.

Nelson, M. 2004. *School Meals in Secondary Schools in England*. London: Food Standards Agency and Department for Education and Skills.

Norges Bank. 2019. 'About the fund'. https://www.nbim.no/en/the-fund/about-the-fund/.

Norwegian Ministry of Culture. 2020. 'The Norwegian government's Action Plan against Racism and Discrimination on the Grounds of Ethnicity and Religion 2020–2023'. https://www.regjeringen.no/contentassets/589aa9f4e14540b5a5a6144aaea7b518/action-plan-against-racism-and-discrimination_uu.pdf.

Notaker, H. 2018. 'Adaptation of dishes crossing frontiers: Examples of the American doughnut and the Spanish bacalao', *Anthropology of Food* S12. https://doi.org/10.4000/aof.9135.

Nunes, A. 2018. *Da Revolução de Abril à Contra-Revolução Neoliberal*. Lisbon: Página a Página.

Ochs, E. and M. Shohet. 2006. 'The cultural structuring of mealtime socialization', *New Directions for Child and Adolescent Development* 111: 35–49.

O'Connell, R. 2013. 'The use of visual methods with children in a mixed methods study of family food practices', *International Journal of Social Research Methodology* 16(1): 31–46.

O'Connell, R. and J. Brannen. 2016. *Food, Families and Work*. London: Bloomsbury.

O'Connell, R. and J. Brannen. 2020. 'We're not "all in this together": COVID-19 exposes stark realities of food insecurity'. UCL Europe. https://ucleuropeblog.com/2020/05/12/were-not-all-in-this-together-covid-19-exposes-stark-realities-of-food-insecurity/

O'Connell, R., A. Knight and J. Brannen. 2019a. *Living Hand to Mouth: Children and food in low income families*. London: Child Poverty Action Group.

O'Connell, R., A. Knight, J. Brannen and S. Skuland. 2021. 'Eating out, sharing food and social exclusion: Young people in low-income families in the UK and Norway', in *Austerity Across Europe: Lived experiences of economic crises*, edited by S. M. Hall, H. Pimlott-Wilson and J. Horton, 15–27. London: Routledge.

O'Connell, R., C. Owen, M. Padley, A. Simon and J. Brannen. 2019b. 'Which types of family are at risk of food poverty in the UK? A relative deprivation approach', *Social Policy and Society* 18(1): 1–18.

OECD (Organisation for Economic Co-operation and Development). 1993. *Purchasing Power Parities and Real Expenditures, GK Results*, Vol 2. Paris: Organisation for Economic Co-operation and Development.

OECD (Organisation for Economic Co-operation and Development). 2019. 'Economic survey of Norway'. http://www.oecd.org/economy/norway-economic-snapshot/.

Offer, S. 2012. 'The burden of reciprocity: Processes of exclusion and withdrawal from personal networks among low-income families', *Current Sociology* 60(6): 788–805.

OHCHR (Office of the High Commissioner for Human Rights). 2016. 'Committee on the Elimination of Racial Discrimination considers the report of Portugal'. https://www.ohchr.org/EN/NewsEvents/Pages/DisplayNews.aspx?NewsID=20958&LangID=E.

Øien, C. and S. Sønsterudbraten. 2011. *No Way In, No Way Out? A study of living conditions of irregular migrants in Norway*. Oslo: Fafo Information Office.

Oliveira, C. R. and N. Gomes. 2016. 'Indicadores de integração de imigrantes. Relatório Estatístico Anual 2016', Portuguese Migration Observatory. https://ec.europa.eu/migrant-integration/librarydoc/immigrant-integration-indicators-in-portugal-2016-statistical-report.

Olwig, K., B. Larsen and M. Rytter. 2012. *Migration, Family and the Welfare State: Integrating migrants and refugees in Scandinavia*. London: Routledge.

Onarheim, K., A. Melberg, B. Meier and I. Miljeteig. 2018. 'Towards universal health coverage: Including undocumented migrants'. *British Medical Journal Global Health* 3: e001031.

ONS (Office of National Statistics). 2017. 'People in employment on a zero-hours contract (LFS 2016)'. https://www.ons.gov.uk/employmentandlabourmarket/peopleinwork/earningsandworkinghours/articles/contractsthatdonotguaranteeaminimumnumberofhours/mar2017.

ONS (Office of National Statistics). 2020a. 'Child poverty and education outcomes by ethnicity'. https://www.ons.gov.uk/economy/nationalaccounts/uksectoraccounts/compendium/economicreview/february2020/childpovertyandeducationoutcomesbyethnicity.

ONS (Office of National Statistics). 2020b. 'Estimates of employment, unemployment, economic inactivity and other employment-related statistics for the UK'. https://www.ons.gov.uk/employmentandlabourmarket/peopleinwork/employmentandemployeetypes/bulletins/employmentintheuk/october2020.

Oostindjer, M., J. Aschemann-Witzel, Q. Wang, S. Skuland, B. Egelandsdal, G. Amdam and E. Van Kleef. 2017. 'Are school meals a viable and sustainable tool to improve the healthiness and sustainability of children's diet and food consumption? A cross-national comparative perspective', *Critical Reviews in Food Science and Nutrition* 57(18): 3942–58.

Padley, M. and D. Hirsch. 2017. *A Minimum Income Standard for the UK*. York: JRF.

Padley, M., L. Marshall, D. Hirsch, A. Davis and L. Valadez. 2015. *A Minimum Income Standard for London*. London: Trust for London.

Palmer, V. M. 1928. *Field Studies in Sociology: A student's manual*. Chicago: University of Chicago Press.

Parsons, T. 1943. 'The kinship system of the contemporary United States', *American Anthropologist* 45(1): 22–38.

Patrick, R. 2016. 'Living with and responding to the "scrounger" narrative in the UK: Exploring everyday strategies of acceptance, resistance and deflection', *Journal of Poverty and Social Justice* 24(3): 245–59.

Pearson, R. 2019. 'A feminist analysis of neoliberalism and austerity policies in the UK', *Soundings* 71: 28–39.

Pedroso, P. 2014. *Portugal and the Global Crisis: The impact of austerity on the economy, the social model and the performance of the state*. Berlin: Friedrich-Ebert-Stiftung.

Pember Reeves, M. 1913. *Round about a Pound a Week*. London: Persephone Books.

Penne, T. and T. Goedemé. 2020. 'Can low-income households afford a healthy diet? Insufficient income as a driver of food insecurity in Europe', *Food Policy*. https://doi.org/10.1016/j.foodpol.2020.101978.

Pereira, F. and P. Cunha. 2017. *Referencial de Educacao para a Saude*. Lisbon: Ministerio da Educacao–Direcao Geral da Educacao, Direcao-Geral da Saude.

Pereira, A. L., S. Handa and G. Holmqvist. 2017. 'Prevalence and correlates of food insecurity among children across the globe', Innocenti Working Paper 2017-09, UNICEF Office of Research, Florence. https://www.unicef-irc.org/publications/pdf/IWP_2017_09.pdf.

Pereirinha, J. 1992. *Observatory on Policies to Combat Social Exclusion: Consolidated national report: Portugal*. Lille: European Economic Interest Group.

Pereirinha, J., E. Pereira, F. Branco, I. Amaro, D. Costa and F. Nunes. 2017. 'Rendimento Adequado em Portugal. Quanto é necessário para uma pessoa viver com dignidade em Portugal?', Universidade de Lisboa, Universidade Católica Portuguesa e EAPN – Rede Europeia Anti-Pobreza em Portugal. http://www.rendimentoadequado.org.pt/images/rap/pdfs/Brochura%20raP%20_%20FINAL.pdf.

Perista, P. and I. Baptista. 2017. 'A new model for the food support programme on Portugal?', European Social Policy Network, Flash Report 2017/24.

Perruchoud, R. and J. Redpath-Cross. 2011. *International Organization for Migration Glossary on Migration*. Geneva: International Organization for Migration.

Pires, R. P., C. Pereira, J. Azevedo and A. C. Ribeiro. 2014. *Emigração Portuguesa. Relatório Estatístico 2014*. Lisbon: Observatório da Emigração, Rede Migra, Instituto Universitário de Lisboa, CIES-IUL and DGACCP. http://www.observatorioemigracao.pt/np4/1207.

Polanyi, K. 1944. *The Great Transformation*. New York: Farrar & Rinehart.

Popkin, B. 1993. 'Nutritional patterns and transitions', *Population and Development Review* 19(1): 138–57.

Poppendieck, J. 2012. 'Want among plenty: From hunger to inequality', in *Food and Culture: A Reader*, 3rd edn, edited by C. Counihan and P. Van Esterik, 563–71. New York: Taylor & Francis.

Portes, J., Aubergine Analysis and King's College London. 2018. *The Cumulative Impact of Tax and Welfare Reforms*. Manchester: Equality and Human Rights Commission.

Power, E. 2003. 'De-centering the text: Exploring the potential for visual methods in the sociology of food', *Journal for the Study of Food and Society* 6(2): 9–20.

Przeworski, A. and H. Teune. 1966. 'Equivalence in cross-national research', *Public Opinion Quarterly* 30(4): 551–68.

Pugh, A. 2009. *Longing and Belonging: Parents, children, and consumer culture*. Berkeley: University of California Press.

Pyrhönen, N. and T. Martikainen. 2017. *Nordic Migration and Integration Research: Overview and future prospects*. Oslo: Nordforsk.

Queiroz, M. 2013. 'Portugal's disappearing middle class', Inter Press Service News Agency. http://www.ipsnews.net/2013/01/portugals-disappearing-middle-class/.

Quilgars, D., M. Elsinga, A. Jones, J. Toussaint, H. Ruonavaara and P. Naumanen. 2009. 'Inside qualitative, cross-national research: Making methods transparent in a EU housing study', *International Journal of Social Research Methodology* 12(1): 19–31.

Radimer, K. 1990. 'Understanding hunger and developing indicators to assess it', PhD dissertation, Cornell University.

Radimer, K., C. Olson and C. Campbell. 1990. 'Development of indicators to assess hunger', *Journal of Nutrition* 120: 1544–8.

Radimer, K., C. Olson, J. Greene, C. Campbell and J. Habicht. 1992. 'Understanding hunger and developing indicators to assess it in women and children', *Journal of Nutrition Education* 24: 36S–45S.

Rana, E. A. and M. Kamal. 2018. 'Does clientelism affect income inequality? Evidence from panel data', *Journal of Income Distribution* 27(1): 1–24.

Rathbone, E. 1985. *The Disinherited Family*. London: Edward Arnold.

Ratti, L. 2020. 'In-work poverty in times of pandemic', *Social Europe*, 27 April. https://www.social-europe.eu/in-work-poverty-in-times-of-pandemic

Ray, K. 2004. *The Migrant's Table: Meals and memories in Bengali-American households*. Philadelphia: Temple University Press.

Reeves, A., R. Loopstra and D. Stuckler. 2017. 'The growing disconnect between food prices and wages in Europe: Cross-national analysis of food deprivation and welfare regimes in twenty-one EU countries, 2004–2012', *Public Health Nutrition* 20(8): 1414–22.

Regioplan Policy Research. 2014. *Study on Mobility, Migration and Destitution in the European Union Final Report*. Brussels: European Commission DG Employment, Social Affairs and Inclusion.

Ribbens McCarthy, J., J. Holland and V. Gillies. 2003. 'Multiple perspectives on the "family" lives of young people: Methodological and theoretical issues in case study research', *International Journal of Social Research Methodology* 6(1): 1–23.

Richards, A. 2004. *Hunger and Work in a Savage Tribe: A functional study of nutrition among the Southern Bantu*. Abingdon: Routledge.

Richards, C., U. Kjaernes and J. Vik. 2016. 'Food security in welfare capitalism: Comparing social entitlements to food in Australia and Norway', *Journal of Rural Studies* 43: 61–70.

Riches, G. 2018. *Food Bank Nations: Poverty, corporate charity and the right to food*. London: Routledge.

Riches, G. 2020. 'Foreword', in *The Rise of Food Charity in Europe*, edited by H. Lambie-Mumford and T Silvasti, xi–xviii. Bristol: Policy Press.

Riches, G. and T. Silvasti. 2014. *First World Hunger Revisited: Food charity or the right to food?*. Basingstoke: Palgrave Macmillan.

Ridge, T. 2002. *Childhood Poverty and Social Exclusion: From a child's perspective*. Bristol: Policy Press.

Ridge, T. 2007. 'Children and poverty across Europe: The challenge of developing child centred policies', *Zeitschrift für Soziologie der Erziehung und Sozialisation* 27(1): S28–42.

Ridge, T. 2009. *Living with Poverty: A review of the literature on children's and families' experiences of poverty*. London: DWP.

Ridge, T. 2011. 'The everyday costs of poverty in childhood: A review of qualitative research: Exploring the lives and experiences of low-income children in the UK', *Children and Society* 25(1): 73–84. https://doi.org/10.1111/j.1099-0860.2010.00345.x.

Rippin, H., J. Hutchinson, J. Jewell, J. Breda and J. Cade. 2017. 'Adult nutrient intakes from current national dietary surveys of European populations', *Nutrients* 9(12): 1288.

Rippin, H., J. Hutchinson, J. Jewell, J. Breda and J. Cade. 2018. 'Child and adolescent nutrient intakes from current national dietary surveys of European populations', *Nutrition Research Review* 32(1): 38–69.

Rodrigues, C., R. Figueiras and V. Junqueira. 2016. *Desigualdade do rendimento e pobreza em Portugal: As consequências sociais do programa de ajustamento*. Lisbon: Fundação Francisco Manuel dos Santos.

Rowntree, B. S. 1901. *Poverty: A study of town life*. London: Macmillan.

Royston, S., L. Rodrigues and D. Hounsell. 2012. *Fair and Square: A policy report on the future of free school meals*. London: Children's Society.

Salonen, A. and T. Silvasti. 2019. 'Faith-based organisations as actors in the charity economy: A case study of food assistance in Finland', in *Absolute Poverty in Europe: Interdisciplinary perspectives on a hidden phenomenon*, edited by H. Gaisbauer, G. Schweiger and C. Sedmak, 267–89. Bristol: Policy Press.

Saunders, P. 1990. *A Nation of Home Owners*. London: Unwin Hyman.

Saunders, P. 2013. *Down and Out: Poverty and social exclusion in Australia*. Bristol: Policy Press.

Sayer, A. 2001. 'Reply to Holmwood', *Sociology* 35(4): 967–84.

Sayer, A. 2017. 'Responding to the Troubled Families Programme: Framing the injuries of inequality', *Social Policy and Society* 16(1): 155–64.

Schäfer, A. and W. Streeck. 2013. 'Introduction: Politics in the age of austerity', in *Politics in the Age of Austerity*, edited by A. Schäfer and W. Streeck, 1–26. Cambridge: Polity Press.

Schofield, J. 2000. 'Increasing the generalisability of qualitative research', in *Case Study Method*, edited by R. Gomm, M. Hammersley and P. Foster, 69–98. London: SAGE.

Schütz, A. 1964. 'The stranger: An essay in social psychology', in *Collected Papers*, Vol. 2, edited by A. Brodersen, 91–106. The Hague: Martinus Nijhoff.

Scott, G., A. McKay, C. Sawers and R. Harris. 1999. *What Can We Afford? A woman's role*. Glasgow: Scottish Poverty Information Unit.

Scottish Government. 2015. 'What do we know about in-work poverty? A summary of the evidence', Communities Analytical Services, Scottish Government Social Research.

Section 7, Healthy Eating in Schools (Wales) Measure 2009. National Assembly for Wales, Cardiff.

Section 8, Schools Health Promotion and Nutrition (Scotland) Act 2007. Scottish Parliament, Edinburgh.

Sen, A. 1981. *Poverty and Famines: An essay on entitlement and deprivation*. Oxford: Oxford University Press.

Sen, A. 1992. *Inequality Re-examined*. Oxford: Clarendon Press.

Sen, A. 1999. *Development as Freedom*. Oxford: Oxford University Press.

Sennett, R. 1998. *The Corrosion of Character: The personal consequences of work in the new capitalism*. New York: W.W. Norton.

Serrano, A. 2013. 'Introducción: Heterogeneización y Nuevas Formas de Pobreza', *Cuadernos de Relaciones Laborales* 31: 275–80.

Shildrick, T., R. MacDonald, C. Webster and K. Garthwaite. 2010. *The Low-Pay, No-Pay Cycle: Understanding recurrent poverty*. York: JRF.

Shorthouse, R. 2013. *Family Fortunes: The bank of mum and dad in low income families*. London: Social Market Foundation.

SIFO. 2015. 'Reference budget for consumer expenditures'. https://www.hioa.no/eng/About-HiOA/Centre-for-Welfare-and-Labour-Research/SIFO/Reference-Budget-for-Consumer-Expenditures/Reference-Budget-for-Consumer-Expenditures-2015.

Sigona, N. and V. Hughes. 2012. *No Way Out, No Way In: Irregular migrant children and families in the UK*. Oxford: Oxford University Press.

Silva, F. C. 2013. *O futuro do estado social*. Lisbon: Fundação Francisco Manuel dos Santos.

Simmel, G. 1997. 'The sociology of the meal?', in *Simmel on Culture: Selected writings*, edited by D. Frisby and M. Featherstone, 130–6. London: SAGE.

Simon, A., C. Owen, R. O'Connell and F. Brooks. 2018. 'Changing trends in young people's food behaviour and well-being in England in relation to family affluence between 2005 and 2014', *Journal of Youth Studies* 21(5): 687–700.

Sivoplyasova, S. 2019. 'Influence of the state social policy on consumer behaviour of family with different number of children', paper presented at the ESA conference 'Families in the Context of Economic Problems and Crises', Manchester, August.

Skevik, A. 2006. 'Fairness in child support assessments: The views of non-resident fathers in Norway', *International Journal of Law, Policy and the Family* 20(2): 181–200.

Skuland, S. 2018. *Final Report for Norway in Families and Food in Hard Times*. Oslo: Oslo Metropolitan University.

Skuland, S. 2019. 'Packed lunch poverty: Immigrant families' struggles to include themselves in Norwegian food culture', in *Inclusive Consumption: Immigrants' access and use of public and private goods and services*, edited by A. Borch, I. Harsløf, K. Laitala and I. G. Klepp, 39–59. Oslo: Universitetsforlaget.

Smith, N. and S. Middleton. 2007. *A Review of Poverty Dynamics Research in the UK*. York: Joseph Rowntree Association.

Snape, D., M. Otley and M. Kumar. 1999. *Relying on the State, Relying on Each Other*. London: DSS.

Sobral, J. 2014. 'The high and the low in the making of a Portuguese national cuisine in the nineteenth and twentieth centuries', in *Food Consumption in Global Perspective: Essays in the anthropology of food in honour of Jack Goody*, edited by J. Klein and A. Murcott, 108–34. Basingstoke: Palgrave Macmillan.

Søholt, S. and T. Wessel. 2010. 'Contextualizing ethnic segregation in Norway: Welfare, housing and integration policy', in *Immigration, Housing and Segregation in the Nordic Welfare States*, edited by R. Anderson, H. Dhalmann, E. Holmquist, T. M. Kauppinen, L. M. Turner, H. S. Anderson, S. Søholt, M. Vaattovaara, K. Vilkama, T. Wessel and S. Yousfi, 127–94. Helsinki: University of Helsinki.

Solomos, J. 2003. *Race and Racism in Britain*, 3rd edn. Basingstoke: Palgrave Macmillan.

Sørvoll, J. 2015. 'The Norwegian welfare state 2005–2015: Public attitudes, political debates and future challenges'. https://doi.org/10.13140/rg.2.2.10481.33123.

SOS Racismo, ed. 2002. *Sastipen ta li saúde e liberdade, ciganos: números, abordagens e realidades*. Lisbon: SOS Racismo.

Sosenko, F., M. Littlewood, G. Bramley, S. Fitzpatrick, J. Blenkinsopp and J. Wood. 2019. 'State of hunger: A study of poverty and food insecurity in the UK November 2019', Trussell Trust. https://www.stateofhunger.org/wp-content/uploads/2019/11/State-of-Hunger-Report-November2019-Digital.pdf.

SPC (Social Protection Committee). 2014. *Social Europe – Many Ways, One Objective – Report of the Social Protection Committee*. Luxembourg: Publications Office of the European Union. http://ec.europa.eu/social/main.jsp?catId=738&langId=en&pubId=7695&type=2&further-Pubs=yes.

Sperling, J. 2018. *A Writer of Our Time: The life and work of John Berger*. London: Verso.

Spring Rice, M. 1981. *Working-Class Wives: Their health and conditions*. London: Virago.

Statistics Norway. 2014. 'Flere innvandrerbarnefamilier med lavinntekt'. 18 March. https://www.ssb.no/inntekt-og-forbruk/artikler-og-publikasjoner/flere-innvandrerbarnefamilier-med-lavinntekt

Statistics Norway. 2017. 'Innvandrere og norskfødte med innvandrerforeldre'. https://www.ssb.no/befolkning/statistikker/innvbef/aar/2017-03-02.

Statistics Norway. 2018a. 'Table 12599: Personer i husholdninger med lavinntekt (EU- og OECD-skala), etter ulike grupper. Antall og prosent 2008 – 2018'. https://www.ssb.no/statbank/table/12599/tableViewLayout1/.

Statistics Norway. 2018b. 'Table 06947: Persons in private households with annual after-tax income per consumption unit, below different distances to the median income. EU-scale and OECD-scale (M) (UD) 2005–2018'. https://www.ssb.no/en/statbank/table/06947.

Stewart, S. 2013. *A Sociology of Culture, Taste and Value*. Basingstoke: Palgrave Macmillan.

Stone, D. 1988. *Policy Paradox and Political Reason*. Glenview, IL: Scott Foresman.

Sung, S. and F. Bennett. 2007. 'Dealing with money in low- to moderate-income couples: Insights from individual interviews', in *Social Policy Review 19: Analysis and debate in social policy*, edited by K. Clarke, T. Malby and P. Kennett, 151–75. Bristol: Policy Press.

Sweetman, P. 2009. 'Revealing habitus, illuminating practice: Bourdieu, photography and visual methods', *Sociological Review* 57(3): 491–511.

Tarasuk, V. 2001. 'Discussion paper on household and individual food insecurity', Health Canada.

Tavora, I. and Rubery, J. 2013. 'Female employment, labour market institutions and gender culture in Portugal', *European Journal of Industrial Relations* 19(3): 221–37.

Taylor-Gooby, P., Larsen, T. and Kananen, J. 2004. 'Market means and welfare ends: The UK welfare state experiment', *Journal of Social Policy* 33(4:) 573–92.

Thompson, C., Ponsford, R., Lewis, D. and Cummins, S. 2018a. 'Fast-food, everyday life and health: A qualitative study of "chicken shops" in East London', *Appetite* 128: 7–13.

Thompson, C., D. Smith and S. Cummins. 2018b. 'Understanding the health and wellbeing challenges of the food banking system: A qualitative study of food bank users, providers and referrers in London', *Social Science & Medicine* 211: 95–101.

Thomson, R. 2009. *Unfolding Lives: Youth, gender, change*. Bristol: Policy Press.

Thorne, B. 2012. 'Pricing the priceless child as a teaching treasure', *Journal of the History of Childhood and Youth* 5(3): 474–80.

Tinson, A., C. Ayrton, K. Barker, T. Born, H. Aldridge and P. Kenway. 2016. *Monitoring Poverty and Social Exclusion*. York: JRF and New Policy Institute.

Tirado, L. 2014. *Hand to Mouth: The truth about being poor in a wealthy world*. London: Virago.

Townsend, P. 1954. 'Measuring poverty', *British Journal of Sociology* 5(2): 130–7.

Townsend, P. 1979. *Poverty in the United Kingdom: A survey of household resources and standards of living*. London: Penguin.

Townsend, P. 2010. 'The meaning of poverty'. *British Journal of Sociology* 61(S1): 85–102.

Truninger, M. 2013. 'The historical development of industrial and domestic food strategies', in *The Handbook of Food Research*, edited by A. Murcott, W. Belasco and P. Jackson, 82–97. London: Bloomsbury.

Truninger, M., S. Cardoso, V. Ramos, F. Augusto and M. Abrantes. 2018. *Families and Food Poverty: Qualitative report – Portugal*. Lisbon: ICS, University of Lisbon.

Truninger, M. and R. Sousa. 2019. 'School meals reform and feeding ordering in Portugal conventions and controversies', in *Feeding Children Inside and Outside the Home: Critical perspectives*, edited by V. Harman, B. Cappellini and C. Faircloth, 42–62. London: Routledge.

Truninger, M., J. Teixeira, A. Horta, V. da Silva and S. Alexandre. 2013. 'Schools' health education in Portugal: A case study of children's relationships with school meals', *Educação, Sociedade & Culturas* 38: 117–33.

TUC (Trades Union Congress). 2019. *Unsecured Debt Hits New Peak*. London: Trades Union Congress. www.tuc.org.uk/news/unsecured-debt-hits-new-peak-%C2%A315400-household-%E2%80%93-new-tuc-analysis

Tucker, J. 2017. *The Austerity Generation: The impact of a decade of cuts on family incomes and child poverty*. London: Child Poverty Action Group.

Tucker, J. and A. Stirling. 2017. *Analysis Commissioned from the Institute for Public Policy Research*. London: Institute for Public Policy Research.

Tuomainen, H. 2009. 'Ethnic identity, (post)colonialism and foodways', *Food, Culture & Society* 12(4): 525–54.

UKVI (UK Visas and Immigration Service). 2016. *Public Funds*. London: Home Office. https://www.gov.uk/government/publications/public-funds.

UN (United Nations). 2011. *The Great Recession and the Jobs Crisis*. New York: United Nations.

UN (United Nations). 2012. 'UN Human Rights Council twenty-first session agenda item 9: Racism, racial discrimination, xenophobia and related forms of intolerance, follow-up and implementation of the Durban Declaration and Programme of Action. Report of the Working Group of Experts on People of African Descent on its eleventh session. Addendum. Mission to Portugal'. https://www.ohchr.org/Documents/HRBodies/HRCouncil/RegularSession/Session21/A-HRC-21-60-Add2_en.pdf.

Underlid, K. 2007. 'Poverty and experiences of insecurity', *International Journal of Social Welfare*, 16: 65–74.

UNHRC (United Nations Human Rights Council). 2015. *Global Trends: Forced displacement in 2015*. Geneva. https://www.unhcr.org/uk/statistics/unhcrstats/576408cd7/unhcr-global-trends-2015.html.

Van Meeteren, M. and S. Pereira. 2013. *The Differential Role of Social Networks: Strategies and routes in Brazilian migration to Portugal and the Netherlands*. Oxford: International Migration Institute.

Veit-Wilson, J. 1987. 'Consensual approaches to poverty lines and social security', *Journal of Social Policy* 16(2): 183–211.

Veit-Wilson, J. 2019. 'Causes, not consequences: Abolishing the causes of poverty will not cost the country more money than it has or can afford, but political will is essential', Fabian Society, 6 February. https://fabians.org.uk/causes-not-consequences/.

Venn, D. 2009. 'Legislation, collective bargaining and enforcement: Updating the OECD employment protection indicators', OECD Social, Employment and Migration Working Papers 89. http://www.oecd-ilibrary.org/social-issuesmigration-health/legislation-collective-bargaining-and-enforcement_223334316804

Vogel, D., V. Kovacheva and H. Prescott. 2011. 'The size of the irregular migrant population in the European Union: Counting the uncountable?', *International Migration* 49: 78–92.

Voices of the Hungry. 2016. *Methods for Estimating Comparable Prevalence Rates of Food Insecurity Experienced by Adults throughout the World*. Rome: Food and Agriculture Organisation. http://www.fao.org/3/a-i4830e.pdf.

Walker, R. 1987. 'Consensual approaches to the definition of poverty: Towards an alternative methodology', *Journal of Social Policy* 16(2): 213–26.

Walker, R. 2014. *The Shame of Poverty*. Oxford: Oxford University Press.

Walker, R. and E. Chase. 2014. 'Adding to the shame of poverty: The public, politicians and the media', *Poverty* 148: 9–13.

Wall, K., S. Aboim, V. Cunha and P. Vasconcelos. 2001. 'Families and informal support networks in Portugal: The reproduction of inequality', *Journal of European Social Policy* 11(3): 213–33.

Wall, K. and S. Correia. 2014. 'Changes in family policies since 2010: Country overview Portugal', Eurofound Project. https://repositorio.ul.pt/bitstream/10451/22555/1/ICs_KWall_EUROFOUND_%20PortugalTask6a6b_RelatorioFinal-1.pdf.

Wall, K., S. Samitca and S. Correia. 2013. 'Negotiating work and care in a changing welfare regime: The case of Portugal', in *Work and Care under Pressure: Care Arrangements across Europe*, edited by B. Le Bihan, C. Martin and T. Knijn, 125–49. Amsterdam: Amsterdam University Press.

Wandel, M. 1995. 'Dietary intake of fruits and vegetables in Norway: Influence of life phase and socio-economic factors', *International Journal of Food Sciences and Nutrition* 46(3): 291–301.

Warde, A. 1997. *Consumption, Food and Taste*. London: SAGE.

Warde, A. 2014. 'Budge up Nudge', *Discover Society*, 2 September. https://discoversociety.org/2014/09/02/focus-budge-up-nudge-policy-fashions-and-the-demise-of-an-intervention/.

Warde, A. 2016. *The Practice of Eating*. Cambridge: Polity Press.

Warde, A. and L. Martens. 1997a. 'Eating out and the commercialisation of mental life', *British Food Journal* 100(3): 147–53.

Warde, A. and L. Martens. 1997b. 'Urban pleasure? On the meaning of eating out in a northern city', in *Food, Health and Identity*, edited by P. Caplan, 131–51. Routledge: London.

Warde, A., S. Cheng, W. Olsen and D. Southerton. 2007. 'Changes in the practice of eating: A comparative analysis of time-use', *Acta Sociologica* 50(4): 363–85.

Warde, A., J. Paddock and J. Whillans 2019. *The Social Significance of Dining Out: Continuity and change*. Manchester: Manchester University Press.

Weber, M. 2012. 'Science as a profession and a vocation', in *Max Weber: Collected methodological writings*, edited by H. Bruun and S. Whimster, 335–53. London: Routledge.

Wendt, M. 2019. 'Comparing "deep" insider knowledge: Developing analytical strategies for cross-national qualitative studies', *International Journal of Social Research Methodology* 23(3): 241–54.

WFP (World Food Programme). 2020. 'World Food Programme insight: Risk of hunger pandemic as coronavirus set to almost double acute hunger by end of 2020'. https://insight.wfp.org/covid-19-will-almost-double-people-in-acute-hunger-by-end-of-2020-59df0c4a8072

Whitehead, A. 1984. *I'm Hungry Mum: The politics of domestic budgeting*. London: Routledge.

Wilk, R. 2010. 'Power at the table: Food fights and happy meals', *Cultural Studies: Critical Methodologies* 10(6): 428–36.

Wills, W., K. Backett-Milburn, E. M. Roberts and J. Lawton. 2011. 'The framing of social class distinctions through family food and eating practices', *Sociological Review* 59(4): 725–40.

Wills, W. and R. O'Connell, eds. 2018. 'Children's and young people's food practices in contexts of poverty and inequality', *Children & Society* 32(3): 169–73.

Wills, W., G. Danesi, A. Kapetanaki and L. Hamilton. 2019. 'Socio-economic factors, the food environment and lunchtime food purchasing by young people at secondary school', *International Journal of Environmental Research and Public Health* 16(9): 1605.

Windebank, J. and A. Whitworth. 2014. 'Social welfare and the ethics of austerity in Europe: Justice, ideology and equality', *Journal of Contemporary European Studies* 22(2): 99–103.

World Bank. 2018. 'Urban population (% of total population). United Nations Population Division. World urbanization prospects: 2018 revision'. https://data.worldbank.org/indicator/SP.URB.TOTL.IN.ZS.

Wright, O. 2014. 'Tory attitudes to poverty under fire over benefit sanctions and Baroness Jenkin comment that poor "don't know how to cook": Baroness Jenkin forced to apologise after blaming food bank use on culinary incompetence', *The Independent*, 8 December. https://www.independent.co.uk/news/uk/politics/tory-attitudes-poverty-under-fire-over-benefit-sanctions-and-baroness-jenkin-comment-poor-don-t-know-how-cook-9911580.html.

Yin, R. 2003. *Case Study Research: Design and methods*. 3rd edn. London: SAGE.

Yuval-Davis, N., G. Wemyss and K. Cassidy. 2017. 'Everyday bordering, belonging and the reorientation of British immigration legislation', *Sociology* 52(2): 1–17.

Zhang, L.-C. 2008. *Developing Methods for Determining the Number of Unauthorized Foreigners in Norway*. Oslo: Statistics Norway.

Index

Lightning Source UK Ltd.
Milton Keynes UK
UKHW052318120521
383600UK00001B/13